Desert Duty

ON THE LINE WITH THE
U.S. BORDER PATROL

Bill Broyles and Mark Haynes

FOREWORD BY CHARLES BOWDEN

 UNIVERSITY OF TEXAS PRESS
Austin

Requests for permission to reproduce material from this work should
be sent to:
    Permissions
    University of Texas Press
    P.O. Box 7819
    Austin, TX 78713-7819
    www.utexas.edu/utpress/about/bpermission.html

⊗The paper used in this book meets the minimum requirements
of ANSI /NISO Z39.48-1992 (R1997) (Permanence of Paper).

LIBRARY OF CONGRESS CATALOGING-IN-PUBLICATION DATA
Broyles, Bill.
Desert duty : on the line with the U.S. border patrol / Bill Broyles
and Mark Haynes ; foreword by Charles Bowden. — 1st ed.
        p.   cm.
Includes bibliographical references.
ISBN 978-0-292-72283-5 (cloth : alk. paper) —
ISBN 978-0-292-72320-7 (pbk. : alk. paper)
    1. Border patrols—United States.   2. U.S. Customs and Border
Protection.   I. Haynes, Mark.   II. Title.
JV6483.B78 2010
363.28'50973—dc22
                                                        2010019948

Honor First.
— Motto of the United States Border Patrol

With special thanks to Ronald S. Colburn, Deputy Chief, U.S. Border Patrol; Paul A. Beeson, Chief of Yuma Sector; Carla L. Provost, Patrol Agent in Charge, Wellton Station; Stephen K. Johnson, Patrol Agent in Charge, Yuma Station; and agents past and present of the "old" Border Patrol and the "new" Customs and Border Protection Agency of the Department of Homeland Security.

CONTENTS

Charles Bowden

Foreword SILENT LONG ENOUGH

I first met the Border Patrol in the early 1980s because
I had decided to break the law. At the time, I worked for a daily paper
in Tucson, Arizona, and I was dismayed by scant coverage of Mexican
migrants who died crossing the desert in summer. I decided to learn how
the Border Patrol worked and started hanging with the agents at Tacna, an
isolated station in western Arizona that faced an uninhabited zone of thousands of square miles that ran up against the border. That is when I came
to know some of the people in this book. And I decided I needed someone
to go with me on my journey. So I called the man who created this book,
Bill Broyles. On the night of June 21 we crossed from Sonora with a bunch
of Mexicans, a walk that totaled forty-five miles. We staggered out of the
desert the next morning and we felt deep pain. The Mexicans had to keep
going toward their dreams of jobs and a future, and they had to keep hiding
from the Border Patrol.

Since then, the Border Patrol has grown huge, the migration has become the largest one on earth, and the work done by the Border Patrol has
remained a mystery to the public. This book should clear up what it feels
like to patrol the border and give the reader a real sense of the people who
do this work. It has been a labor of love on the part of Broyles and Mark
Haynes and, to my knowledge, it is unique. Here you meet the people
of the Border Patrol without anything standing between you and their
stories.

They are decent people doing a thankless job, mainly trying to stop a
migration of the poor from the utter ruin of Mexico. Sometimes they get
hurt and sometimes they save people from death in the desert. But almost
always, they are props used by proponents and opponents of the migration. Because of the discipline of the service, they are seldom allowed to
speak out.

Now we can hear their voices. And I guarantee you are going to be

U.S. Border Patrol pilots Hank Hays, Joe Dunn, and Howard Aitken near the line. Photo by Bill Broyles, 1995.

surprised by what they say. You'll meet an agent whose father used illegal labor on his farm and cut his son off for years when he joined the Border Patrol. You'll brush against the craft of tracking. You'll find a bunch of people who took the federal job because they needed the money and then discovered the job became their very life.

It is a strange kind of work where you are there alone and you are hunting people—men, women, and children—who are seeking to escape the doom of failing economies. And I can tell you from personal experience, regardless of your views on borders or the migration, you get caught up in the hunt. And you eventually get caught up in the fragments of lives that you meet in the deserts and mountains, the slivers of facts that people tell you about where they have come from and where they are heading. I remember when I first hooked up with the Border Patrol they caught two teenage boys who had walked fifty miles across the desert in flip-flops. At such moments, you ask yourself if you could possibly pull off such a trek and you suddenly realize how fierce the conditions must be at home to propel a couple of kids into such a journey.

Now the world is changing. There are almost twenty thousand people in the Border Patrol, surveillance drones fly in the sky, a huge wall is going up on the line. Mexico is convulsed with poverty and violence, and at least 10 percent of its people now live illegally in the United States. And the same thankless job goes on all along the line. It's time to learn what it takes to police our border and what it costs the people who do the work.

They've been silent long enough.

Charles Bowden is the author of five books published recently by the University of Texas Press: *Inferno, Exodus, Trinity, Dreamland,* and *The Charles Bowden Reader.* Or you may know him from his numerous articles in *Harper's, GQ, Esquire, Texas Monthly, Arizona Highways,* and newspapers, or his two dozen other books, including *Killing the Hidden Waters* (1977), *Blue Desert* (1986), *Juárez: The Laboratory of Our Future* (1998), and *Some of the Dead Are Still Breathing* (2009).

DESERT DUTY

Introduction ON EDGE

I f you have traveled or lived near America's southern border, you have seen the forest green uniform, the white vehicle with a green slash and bold letters, and the agents wearing ball caps. They are the men and women who run highway checkpoints, eye passing cars, and pursue groups of smugglers and undocumented aliens across open country. But have you met the agents themselves, those people behind the sunglasses, the humans at the wheel of the patrol truck, your neighbors down the street who shop at your mall and coach your kids' peewee teams, the fathers and mothers who live and work near the border and wear the green uniform of the U.S. Border Patrol?

They are the mobile, uniformed arm of the federal government charged with patrolling between the official borderline ports of entry. Their authority to enter private lands to patrol for illegal aliens extends twenty-five miles from the border, and they may legally stop all vehicles to check for aliens as far as one hundred air miles from the border. Based upon reasonable suspicion of the commission of a criminal act or upon procurement of a warrant, they may investigate immigration offenses anywhere in the country.

They are the border police, and like your hometown force, they both protect and serve. In a day's work they may catch a load of narcotics, apprehend groups of people entering the country without permission, and intercept a potential terrorist. The day undoubtedly will include rescuing aliens from death by thirst or murder by border bandits, preventing neighborhood assaults and burglaries, and administering first-aid to accident victims, and may involve delivering an untimely baby or helping stranded motorists. If you don't know them, you should.

What follows is a set of interviews documenting the trials and triumphs of U.S. Border Patrol agents who have worked the southwest border between the United States and Mexico. They represent two-thirds of the

Peligro *(danger)* on the border. Photo by Bill Broyles, 2005.

patrol's history, which dates back to 1924. It is written as told by those who have "walked the line" and is dedicated to their often unsung achievements. We relay the stories in historical sequence, from the older guard now retired to those still wearing the badge, for one name leads to another, policies progress, and equipment evolves. The common theme is duty to country.

These are self-told stories of working folks doing desert duty at Wellton Station, just as they are at dozens of other Border Patrol stations along America's borders. Names like Eagle Pass, Laredo, Fort Stockton, Douglas, Ajo, Calexico, and Campo signal stations with proud histories. The agency's motto is Honor First, and uncommon dedication is required. The work is rigorous and dangerous. Agents must be vigilant, self-sufficient, and honest. As you will read, the stories of these law officers reflect the fact that they are actual people with smiles and frowns.

Whether you are an alien downed by fatigue, battered by heat, or threatened by thirst or border bandits; a fellow agent in hot pursuit of drug smugglers or holding suspects at gunpoint; or a citizen lost in the wild borderlands, these are the people you'd pray were on your trail and on their way. If you are a smuggler evading the law, these are the relentless forces you fear.

In their own words, these are the stories of men and women working the border where, before you had breakfast this morning, someone crossed the line and now someone is looking for them.

THE DUTY

Since the expansion of our nation into the American Southwest, the unenviable task of policing the nation's southwest border has fallen on a thin line of hardy individuals dressed in blue or khaki, in denim and chambray, in green or blue wool, or in modern rip-stop nylon. Through the years, the U.S. military and federal law enforcement entities have shared the task of protecting the nation's borders from foreign enemies, economically motivated migrants, and opportunistic criminals. The working conditions were generally wretched and tasks were rigorous and mostly thankless. On many occasions, however, the men protecting the border were placed into the role of rescuer, delivering innocent citizens and wrongdoers alike from captivity, injury, or death.

The earliest effort at providing security to the borderlands of the Southwest came in 1849, with the establishment of Camp Calhoun at the confluence of the Gila and Colorado rivers, near present-day Yuma, Arizona. This military post eventually became Fort Yuma, and served the dual purposes of protecting this important river crossing into California from hostile Native Americans and projecting the influence of the United States into a region that was newly won from Mexico in the Mexican War.

Between the establishment of Camp Calhoun and the surrender of Geronimo in 1886, the U.S. Army was active throughout the Southwest, particularly along the present-day border between Arizona and Mexico. Native Americans, and Apaches in particular, did not recognize national borders. They soon discovered, however, that crossing the imaginary line could give them sanctuary from retribution for their transgressions. The raiding parties of the tribes crossed between the countries on long-established trails, committing depredations in an attempt to drive all whites from the region.

The military built forts at strategic locations and employed infantry and cavalry units, as well as Native American scouts, to patrol the border region. They worked to detect the movement of raiders between the countries, vigorously pursued them, and engaged them in combat whenever possible. These pursuits sometimes crossed the international border, with or without the appropriate governmental sanction. The incidents were not always merely about combat, but often involved a humanitarian aspect. Historical accounts record many instances where soldiers were able to intercept war parties and release innocent captives. Eventually, the wayward bands were brought into the reservation system, and many were exiled from the region.

During this time the movement of citizens of both countries across the frontier was virtually unimpeded by governments of the United States or Mexico. The treaty of Guadalupe Hidalgo, concluded in 1848, had made U.S. citizens of approximately 80,000 Mexican residents of the Southwest. Economically and as a matter of national policy, neither Mexico nor the United States had any overriding interest in limiting peaceful cross-border trade or interaction.

The laissez-faire approach to immigration into the United States in this era was not to last. When distinguished jurist Oliver Wendell Holmes commented that "the life of the law has not been logic, it has been experience," he might well have had the Immigration and Nationality Laws of the United States in mind. Throughout the history of the nation, the laws regarding the admission of persons into the United States have at times been nonexistent, at other times defied logic, and at other times been outright racist or unenforceable.

Beginning in 1870, isolationism and economic downturns created an anti-immigrant sentiment that resulted in Congress's enacting laws to protect the country from uncontrolled immigration. The "Exclusion Acts" began in 1875, with a prohibition on the legal entry of convicts and "immoral women." This was followed in 1882 by an act that excluded idiots, lunatics, and paupers, and the more imposing Chinese Exclusion Act. The latter act was prompted by the fear of a glut of cheap labor. Uncontrolled Chinese immigration, brought on as a result of the large numbers of Chinese laborers imported to build the transcontinental railroad, created alarm in organized labor and governmental circles. The act suspended the immigration of all but a few limited professionals from China for a period of ten years. In 1902 the exclusion was made permanent, and some form of bar on immigration based upon Chinese or oriental derivation existed until 1943.

The enactment of legislation alone was not entirely effective. Chinese were able to embark from China and enter into Mexico. From there, they could enter the United States across its southern border. Many individuals residing on the frontier were familiar with the historic routes transecting the border, and many were more than ready to step into the lucrative business of human smuggling. Officers employed by the national government were sorely needed to augment the meager military resources on the border, which were steadily declining with the end of the Indian Wars.

Initially, the role of patrolling the border to curtail Chinese smuggling fell on the Customs Service. One of the earliest civilians to be assigned to patrol the southwest border was professional lawman Jefferson Davis Milton. Formerly a Texas Ranger, he entered on duty on March 11, 1887, as a U.S. Customs Line Rider, or Mounted Inspector, the forerunner of the Immigration Riders. Reporting to the El Paso Collector of Customs, Milton performed the duties of immigration and customs officer. One of only eleven border guards stationed between El Paso and the Pacific Ocean, Milton's job entailed patrolling alone on horseback. Leading a pack horse, he rode from Nogales, Arizona, along the border to the Colorado River below Yuma. The primary mission of Milton and his fellow officers was the collection of customs duties on goods brought into the country, but they also prevented the smuggling of cheap, untaxed liquor and Chinese aliens into the United States.

For a time, Mounted Inspectors, employed by the Chinese Bureau within the Customs Service, and line riders, employed by the newly established Immigration Bureau, shared enforcement of the Chinese exclusion laws. To eliminate confusion near border cities and reduce the chance of mistaking fellow officers for smugglers, the officers in charge of the respective units would alternate areas of coverage on the border. Sometimes, however, the units would pair up or work together in one area in response to specific intelligence information.

A change in presidential administrations resulted in a wholesale purge of the Customs Service in 1899, costing Milton and others their jobs. Ultimately, Customs relinquished its role on the border, and the Chinese Bureau within Customs was disbanded around 1900.

The Chinese Exclusion Act also created an Office of the Superintendent of Immigration, which was established within the Treasury Department in 1891. The new Bureau of Immigration oversaw the U.S. Immigrant Inspectors stationed at the ports of entry. By 1904 Immigration line riders, often referred to as "mounted guards" or Chinese Inspectors, were hired and assigned to positions along the southern border. Their role would be to provide border security between the ports of entry from El Paso, Texas, to California. Jeff Milton returned to border work as one of the new Mounted Chinese Inspectors in April 1904. Never numbering more than seventy-five men, they were an enforcement presence along the border whenever resources permitted. As an inspector "at large," Milton primarily worked the border between Nogales and Yuma, Arizona.

As dedicated as this small number of patrol officers was, criminal activity was on the rise in Arizona, particularly along the southwest border. Fearing that lawlessness would stymie the attainment of statehood, in 1901 the Territorial Governor of Arizona organized the Arizona Rangers to protect Arizona from outlaws and rustlers. Similar to the conditions during the Indian Wars, much of the criminal activity involved rustling and raiding across the U.S.-Mexican border. To combat the problem, a cooperative agreement was reached between the Rangers and the Mexican Rurales that allowed cross-border pursuit of outlaws. The Rangers continued their work until 1909, by which time the governor had determined that they were no longer needed, and they were disbanded.

Although the general lawlessness rampant along the border at the time was an issue, the primary driving force behind congressional action on immigration was the protection of American workers. In recognition of this fact, in 1903 Congress transferred the Bureau of Immigration to the newly created Department of Commerce and Labor. Naturalization functions were added in 1906 and the agency was renamed the United States Immigration Service, or "USIS."

Line riders were gradually replaced by Chinese Inspectors of the USIS Chinese Division. These were the first uniformed civilian law enforcement officers employed on the border, and they were required to purchase olive drab wool tunics out of their own wages. By 1913, the bureaus of Immigration and Naturalization were transferred as separate entities into the U.S. Department of Labor, and Chinese Inspectors reverted to the title "Immigration Inspectors."

In 1910, the border region faced a new security threat. Revolutionaries led by Emiliano Zapata began an insurgency against the dictatorship of Porfirio Díaz. U.S. Cavalry units were once again assigned to patrol the border as a stabilizing influence. By 1913, the forces of one of Zapata's lieutenants, Pancho Villa, had forced their way north through Chihuahua. The revolutionaries under Villa were occupying Ciudad Juárez, just across the Rio Grande from El Paso.

When the revolutionaries under Pancho Villa raided Columbus, New Mexico, on March 9, 1916, the attack triggered the last large-scale cavalry operation in U.S. history. A force consisting of three cavalry regiments, two infantry regiments, and a contingent of artillery crossed into Mexico in two columns. They spent a total of eleven months following the raiders and attempting to punish them for the incursion into the United States. Some minor skirmishing occurred, and some of the raiders were killed or captured, but beyond disrupting the revolutionaries' lines of supply and communication, the Punitive Expedition had little long-term impact on the border.

A new group of mounted guards or inspectors was authorized by Congress in March 1915. At this time most continued to patrol on horseback, but a few automobiles were being used. By 1918, Immigration Inspector Jeff Milton was assigned to work alongside a Customs Inspector at Indian Oasis, a Tohono O'odham Indian (Papago) town 65 miles southwest of Tucson. Milton utilized a stripped-down Model T Ford for some of his patrols. Although he possessed a broad authority as an Immigration Inspector, he still was concerned mostly with the illegal entry of Chinese immigrants.

During and immediately following the Punitive Expedition, the U.S. military continued to perform intermittent patrols along the southwest border. By 1916, political turmoil in Mexico and the termination of steamship travel between China and Mexico had slowed illegal immigration from China to a trickle.

The comings and goings of Mexican nationals across the border seldom merited any attention. Thousands crossed daily or with the crop seasons to obtain laborer jobs. This changed significantly, however, when Congress passed the Literacy Act in 1917. It required any person crossing the border for work to be able to read and write in some language. Many of the laborers who had crossed from Mexico could not meet these requirements. The result was a big increase in illegal entry between the ports of entry.

The United States entered into World War I by declaring war on the Central Powers in April 1917. The next year Congress enacted the Passport Act to deter the entry of enemy agents and spies into the country. Once again, U.S. cavalry units were assigned to patrol the southwest border to augment civilian interdiction efforts. Civilian law enforcement professionals continued their work on the border alongside the cavalrymen. They were variously referred to as mounted guards, mounted watchmen, or mounted inspectors. They were hired under a mix of civil service standards, and were paid by various agencies. Employed at grade levels below those of existing patrol officers and lacking civil service protections, many were released at the end of World War I.

Customs line riders, later called Customs Patrol Inspectors, continued to be an on-and-off presence on the border. They were especially active for several years after 1920, when the Volstead Act was enacted to enforce the prohibition on liquor brought about by the Eighteenth Amendment to the Constitution. The Customs Patrol was officially disbanded after the formation of the U.S. Border Patrol in 1924, but was, from time to time, resurrected. Until the early 1980s, when they were again disbanded and converted to Sky Marshals or Customs Investigators, Customs Patrol officers were assigned to work the same border areas worked by Border Patrol agents. Ostensibly, the officers with Customs interdicted goods, while the Border Patrol officers interdicted persons.

In 1921, quota laws enacted by Congress severely limited the numbers of certain nationalities who could apply for legal residence in the United States. The impact of these laws was felt most acutely in many of the northern European nations, the source of much of the earlier migration into the United States. The result was an increase in the smuggling of Europeans into the country to join friends and relatives already living in the United States.

A major overhaul of immigration laws in 1924 reunited the separate bureaus of Immigration and of Naturalization within the Department of Labor to form the modern-day Immigration and Naturalization Service (INS). This new INS was charged with administering all of the laws relating to foreign nationals and with patrolling the U.S. borders. The United States Border Patrol was founded by Congress on May 28, 1924, and in June of that year Border Patrol Inspectors assumed the duties of the USIS (Chinese Division) Immigration Inspectors. The changeover was not immediate, however. Jeff Milton continued performing his duties as an Immigration Inspector in various parts of Arizona and California up until 1931, when he finally took a well-deserved retirement.

An early recruitment effort for Border Patrol included the following announcement in the *Daily International* newspaper from Douglas, Arizona, on March 16, 1925:

> The newly organized border patrol is looking for new men and an examination for positions will be held at Douglas and at centrally located places in the state some time after April 11. The patrol, which is a branch of the immigration service, will accept no man unless he is big and strong and fearless. He must have experience in cowboy work; tracking and general border occupations and he must have had service in some highly organized police unit or in some regular army. They must be between 23 and 45 years of age and must have had at least three years' experience in general ranch work along the border. This qualification is necessary because the principal work of these men is border riding, which is done

mainly on horseback. Applicants must measure at least 5 feet 7 inches in height and be well proportioned, they must be of good moral character, honest and courageous.

At times during our nation's history, the border between the ports of entry has been patrolled other than by military or law enforcement officers. Outbreaks of diseases, such as "hoof and mouth disease" during the last two centuries, prompted assignment of agricultural specialists along the border. Known as "tick riders," or mounted agricultural inspectors, they were assigned to patrol the border for foreign livestock. They exterminated animals crossing the border to eliminate the potential for the spread of disease to U.S. livestock herds.

In 1933 the United States Border Patrol and its parent agency, the Immigration and Naturalization Service (INS), became part of the U.S. Department of Justice. INS continued as the lead agency for border enforcement between official ports of entry until it was disbanded in March 2003.

Following a reorganization triggered by the attacks by foreign operatives on the World Trade Center and the Pentagon on September 11, 2001, Border Patrol was given a new look. Operational activities of INS and Customs were moved into the newly established cabinet-level Department of Homeland Security (DHS), which was further divided into branches. Both Border Patrol and Customs are branches within the Customs and Border Protection Agency. Immigrants coming into the country illegally through ports of entry are the responsibility of Customs. Border Patrol agents retain responsibility for aliens entering illegally between the ports.

Within DHS, Border Patrol stands alongside twenty-two other federal agencies, including the Coast Guard, Secret Service, Federal Emergency Management Agency (FEMA), Transportation Security Administration (TSA), and Immigration and Customs Enforcement (ICE), which handles undocumented aliens already within the United States. Foreigners coming to the United States legally are processed by Citizenship and Immigration Services (CIS). Border Patrol is assigned 5,000 miles of the Canadian border, 1,900 miles of the Mexican border, and the coastal waters of Florida and Puerto Rico. The U.S. Coast Guard patrols for illegal entries coming by sea or air to the Atlantic, Pacific, and Gulf of Mexico coasts. At America's 327 borderline ports of entry, other U.S. officers, Customs agents, check incoming traffic for contraband, illegal entrants, and terrorists.

But Border Patrol's mission remains largely the same as it always was: to manage, control, and protect the nation's border between ports of entry and to keep terrorists and their weapons out of the country. It has largely been forgotten, but during World War II agents kept an eye out for Nazi and Japanese infiltrators and spies coming across the border. Now they watch for terrorists. With the projected levels of manpower, increased effectiveness of technology, and expanded legal remedies, Border Patrol, along with its sister agencies, may be able to effectively control the border for the first time in its history. Time will tell if America's lawmakers and voters sustain the support to let them.

THE TRADE

Agents receive basic training at a police academy. Over its history, Border Patrol has used several locations, including the Federal Law Enforcement Training Center (FLETC) in Glynco, Georgia, but today it employs its own academy at Artesia, New Mexico. The curriculum at the Border Patrol academy includes Immigration and Nationality Law, Criminal Law and Statutory Authority, Spanish, Border Patrol Operations, Care and Use of Firearms, Physical Training, Operation of Motor Vehicles, and Anti-Terrorism. Standard federal law enforcement courses are Communications, Ethics and Conduct, Report Writing, Introduction to Computers, Fingerprinting, and Constitutional Law. Increasingly agents must master computers, remote cameras, and other complex tools. One of the slogans currently used in recruiting new agents proclaims "This isn't the old Border Patrol," but in some cases, sons and daughters follow their parents in uniform. At least one family, the Colburns, boasts four generations of Border Patrol agents.

Probationary agents—probies, trainees, or more recently, interns—are assigned to any of 144 stations along the southern border with Mexico or the northern border with Canada. Their training is periodically supplemented, updated, and upgraded with special classes and schools for journeymen agents. They may also volunteer for collateral duties and assignments. For example, they may elect to train for BORSTAR, the agency's search, trauma, and rescue team. Others become dog handlers, range officers, air observers, intelligence officers, or color guard members. Many will be assigned to undercover operations within the agency or in other federal entities such as the Drug Enforcement Agency or the Federal Bureau of Investigation. Others will add their unique experience and their authority to enforce certain federal statutes to specialized task forces comprising federal, state, and local officers.

Like any job, especially those demanding quick and decisive staccato bursts of information and commands on the police radio, Border Patrol has its own blunt, single-syllable lingo. A typical transmission might sound like, "Whiskey 5. Yankee 9. The lower drag is cut," meaning that Yuma ground unit 9 is telling Wellton unit 5 that he has finished checking—cutting—a dirt road for footprints. "Apps" are apprehensions, persons in custody. "Bodies" are the number of people in sight or custody. "Sign" can be any clues to the movement of people or vehicles, such as footprints, litter, or tire tracks. Air units, either a helicopter or plane, use the radio call-sign "Omaha" and pilots are known as "X-Ray units." Agents from Wellton use the call sign "Whiskey," while those from Ajo use "Alpha," Yuma units are "Yankee," and Blythe agents use "Bravo" to identify themselves.

A casual listener of radio traffic from Border Patrol trackers may think he has tuned into shop talk at a shoe store. Shoe prints must be described in sufficient detail to allow other agents to identify the same "sign" sight-unseen at another location. Common shoes may be described by type, such as pointed-toe cowboy boot, lugged work boot, running shoe, flip-flop, *huarache*, or irrigator boot. Too, they may be described by manufacturer, such as "Converse" or "Nike," or they may be described as having a herring-bone or diamond pattern, ball bearings in the sole, or a sonar pattern in the heel or toe. The combination of shoe prints in a particular group—a cowboy boot, running shoe, and a lug sole, for example—provides a distinctive signature almost as defining as a license plate. And, as unbelievable as it may sound, groups composed of aliens from outside North America could often be identified before they were caught by the fact that their collective foot sign contained few of the types common to Mexicans and Central Americans. This foot sign might be described to others as "Chinese," "Japanese," or "weird" tennis shoes.

People who cross the border without permission or papers have been referred to as illegal aliens, illegal immigrants, UDAs (undocumented aliens), and "wets," which is short for "wetback." Agents from past eras used the word "wet" or "wetback" when referring to undocumented aliens, with no derision intended. The term comes from the language aliens used to describe themselves, a Spanish-to-English translation of *mojado*, which means wet and refers to the fact that the aliens often crossed rivers or canals during their journey from Mexico into the United States and were still damp at the time of their apprehension. Some today refer to themselves as *alambristas*, which means fence jumpers. Agents call Mexicans who are in the country legally "Mexicans," reflecting their nationality or country of origin.

Because of America's common border with Mexico and the disparity in economic levels in the two countries, a very high percentage of illegal aliens come from Mexico. Illegal aliens from other countries are OTMs (other than Mexicans), and they may represent any other country in the world. According to the U.S. Office of Immigration Statistics, Mexicans comprised 91.4 percent of all aliens apprehended in 2008, with 7 percent from Central America and 0.6 percent from Caribbean nations. Where did they enter the United States? The vast majority, 97.4 percent, were apprehended in the Southwest, 1.5 percent on the coasts, and 1.1 percent on the northern border. From a decade high of 1,189,031 apprehensions in 2005, the total fell to 723,840 in 2008, with 83.8 percent of those being male and 70.9 percent between the ages of 18 and 34.

Mexicans call the Border Patrol *La Migra*, from the Spanish word for "immigration police." In this book we use "alien" and "agent" throughout, except where quoted from a conversation. Any foreigners, Mexican or other nationalities, are aliens. Those who hold legitimate papers such as visas, passports, and green cards fall into a couple of dozen categories ranging from ambassadors to students, businessmen to tourists, guest workers to entertainers, and resident aliens to refugees seeking asylum. The job of Border Patrol is to sort out who has valid papers and who doesn't.

In Mexico, aliens crossing the border without visas or passport papers are called *pollos* (chickens) in counterpoint to the human smugglers, who are called *polleros* or *coyotes*. *Pollero* on one level means chicken farmer but has come to mean guide for pollos, illegal aliens. The predator-prey relationship of coyotes and chickens should not be taken humorously, for the coyotes are as likely to pluck or devour the pollos as to guide them. It is a ruthless trade, where humans are shuttled like cargo, held for payment—ransom, really—in filthy "safe-houses" (which are anything but safe), or stolen by rival smugglers. Sometimes pollos are discarded in the desert to die if they can't keep pace with the fast-moving groups. The bottom line is profit margin, and deaths or injuries are seen by smugglers simply as costs of doing business.

For many decades, patrolling the border involved a minimal amount of technology. Cavalry and law enforcement officers alike relied mostly on a good mount, a handgun, and a rifle. An expansion of technology generally followed the end of each war fought by U.S. forces. After World War I, automobiles began to replace animals as the primary form of transportation for border lawmen. The end of World War II saw the introduction of two-way radios into border enforcement. The Korean War brought the large-scale introduction of aircraft into Border Patrol efforts, and the Vietnam War introduced helicopters, remotely monitored sensors, and computer databases into common usage. In the post–9/11 world, vast improvements have been made in identification methodology, available bed space for detainees, weaponry, and border fences and ports of entry.

Despite the vast gains made in technology, one of the stocks in trade for border law officers remains the ancient art of "sign cutting." It involves detecting the physical clues to the passage of a living thing and following that living thing by using those clues as a guide. First used by humans in prehistoric times, the ability to track aided in hunting, in self-protection, and in conducting war. This skill, honed by daily practice through the decades, is one common link between all the various entities and individuals who have worked the border. Native American scouts for the U.S. Army, Jeff Milton and his coworkers, and present-day agents all have used sign cutting to accomplish their mission.

Through the years the tracking art has served many functions. It has been used to document the trails used by marauders and allowed a count to be made of the offenders. It has provided officials with a gauge of illicit activity and precipitated a call to action when large numbers of smugglers and crossers were detected. Frequently, it has been used as a means of following and intercepting offenders. And last but not least, when done by skilled professionals, it has been utilized as a means for finding individuals in distress and saving their lives. A large number of individuals, illegal border crossers and innocent civilians alike, owe their lives to the tracking art used by border law officers.

AN OUTPOST OF TRACKERS

In this book about border patrolmen we focus on one Arizona station that watches over what is arguably the most perilous crossing along the U.S. border. Here undocumented immigrants attempt to negotiate sixty-four miles of the line. It is hot, dry Sonoran Desert, a land with few waterholes and summer temperatures routinely topping 110 degrees Fahrenheit.

At times the Border Patrol station has been located in the small farming town of Tacna. The owner of a roadside gas station and soda stand on the highway from Yuma to Phoenix or Tucson contrived to call it Tachnopolis, after an imaginary Greek priest, but the actual town never was

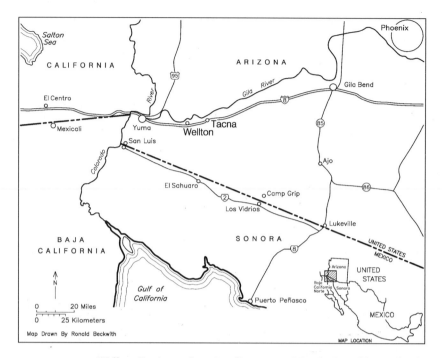

Wellton Station and surrounding region. Map by Ronald J. Beckwith.

very big and the signpost has moved several times. Since 1990 the Border Patrol station has been located at Wellton, eleven miles down the road from Tacna. When wells were dug here for the southern transcontinental railroad that arrived in 1879, the spot was named Welltown and later shortened to Wellton.

Now Interstate 8 serves both Tacna and Wellton. The enormous swath of land lying south from the interstate to the border is virtually unpopulated, a *despoblado*, an area with no real roads and few jeep trails. Much of it is administered by the U.S. military as the Goldwater Range, where Marine, Navy, and Air Force fighter pilots learn to strafe, bomb, and dogfight. A large section is the Cabeza Prieta National Wildlife Refuge and Wilderness Area. Another sizeable portion is Organ Pipe Cactus National Monument, and it too is largely federally legislated wilderness. Public entry to these lands requires a permit and, even then, access to much of the area is limited or closed. Perimeter signs state: "Danger. Military reservation. Unexploded ordnance. Permit required. Peligro. Municiones vivas. No entre." South of the border, in Mexico, lies the enormous Pinacate Biosphere Reserve, featuring drifting dunes and rugged volcanic flows and

The message: zona Despoblada, *desert wilderness. Photo by Bill Broyles, 2005.*

The reality: the worst is yet to come, Mohawk Dunes ahead. Photo by Bill Broyles, 1983.

cinder cones; it is bounded by modern roadways. Fewer people live in this twelve-thousand-square-mile region today than when the first European explorers passed this way in 1540.

This is the landscape crossed by the infamous El Camino Diablo—the Devil's Highway—where Spanish pioneers from the interior of Mexico and from Spain migrated by land to settle San Diego, Los Angeles, and San Francisco, and where miners raced to California's Gold Rush of 1849. Many hundreds died here, most of thirst. One observer, Lt. Nathaniel Michler, in 1857 reported that the land was scorching hot and blindingly bright, and travel here was a "torment." And of the road he wrote, "All traces of the road are sometimes erased by the high winds sweeping the unstable soil before them, but death has strewn a continuous line of bleached bones and withered carcasses of horses and cattle, as monuments to mark the way." This area is the setting for Charles Bowden's *Blue Desert*, John Annerino's *Dead in Their Tracks*, Aron Spilken's *Escape!*, and Luis Urrea's *The Devil's Highway*.

Signs sponsored by both the United States and Mexico have been posted along the border, alerting illegal aliens to the danger. The signs face south to greet America-bound aliens and carry such messages as "Peligro. Zona Despoblada" with a drawing of cactus, the sun, and no dwellings. Another sign has a you-are-here map showing 100 kilometers to go, with a cactus, scorpion, rattlesnake, and skeleton lying under a large red sun symbol; a skull and crossbones and a stop sign punctuate the urgency of the message. Advertisements in Sonoran newspapers and on Spanish-speaking airwaves warn of the dangers of crossing this desert. Scattered emergency-beacon towers invite aliens to push a red button and wait for rescue. Still aliens come.

Though most of the action is in the southern half, the Wellton Station's arena of responsibility comprises 7,995 square miles. That is an area larger than the entire state of Massachusetts, or New Jersey, or Connecticut plus Rhode Island. Imagine trying to detect and then follow a group of walkers, or even a single set of footprints, across an entire state. That is what this job requires. In days gone by, you might be the only agent on duty, and even today the lives of those walkers, facing fatal fatigue and heat stroke, could literally be up to you. If you find and save them, they live. If not, they die.

The old Tacna Station sometimes consisted of only one Border Patrol agent operating out of his home, a two-drawer file cabinet, and a Jeep. In Border Patrol lore, Tacna was a place you *never* wanted to work. Agents used to mention Tacna in the same breath with Presidio and Sierra Blanca, Texas, as the absolute worst places to live, but many who were assigned to Tacna enjoyed both the area and the work. A new station was opened in Wellton in 1990 to accommodate several dozen agents instead of the handful who had served at Tacna from the 1960s into the 1980s. A newer station is being built for up to 350 agents. The number of agents nationwide is expected to swell to 20,000 in 2010.

A multipronged effort at Wellton has begun to pay dividends, though many observers doubt the flow of attempted crossings can be cut to absolute zero, meaning there will always be a need for Border Patrol here, as a deterrent if nothing else. From May 2007 to May 2008 alien apprehensions at Wellton dropped 88 percent and the number of smuggling vehicles crossing the desert was virtually nil after rising to several hundred a few years before. As of 2008, a number of factors have come into play. A stout barrier along the borderline inhibits vehicles. Yuma Sector adopted a zero-tolerance policy: instead of being returned immediately to their home country, every crosser now faces "delivered consequences," and most are prosecuted. The state of Arizona has passed an employer sanctions law that punishes businesses that knowingly hire undocumented aliens. The United States and Arizona economies sometimes sputter, so fewer unskilled jobs in construction and service industries are available.

In addition, Border Patrol has established an encampment near the border; it is called Camp Grip, as in "get a grip on the border," and it is manned 24/7, drastically reducing the time required for agents to intercept crossers. Too, Wellton Station now increasingly mans permanent checkpoints on the highway. In the field, remote sensors detecting vehicles and people are more widespread and sophisticated; these include ground radar units mounted on trucks. Ironically, the electronic age is also a boon for crossers, who can now more easily obtain phony identification and attempt to enter through ports of entry instead of the open desert, and who can communicate with their "pick-up" cars by disposable cell phones.

Wellton Station is one of three stations within the Yuma Sector, which is headquartered in Yuma. The scope of the problem and the vision for solution is explained by Chief Patrol Agent of Yuma Sector Paul A. Beeson, who says that by all accounts 2005 was the high-water mark in terms of smuggling and illegal alien activity, as Yuma Sector agents caught over 138,000 aliens without papers, smugglers, and other criminals and intercepted 2,700 vehicles—over 7 a day—illegally trying to cross 118 miles of borderline. With a doubling of the number of agents, a commensurate increase in the amount of equipment, and improvements in policy and tactics, Yuma had only 8,363 arrests in 2008, a drop of 94 percent. In the first few months of 2009 the trend showed a further decline of 40 percent from the previous year. The heightened number of agents also lowered the number of fatalities. The number of aliens known to have died in the desert in 2005 was 51, but fell to 5 in 2008, not counting the remains found of persons who had died in previous years. Vehicle crossings have fallen over 90 percent, to 240. Chief Beeson notes, "While we have experienced a tremendous level of success here, we know that there are still weaknesses. We have a pretty good handle on what is traversing our area, and some do manage to evade arrest. We know that number is relatively small, but I hate to lose even one."

These declines in alien deaths, apprehensions, and attempts to cross illegally in vehicles indicate major improvements for the health and safety of not only aliens but also borderland citizens and Border Patrol agents. In America before 9/11 the new numbers might be cause for celebration, slowing the pace, or taking a day off. However, Yuma is but one sector of many, and 2008 is but one year of many. America's border history is a cautionary tale of hard-earned gains easily eroded or summits not quite reached. Chief Beeson reminds us, "We still have threats. We still have vulnerabilities. We are better positioned today than we were a few years back and we've seen some tremendous benefits as a result, but we're not done. We still have to have as part of our strategy the ability to detect, iden-tify, classify, respond, and resolve any cross-border incursions. We are well-situated here to do a good portion of that, but we're not there yet. I will tell you that I say we have operational control over a good portion of our border but it's not at the level where we're satisfied that we've addressed all the threats and vulnerabilities in this area."

Air support for Wellton is based at Yuma International Airport and shares its runways with Yuma Marine Corps Air Station, which specializes in pilot training for U.S. Navy and Marine Corps attack and fighter jets, as well as combat helicopters. Yuma's Border Patrol "air force" started with one secondhand airplane fifty years ago and now includes eleven sophis-ticated aircraft. The pilots match their missions with EC-120 Eurocopters, AS-350B3 Eurocopters, Piper Super Cubs, a UH-1H Huey, and a Cessna 182. The pilots spend significant time patrolling the Wellton area, for it presents the most challenging tracking, pursuits, and rescues.

Aircraft are a very effective tool. Nationwide in the fiscal year 2004, for example, Customs and Border Protection aircraft flew almost 46,000 hours while apprehending 96,341 persons and assisting in seizing $103.6 million of illegal drugs. This works out to 2.1 arrests and $2,259 of contra-band for each hour flown. The number of rescues and prevented deaths are not officially tallied but number in the thousands, especially in the

Wellton arena, where in 2005 pilots apprehended 2.3 aliens per hour and seized over two tons of drugs and 92 vehicles. By 2008 at Yuma the program's success rose dramatically as the numbers fell about 90 percent to 0.3 aliens per hour and seven vehicles seized during the year; the amount of drugs seized per hour remained constant.

Total success would be zero apprehended, not millions: no aliens, no drugs, no vehicles, no terrorists. In the words of Yuma's chief pilot, Howard Aitken, "The aircraft are another tool in the tool box that is utilized to deter and provide certainty of arrest. If an alien, smuggler, or terrorist knows that he cannot enter in Yuma without being caught, he tends to try other places or not come at all. The other tools are tactical infrastructure, more boots on the ground, and Operation Streamline. The deterrence factor is big." Operation Streamline is a program used to prosecute nearly all persons caught entering the country illegally within the Yuma Sector's area of responsibility.

But the denominator in this story is the border agents themselves. They are common folks doing an uncommon job. Like police work anywhere, days of humdrum patrol and investigation are interspersed with moments of fear and heroics. Shots have been fired here, but the real count is in persons rescued from heat and fatigue, aliens apprehended, and tons of drugs confiscated. There is a toll of human life. Hundreds of aliens are known to have died in this crossing, but the total is unknown. Plane crashes have killed three Border Patrol pilots and an agent on duty in the region, and four ground agents have died, two in car crashes, one run down by a smuggler fleeing to Mexico, and one drowned as he attempted to save aliens caught in the swirling Colorado River.

Sometimes public attitudes toward agents are wary or even hostile. Expecting the worst, author Aron Spilken approached Border Patrol for information while writing his account of the Salvadorans who were rescued or died in the southwestern Arizona desert early in July of 1980. He assumed that "[p]eople who did such work must be harsh and insensitive. . . . What I found instead were public-spirited people with a difficult job. . . . Certainly the desperate energy that [the agents] invested in saving the Salvadorans' lives could only have come from a certain nobility of spirit" (*Escape!*, page 4).

Time at a Border Patrol station is measured in daily logs and monthly reports, but it is remembered by traumatic events. At Wellton, agents remember those thirteen deaths and the rescues of those Salvadorans in 1980. Even though the massive search, rescue, and recovery occurred in a neighboring station's area, Wellton agents were called to help. They also mourn the death of junior pilot Lester Haynie on June 14, 1985, when his small patrol plane clipped a power line. Then five Salvadoran women and children perished in the Mohawk Dunes a few days later. Four years later pilot David F. Roberson died in an early morning plane crash. Without warning his Husky A-1 plunged straight into the ground from less than one hundred feet, and he died instantly, even before the plane was destroyed by fire. That was July 14, 1989, but it still haunts those who knew him. In May of 2001, a group of twenty-six aliens followed their coyotes across the border. For days they wandered west of the Granite Mountains. Fourteen died. Agents have that tragedy posted on their mental calendar, too, whether they were on duty then or not.

And each agent will remember the time he or she first rescued an alien from the desert or the clutches of a smuggler, or discovered the remains of someone long dead, or administered a drink to a heat-exhausted child or first aid to a terrified alien injured by a smuggler.

It takes special people to confront the desert daily, to ride out to meet armed smugglers, to retain compassion when threatened, to remain calm when situations fly out of control, and to serve with honor. Welcome. Meet the agents at Wellton Station who have chosen desert duty.

On the Line

Glen Payne cutting sign (looking for tracks). Photo by Bill Broyles, 1984.

CHET WILSON

Chester "Chet" Wilson served in the U.S. Border Patrol from 1954 to 1980, including Tacna Station from 1956 to 1959. He currently lives in Alpine, Texas, where he served as a justice of the peace for Brewster County for thirteen years.

The way I was raised, if you work for somebody, you're riding for the brand. You either work for them or get out. I'm from Del Rio, Texas—I was raised there, though I wasn't born there. I was born out on the Nueces River, way up north of Uvalde in Edwards County. I was born premature—three pounds, three ounces, but mother was a registered nurse and I survived. Pa, my dad, got killed in '43, and I didn't have anything but my grandparents. As far as what I learned to do and what to do, I danged sure didn't like working on a ranch. Years ago, I remember coming into my grandparents' ranch one night after church—I went with my grandma—and we found aliens sitting outside the yard. We had about a half-acre around the house, had a garden and fruit trees and all. A couple immigrants were hungry and wanted something to eat, but they hadn't even been in the yard. They were sitting politely by the gate, waiting for somebody to come back.

Eventually I went in the military service. Then the Korean War started. I went to Korea and came back. They had a big push for border patrolmen back then. Eisenhower got elected and had appointed General Swing for the Commissioner of Immigration, so the Patrol had all this stuff going on in 1954.

I thought I might like it, because I had neighbors that were Border Patrol. Then I knew of several other Border Patrolmen, and I'd had a—oh, I wouldn't exactly say a run-in—with them, when my buddy and I were

Chet Wilson. Photo by Bill Broyles, 2006.

about thirteen years old down on the river fishing. Of course we was naked as jaybirds. A guy on the Mexico side took a shot at us and hit the sand right there and kicked it up. It burnt my naked butt. We got over to our bicycles, and we was gonna go home, get our guns, come back, and shoot that son of a bitch.

While we were putting our clothes on, out stepped two Border Patrol-men. "What you boys doin' here?" Gawdang scared the hell out of us, two uniformed Border Patrolmen. "Well, we *were* gonna fish. We're settin' a trot line across this little place." They said, "What was that shot?" And I said, "That gawdang son of a bitch shot at us," and you could see him up on the bluff over there that's just north of the bridge there at Del Rio, a mile or so up there. One of the patrolmen had a rifle, so I said, "Lend me that rifle, I'll shoot that. . . ." They said, "No. You boys get on your bicycles and get home." They'd hide by the river and slip down there looking for aliens. I thought, "Well, that might be fun." So I went ahead and gave it a try. I liked it, and here I am!

I reported in at El Paso in 1954. From El Paso, they sent me to Fort

Hancock Station that had four or five men then. I stayed there for a while, and then I went to the Border Patrol Academy. I was born and raised on a ranch, and we didn't get electricity until, oh, about 1945, just before the war was over, and REA, the Rural Electrification Administration, came through and we had electricity. The only light we had had was kerosene lanterns, so I learned how to wash them globes without breaking them, and trimmed the wicks and filled the lamps full of oil. They didn't call it kerosene; they called it coal oil. When I was a trainee there at Fort Hancock, we had this patrol car, and in the trunk was a wooden box somebody built, with six lanterns in it, with red lenses on them. So my primary duty, no matter what shift I was working, was to get that ready before sundown, before the four-to-midnight crew went to work. I had to make sure the lanterns were full of oil and had to clean the chimneys and trim the wicks. I had to do that extra duty, but I didn't argue with them.

In fact, back in those days, it seemed to me like every now and then some of the supervisors—seniors, as they called them—had contests over who could fire the most probies, new guys on probation. I was fortunate. There was a classmate there that caused a little bit of problem, and they got after him. That gave me a break. They were too busy trying to fire *him*.

Then I got transferred over here to Tacna, Arizona, in September of 1956. I was patrol inspector in charge of one man, name of Glendon "Bud" Pagett. When Bud transferred back to Yuma, they sent Ed Tuffly out here. Bud later went to Customs and went to Del Rio. I was the best man at Ed's wedding. He married Shirley Kelland, Roy Kelland's daughter. Roy owned the whole town of Tacna, nearly. He had the water company and had a real estate office, and little businesses. He had bought a whole bunch of land way back a long time ago, for ten, fifteen cents an acre. He was a good ol' boy.

Anyway, Tacna Station was really Wellton Station back then, because the station was in my house and I happened to live in Wellton. When the wind blew, the old linoleum floor would puff up because of cracks between the floor boards, and the dust would fog up on each side. Oh, it was terrible! I don't think my place even had a street number or nothin' else. I know right where it was, though.

Leo Dunnigan, a pilot out of Tucson, called me one day on the radio, and he said, "Meet us at the airport," there in Wellton. I asked something about, "Who's 'we'?" "Well, I have General Partridge with me." Frank H. Partridge was one of General Joseph Swing's right-hand men, and "Jumping Joe" Swing ran the Border Patrol. We both got there to the airport about the same time. They were in a Cessna and come in and landed, and Bud Pagett and I drove up there. They got out, and this little general walked around looking at my Jeep.

He said, "We were thinking about going and checking your office. Where's your office located?"

I said, "Right there," pointing at that Jeep. It was dirty. We'd been out working and were covered with dust. We'd been out somewhere off up the country, and I could tell he wasn't wanting to get in that nasty Jeep. It was just a two-seater, you know, canvas top, no doors on it or nothin'. I said, "Well, if you want to go to town, the coffee shop, I'd be glad to take you. Leo can drive, or you can drive, I don't care. Bud and I'll ride in the back."

"Well, what do you do with your reports and all that?"

I said, "Well, sir, I've got a two-drawer filing cabinet."

He said, "Where's that?"

I said, "It's in my bedroom at my house. Do you want to go look at them?" That's one of the first things they want to do, look at your files. And I added, "You're more than welcome."

"Hell, no, I don't want to go in your private residence."

I said, "Well, my wife'll fix us a glass of tea or whatever." He said no, so we visited there a little while, and they took off and went to back to Yuma.

When I came in the Patrol, we wore khakis, and you had to buy them yourself. Later on, they switched to green, and you had to buy your own green uniforms. They didn't furnish us nothin'. I put in a whole year before I ever got a badge. The only thing they furnished you was a pistol and the ammunition. You had to buy your own belt, holster, and handcuff case. They issued you handcuffs, and I've still got my original pair. All of that came out of your pocket, this $3,675 a year salary, which really wasn't much.

I got acquainted with everything, and I guess sometime in '57 there was a cinder block house, pretty nice, up there in Tacna, owned by a family named Farr, and they had a service station there, so they were taking care of the house, renting it out. Ol' Roy Kelland told me about the house, so I moved up there, with the office, which was that little filing cabinet with two drawers. And just like that, a whole Border Patrol station was back in Tacna.

We finally got a sedan. It was a '54 worn-out Ford that didn't even have a radio in it. It had a spotlight on it, though, where you could put a red lens, one of those red lenses with the little spring deal to snap over it. That's the way we stopped traffic. Highway 80 was two lanes: one going west, and one going east. For traffic checks we got a little kit, had three lights in it that had a little swinging reflector deal, and it blinked—battery operated. I think it held like four D-cell batteries. And that was it.

We had canned sardines for emergency rations. In fact, a lot of times when we picked up aliens, they packed cans of sardines. A lot of times they'd go off and leave them in the Jeep. We'd find them after we done booted them out over there at Yuma. Everyone we caught we had to take to Yuma. We barely even had an office let alone a cell here at Tacna. I don't remember what year or how many aliens we caught, but Ed Tuffly and I caught more aliens than what the whole damned Yuma Station did, so we were doing our job.

Tacna was a relief from Yuma. I'm sure the old man is dead now who threatened me over there, but according to the FBI report the only thing I did wrong is threaten him back. Threatening me is one thing—threatening my family, that's something else. I told him, "Mister, I'm gonna tell you one damned thing. If anything ever happens to any of my family that I can remotely connect to you, any of your men, or anything else"—and he had hundreds of *braceros*—"you'd better give your soul to God, because I'm gonna get your ass. You understand me?" At least that's what the report said I said.

When I was working at San Luis, south of Yuma, we had a drag road that came all the way out to the mountains. At that time, you had to carry extra gas with you and everything, because you could run out of gas. With the drag road, you got in the sand dunes. You burn fuel pretty fast in them old military-style Jeeps. You had to put it in four-wheel drive, sometimes low range. I've been to the far end of that fence and nearly ran out of gas, so I got permission from the Mexican Customs to come to the end of the fence and get out on the paved Mexican highway and come back to the United States right through the port of entry.

One time I come out the end of the fence and made the circle, got on the Mexican Highway, paved road, going back in, and lo and behold, "Wooo!" sirens and red lights, a Mexican highway patrolman pulled me over. The first thing he wanted was my gun. "No, señor." He said, "Well, you don't have any right over here." I said, "Oh, yeah, I got permission. If you want to find out, you just follow me." I knew better than to argue with him. I didn't want to have to kill him, and I certainly didn't want him shooting me. So I just walked over, got back in my Jeep, and cranked it up. He's got his red light going, so I just told him, "Follow me." We went right through San Luis Rio Colorado, and right up to the port and stopped. He was kind of embarrassed, because the Mexican officer in charge there had given me permission. It wasn't written or nothin', he just told me. I was well acquainted with him, because anytime there was a problem there they called me.

At Tacna usually we'd go to work early in the morning, like six o'clock in the morning, and we'd drive the canal looking for tracks. If we didn't have anything there, we'd come down and cut sign on the drag road. And if we didn't have nothin' going on, then we'd go back up the other way. Some of the supervisors, sector supervisors, felt like we ought to be doing more diverse activity, like check the train once in a while, and do traffic check. We varied our days and many a time we'd work on the highway at night.

A lot of times we wouldn't come south unless the pilot cut sign on somebody on the other side. Tommy Tomlinson, a Yuma Border Patrol pilot, would come out. He'd come over in a Super Cub. In fact, one time I was at home so asleep that I never did hear him, and Mrs. Farr, a neighbor lady, come banging on the door, saying, "I think that man in the airplane wants to talk to you." He'd land right across the highway. And sometimes I'd bring him to the house and we'd have coffee or we'd stop at a coffee shop, depending what day of the week it was, and if the coffee shop was open.

He was a very small man, and I think one time they tried to wash him out because of his height. Pilots were supposed to be five-foot-eight, and he was like five-foot-five or six. They gave him a hard time, but they put him on, and he made a danged-good pilot. He was already a good pilot, a World War II fighter pilot, evidently. But I enjoyed working with him, because he didn't just put in his five hours and then go home.

I've seen some of them pilots that could run out of gas in two and a half hours, if they didn't want to work. They just sat in the hangar. I've seen several of them like that. In fact, I told one guy, "If you're gonna work like that, we don't want you to come over here no more. We don't need you." Hell, they do more harm than good. When the aliens happen to see the plane, and then the plane pulls off and goes home, they get up and they scatter. Then you'll find one over here, and one way up over yonder, and one back up over here. When the plane is still around, they bunch up in one spot—even if the pilots don't see them.

Tomlinson was darned good. He found an airplane that cracked up down there, and led us to it. We picked up the pilot, and hauled him and his passengers out. He was the vice-president of the National Cash Register Company. They hadn't had no water, and they'd been there a day and a half. We had one of these desert cooler canvas water bags. I gave them that to drink, and they took big swigs, "Hoo-wee! Salida! Salty!" And spit it out. Hell, it was just ol' Tacna tap water that we drank every day.

If you're gonna try to catch aliens, in my opinion, you need to get out early, and a lot of times you're gonna stay late. There was no such thing as a Fair Labor Standard Act for agents. In fact, in my opinion, if you're running a trail or working somebody or just investigating, you can't be looking at the clock to see what time you're gonna get off. You get off when the job's done. One time when I was over there at Yuma, we worked seventy-two hours before we got home. Of course, my wife was on pins and needles, and she called in to check on us but they hadn't heard from us, and then they started a big search. Well, hell, the radio didn't work worth a hoot.

Our walkie-talkies weren't too well developed back in them days either. The first Jeep I got over here, it had a radio in it, but it didn't work half the time. And then when we got a sedan to work traffic check, it didn't have a radio in *that*, period, no radio. It was a '54 hand-me-down sedan. And of course it had I don't remember how many miles, but umpteen jillion miles. They wanted us to work nights. I had a deputy sheriff ask me one time, "Damn! Have all your bosses been vaccinated with the same needle?" And I looked at him, "What do you mean?" He said, "The dumbass needle!" That's a little embarrassing, when you have another law enforcement agency ask you somethin' like that.

One time on traffic check, three o'clock in the afternoon, probably 115 degrees, there we were in dress uniform, with wool shirts, dress trousers, and everything, Smokey Bear hat, and the sweat just a-pourin'. This game warden pulled up there, stopped, and visited. We batted the breeze a little bit, and he said, "What stupid son of a bitch has y'all workin' out here in those type uniforms?!" We had a rough duty uniform then, but when you're checking traffic, meeting tourists and everything, you'd be in *dress* uniform. And I said, "Oh, Officer So-and-So, do you know our Chief?" The chief was standing right there.

That chief was somethin' else. I never saw him in a rough-duty uniform. He'd wear a dress uniform all the time, because he sits in an office. Very seldom does he get out and work in the field. I don't figure a man's a good supervisor unless he knows firsthand how it is out there. And that's a problem the Border Patrol's got. Back in those days you had to have experience as an immigrant inspector or investigator before you could get promoted above first-line supervisor, which is what they called a senior patrol inspector then. Nowadays you don't.

Tacna, like I say, was a hardship station, but it was no hardship on me or my wife, Pherba. Ed Tuffly was single then. We always invited him over every now and then, you know, when we were gonna grill a steak or somethin', and watch Friday Night Fights. I had a TV. I don't think he did, but he'd come over there, and my wife would fix us something to eat, and we'd sit there. We didn't ever get drunk.

Pete Newman was the sheriff when I first came. I remember one time they called me. He said, "Hey, c'mon, you're on this jury." We got a coroner's jury together and went out where one of the braceros out there found blond-looking hair, and there was a silk scarf deal around part of it. We just knew it was a murder victim. So we go out there, stopped alongside the highway, and walked off down there. Oh, this Mexican was shook. He'd found a body. Me and another guy got down there and went ahead and uncovered and exhumed it. "Hell, that ain't no human! That's a dog!" It was somebody's dog, some tourist's maybe. Their dog had died, and they stopped and went down there and buried the dog in that soft sand.

One time Bud and I came across three Mexicans in a truck down near Tule Well. We tracked them down, saw where they went across, run them down, got them outta there. I come that close to killing one damned guy. He had a .22 rolling block rifle and pulled that damned thing out when I come around the back of that truck. And I just damned near shot him. But I got the gun away from him, and it was loaded with .22 short. This truck was dual wheeled and had a whole bunch of wood they were stealing. They'd take it back to San Luis and sell it. But they're stealing it over here in the United States, off the gunnery range and Cabeza Prieta Wildlife Refuge.

I've been at Dateland many times. A highway patrolman and I walked in on an armed robbery right there one time. These two punks was robbing this place, and we didn't know it. We come driving up there and got out. Just as they come out, we walked in. They dropped their guns.

We had a very similar incident like that happen over at the checkpoint close to the Salton Sea. Here come a car zooming up, gawdang, a bunch of guys. They stopped a little ways from us. They get out with their hands up. Hell, when they did that, we knew there's something strange goin' on. I grabbed a shotgun and walked down there. In a few minutes, here come a highway patrolman. The robbers must have thought we were a roadblock to get them! They stopped just short and then decided, "We'd better give up. There's some behind us and some in front." They had pulled a big burglary and locked the employees up in the cold storage locker room there in Brawley. We didn't even know about it.

One time down by Roll, Arizona, Bud Pagett and I caught two guys that were wanted men. They had escaped prison and had killed a highway patrolman in a wreck. Bud and I were going down the highway, and I was driving, and a danged car just—shoom!—passed us flying. I could tell he was law enforcement. Directly here come a deputy sheriff—and I don't even remember his name—he was an older guy driving about 40–45 miles an hour, and he just barely caught up with us, with his light going. He was following these others. I flagged him down and asked him, "What the hell is going on?" He said, "You didn't hear about the big deal?" I said, "No. What big deal you talking about?" Here we've got a radio and everything, but it's just strictly Border Patrol.

He told us then, "Two guys escaped from prison." They stole a car, then they wrecked the car, killed the highway patrolman, and then they stole another car over in Buckeye. They bought gas over in Roll, but took off without paying for it. And here they were. I told my partner, "They ain't gonna be on this road. They're gonna get run over if they stay out on this road. Let's get off down in the valley." So we go off down there, and we're going along. I said, "You know, they're hid somewhere." The railroad ran up around there, and a road went under it. "Let's go over here and check." We go over there, see these fresh vehicle tracks turn off. I backed up. I could see the rear end of this car, could tell it was a Chevrolet, and it was blue or green, I don't remember the color.

"That might be them. Let's see." I shut the Jeep off and got out. I walked up there and looked, and one guy was in the front seat, and one in the back. I checked and it looked like them. I got my pistol out, and I told my partner, "They're in there. I'll take the driver; you take the guy in the back seat. And when we bust them," I said, "if he makes the wrong move, you blow his ass off." My partner said, "I don't know if I could do that." I said, "By god, you'd better, or you'll get killed." I go up there, I yanked the door open, and I stuck my pistol right in that guy's ear. He didn't have no gun on him. We got the other one out. They didn't have no gun. They supposedly were considered armed and dangerous. Fine, we got them. We called in and told them where we were. Within a matter of minutes, whew, there's everybody all over us!

But then it comes out in the news that the FBI captured them. It sure wasn't FBI. There was FBI *somewhere*, because they showed up eventually, but Bud had his handcuffs on one, I had mine on the other. Here the FBI comes, of course, big as squat, telling two gawdang stupid Border Patrol-men, "We're gonna take them." I said, "Fine. But I want my damn hand-cuffs back." That happened right here at Tacna Station. And 85 percent of the DEA arrests at one time—I read a consolidated report about it—were made by Border Patrol. "DEA arrested," it said. Well, hell, DEA never arrested nobody!

I enjoyed my stay in Tacna. It was very good, and the only reason I left was a promotion. Tacna was a hardship station; you're supposed to put in two years and then move on. They'd offer you these places like New York, Chicago, Detroit. They did offer me San Francisco, Los Angeles, and Portland, Oregon, but I turned them down. I'm not a big-city man. I wasn't gonna raise my family in that environment. I've been to them. I've been on details all over the place, but I ain't moving my family to a place like that. They finally offered me a supervisor job over in El Centro. That left Ed here by himself. Later I found out they had appointed him to run the Tacna Station, and he was the right man.

I like outdoor work. A lot of times you don't know what you have until you're in a position where you don't have it. After I retired, I didn't have a government vehicle to run around, and I didn't have that government credit card to buy that fuel. But I do a lot of the same things now: I go hunting and tootlin' around everywhere.

I never thought of anything as being a highlight. You tend to remember a lot of good things and forget some of the bad things. I made lots of friends over the time. I'd like for *all* the people to know that most of the agents are dedicated, hard-working, federal employees.

I've been involved in a number of other things—some of them were interesting, some of them wasn't so interesting . . . like finding dead people. I went out south of Tacna, to the dump to clean a bunch of birds, doves or quail, one day after hunting. There was a set of tracks. "That's a wet Mexican," I thought. But it was my day off, and it was in the evening. I got through cleaning them and everything, and I saw where he went. It was getting dark so I thought, "I'll get him in the morning." Next morning Bud Pagett and I tracked him. He went across the canal, right on down, under a big ol' mesquite tree, and we got to looking. There he was, laying there looking at us. We hollered at him to come out, but he didn't come out.

I got me a couple of rocks. "Dang it, you'd better come out of there!" The ol' boy wouldn't even talk to us. He was laying on his stomach, with his hands kind of like that under his chin, looking right at us. Damn, I drawed back and I whopped him with a rock, he just went "Ugh!" I said, "Come out of there!" Shoot, I didn't want to get under there. He wouldn't come out, so I had that other rock, and I whopped him again. He still wouldn't come out. I went around and crawled in the way he'd gone in, and got hold of a foot. He didn't resist. I started backing him out of there, through gawdang mesquite thorns and everything. We got out, and when I cleared,

I just pitched him. He hit the ground and flopped, and I thought, "Oh, shit, something's wrong with him." He was dying.

I went over, and he couldn't hardly talk. I took him up to Ward and Jesse's store and got him an Orange Crush or a Coca-Cola. That's what I used to get them to rejuvenate them. I got him to drink some, and he started talking. I said, "Where's all your buddies?" He just pointed, and then he got to where he could talk a little bit. We loaded him up, come on south, and he'd point out which way. We went up there and found where they split up, and we seen his track goin' this way, and the other went that-a-way. Heck, we didn't go 200 yards, and there his buddy was, *muerto*. Gawdang. That's the way it was.

ED TUFFLY

*Now living in Oklahoma, Edward "Ed" Tuffly was in
the U.S. Border Patrol from 1956 to 1981, and he was
assigned to Tacna Station from 1958 to 1962 and 1967 to
1978. Two of his sons are in the Border Patrol.*

I was first assigned to the Tacna Station in 1958 and served
there until 1962. In those days the desert south of there was almost a virgin
area to explore. The old mines were pretty much the way the old timers left
them, with lots of purple bottles laying around. The old Camino Diablo
was fascinating to explore. Old graves were pretty much untouched. As
more people got four-wheel-drive vehicles and started going down there,
vandals and antique collectors destroyed much of the history of the area.
The old graves of many of the Gold Rush '49ers will probably never be
found again. The old Papago Ranch was pretty much intact. We used to
take extra gas with us to pump water for wildlife. The last time I was there,
vandals and thieves coming from Ajo had pretty much destroyed the place.
They even stole the old engine that was there to run the well. Tule Well
camp was pretty much intact last time I was there, but woodcutters and
other traffic crossing the border were getting pretty close to it.

In 1962 I was replaced by Billy D. Peiser and transferred to Jackman,
Maine, and in 1965 I moved to Brackettville, Texas. In 1964, the Wellton
Station was closed and Billy D. was transferred to Marfa, Texas, where he
still resides. The area was unpatrolled for about three years, until I came
back. During that period several labor-intensive agribusinesses, citrus and
grapes, moved into the Wellton, Tacna, Horn, and Hyder areas. Droves
of illegals started coming through the desert again south of Wellton and
Tacna, many of them dying in the desert. For mostly humanitarian reasons

in 1967 it was decided to reopen a Border Patrol station in Tacna. They wanted somebody who knew this desert. I had already spent time here and knew this damned desert, so I was "selected" to get the station going.

Tacna wasn't a hardship station then. The hardship thing started just before I left in '78. I never thought it was a hardship. Hell, I was a Dryden, Texas, kid. It takes a hundred acres to raise a sheep there. My dad was an Army man, and we lived on Army pay. I liked Tacna. The men always liked to work here, but their wives couldn't stand to live in the isolation, 45 miles from Yuma, and 160 from Phoenix. They didn't like it.

I married a Tacna girl, Shirley Kelland, and I was married to her for twenty-five years. Two of our sons are in Border Patrol. Chet Wilson was my best man. Roy B. Kelland, my father-in-law, owned most of Tacna. He was *very* friendly with Border Patrol. Roy had been a Missouri highway patrolman. As a matter of fact, he damned-near got killed when they killed Pretty Boy Floyd. And then he worked for the Yuma County sheriff here for years and years. I don't know how, honestly, because he had that Ralph's Mill, a roadside gas station and diner. Did you ever hear of Ralph's Mill? He had slot machines in there, and they played a little poker in there, too. Roy died in November of 1981.

The bosses at sector headquarters didn't tell me how to run the station. I knew what to do. I'd already been in the Border Patrol, since 1956, and been at Tacna before, so when they sent me back there, I was already home. When we reopened in '67, I already had eleven years in the Border Patrol. So I pretty well knew what to do. So they just give me the reins and tried to give me what we needed, as finances allowed. We were always broke. The Border Patrol was the bastard stepchild of the Immigration Service. The only boss we ever had that liked us was General Joe Swing. The only president that ever liked us, I think, was Dwight Eisenhower.

The drag roads saved many lives. Often aliens in trouble would wait for us on the drags or, to save face, stop just after crossing a drag so it would look like bad luck rather than surrender. The Hobbs drag road was the first we built, in late 1967 or early 1968. At that time the station consisted of two men, Kenneth Hobbs and me. It was Kenny's assignment to check that drag every workday morning for footprints, so it was natural to call it the Hobbs drag. Kenny was from West Texas. He was a hard worker, willing to work day and night. He was stationed in Yuma and got "volunteered" to serve in Tacna as my partner. In my opinion Kenny

Ed Tuffly. Photo by Bill Broyles, 2006.

was a natural-born border patrolman, very good in his work. He was later transferred to Brackettville, Texas, then later to Rock Springs, Texas, where he retired as Patrol Agent in Charge.

We built the Vidrios drag road, I think in the early 1970s. As the illegals learned to go around the drags to the east, we kept building drags farther to the east. First the Big Pass drag, then the Mohawk, then the Vidrios which ended at the Yuma County line. East of there was the Gila Bend Station's responsibility. Where we broke the crust building drags, lush vegetation grew with every rain. A herd of about fifteen rare Sonoran pronghorn started hanging around the Mohawk drag. We tried to protect them from poachers and predators by not passing up a chance to shoot a coyote and kept pretty close track of vehicular traffic in the area.

We relied on our Border Patrol pilot a lot. Tommy Tomlinson was so good at sign cutting and tracking that he took over patrolling the drags by aircraft. He would detect entries from La Jollita in the La Jolla Wash, and then determine whether they were headed for Wellton or Tacna by cutting their sign through Coyote Wash. He would then run the Hobbs and Big Pass drags. Meanwhile we checked drags near Interstate 8 and the Wellton-

Mohawk canal to determine if anyone had come out of the desert. That pretty well narrowed down the area they were probably in. Many times Tomlinson would track them down, land the airplane, and have them sitting under the wing of the plane when we got there. He was an Army Air Corps pilot who flew P-40s, then P-38s, over Europe during World War II. In my opinion, he was the best pilot the Border Patrol ever had. Then one morning he preflighted his plane, then took off and noticed the engine cowling flapping in the breeze. He told me that very morning it was time to retire, which he did. He saved many lives in that desert. That type of flying is very dangerous. Sign cutting altitude is seventy feet, and we could generally hear his stall buzzer when he keyed his radio.

Pilot Fritz Karl hit a static power line that is practically invisible when seen against the background of the Gila Mountains. Agent John Blue was with him and they crashed in the median of I-8 right at milepost 40. Fritz was a great guy. He was witty and a fun guy to be around. He flew Corsairs off aircraft carriers during the Korean War and, I think, World War II, also. He flew transport aircraft for the Border Patrol airlift until they were all grounded. Those transport aircraft were used for alien removal and transporting prisoners for the U.S. Marshals Service. They were also used to fly "dignitaries"—D.C. and regional big shots. The transport pilots were then transferred to Border Patrol sectors to fly Super Cubs.

Pilot Clair Culver encountered a saguaro cactus and crashed. He was keeping track of a suspect vehicle for us southeast of Raven Butte when he got too low and clipped a saguaro. The plane flipped and crashed on its back. Clair got himself out of the plane and started walking in a daze towards Yuma. He was rescued by a Marine Corps helicopter and flown to the hospital in Yuma. How he survived the crash was really miraculous. Three of the four bolts that held the pilot's seat broke and the cross members over his head were crushed by his helmet. He suffered severe spinal injuries from the crash and was given disability retirement from the Border Patrol. Pilots have told me that winds in the Raven Butte area are very tricky and especially dangerous for low flying.

Clair was an infantry officer in Korea and received the Silver Star for bravery in combat. I don't know how he got into flying, but he had lots of experience flying various aircraft for the Border Patrol. He flew Beavers on the northern border, military-type aircraft during the Cuban situation in Florida, and Beech Barons during "Operation Intercept." He was one of the finest men I have ever met, very modest, charitable, and just an all-around good guy.

The first time I worked at Tacna, Chester Wilson was my boss. I did two years in Yuma before I came here to work with Chester. Bud Pagett wanted to put his kids in a parochial school, and I was tired of working midnight-to-eight train check in Yuma. Ol' Bob Jarrett, sector chief, arranged a transfer on the phone one day. I was single. I put everything I owned in the back of a green '56 Ford car and moved to Tacna, at no expense to the government.

Actually, I guess I took over from Frank Quilter at Tacna in 1960. They had sent him here after Chester Wilson left, but he was soon moved back to Yuma. I had some good guys work for me. The first one was Kenny Hobbs. And then they sent me Jim Woods, fresh out of the Marine Corps. He was a good hand, and I always appreciated his work ethic and loyalty. Then they sent me Danny Walker. He and I are still friends; he was another natural-born agent. Jimmy Reynolds—he's dead. Dale Johnson was a good one. Mike Higgins, now dead, became a senior at Casa Grande. He was the under-sheriff of Cochise County before he came in the Border Patrol, and I think before that he was in the Army. They sent Melvin "Dean" Hall to Tacna for a bit. Dean was a good one. Another fine officer, Fred Gaedke, served in Tacna during this time, too. Richard Ruffel, a hard charger, is now retired. Steve Parker had formal education in law enforcement and was a fine officer. Border Patrol was a stepping stone in his advancement in law enforcement. He and I clashed over my smoking in his presence. After I quit smoking and learned how offensive cigarette smoke is, I realized that I owe him an apology. Other men who worked Tacna Station with me were Bill Carter (son of Commissioner Harlon B. Carter), Jack Weaver, Cliff Erickson, Ray Putnam, Charlie Mazon, and Neil Jensen. We did the job.

The closest we ever came to a shoot-out was a load the DEA (Drug Enforcement Administration) was bringing through, and we almost had a big shoot-out over a load of marijuana. We caught it right up near the end of High Tanks Road. That's where we used to waylay them. We had that sensor down there, and we caught a lot of dope until I had an old boy mess up. I always told them to write on that form, "following routine patrol, we observed traffic coming north on High Tanks Road with lights off." That's all the probable cause you needed. But this one guy did the paperwork and put on there, "responding to sensor." The DEA and U.S. Attorney took that to court, and we lost the case. All those thousands and thousands of dollars we spent down there was for nothin' after that, over a slip of the pen. When word about the sensor got out, we never caught another load of dope in that area.

And, prosecution of drug smugglers was for naught, a waste of tax-payer's money. The courts turned smugglers loose faster than we could catch them, but there're a lot of ways to do justice. I finally told the men, "When you catch a load, just tell the smuggler goodbye, and then let him tell whoever bankrolled that load, 'They caught me.' Then let him explain to the boss why he isn't in jail." We got the load; we got the vehicle—nobody said we had to give those back. The way I ran things is probably why I never got higher than a Grade 11. I didn't generate enough paper-work for upstairs, and DEA had the attitude that if they didn't catch it, they didn't want it caught. They didn't want us catching it either, because we were making them look bad.

After I reopened this place in '67, we caught more aliens than the Yuma Station did. Our area was *full* of aliens. We built the station up to eight men, eight men counting me. We finally got the line under control, but aliens watch and learn. They are smart and know the game we played. They knew how to time us on the drags. They knew at daylight that airplane was gonna cut their sign. And, they had a good word-of-mouth intelligence system. So unless they were really dumb, they knew they had to high-tail it out of here. But you know, these old campesinos who used to come through this desert, we were all buddies. It was a game we played. Some-times we win, and sometimes they win. But these were all good guys, old country boys.

I remember one time they came about two in the morning, pounding on my door, "*Mi compañero está en el desierto. Una víbora lo ha mordido!*" Their friend had been snake bit, and they left him in the desert to come for help. So the aliens and I went down and found him right there at the junction of High Tanks Road and the Hobbs drag. He'd been bitten on the ankle, and they put a tourniquet on his leg but failed to loosen it occasion-ally to allow some circulation. Man, what a horrible-looking mess, and the guy was in agony.

No, he didn't lose his leg. That's a medical miracle. After sun-up Tommy landed his Super Cub on the drag road, because I didn't have the heart to haul him out in that condition in a Jeep. Tommy didn't like to do that kind of stuff, but he strapped that ol' boy in the back seat and flew him to Yuma. Doctors saved his leg. About two months later we caught him again coming out of the desert south of Wellton. I asked him how his leg was and he replied, "Not so good," but he had walked on it from La Jollita almost to Wellton, more than forty miles.

There were many sad things that didn't work out so well. I remember one incident where a father and teenage son tried to cross through Big

Pass. They got in trouble down there south of the Van Waggoner barn. The son must have been some good kid, and I think about that often, how he come rushing out to get help for his father, who was down in the desert. The son died at the damned 1-8 freeway fence, where we found him. That night his father recovered and came out on his own. I said, "Man, that was some damned nice kid that ol' boy raised, killed himself tryin' to save his old man." Americans should thank God for allowing us to be born Americans and not having to endure such hardships to make a living.

A lot of pathetic stories like that in this desert, a lot of death down here. I found more people who have died down here and rotted into the ground. And you could tell, a man died right here, just from the way it all lay, the little pieces of bones and everything that were man-shaped. I guess now that people are dead, we can tell some military secrets. A lot of these skulls that they used back then in research centers, museums, and universities were picked up out in this desert. You couldn't identify them—just a skull of a dead man.

There were a bunch of javelina hanging around the La Jolla Wash down there. And they ain't afraid of people. I've gotten right up on them damned things. One time Neil Jensen was down there and he found a body. He didn't have a body bag and decided to come on out and get a body bag, and take the coroner down the next morning. We went down there next morning, no Mexican, just javelina tracks. They'd ate him up. And, I remember finding pieces of bodies down there eaten. Javelina will eat anything. Buzzards don't eat people. I haven't found anywhere coyotes ate on them either. I'd see where the coyotes had shit all around, but they never come over. Coyotes will start chewing on bones after a body has lain in the desert for more than six months and the human smell has left. The flies lay eggs and worms eat them, but ground squirrels eat the fingernails and the toenails sometimes. That's the first thing they'll eat. Before they're even dead, maybe they'll eat their toenails off, or start eating their toes.

You remember the orders: we were forbidden to pay medical expenses for aliens. That was a direct order. One time there was a whole bunch of aliens got in trouble on the east side of the Mohawk Mountains. They were dying down there. It was a big bunch. So we went down there and gathered up what we could. I had about five or six of them already in the back of my vehicle, a Ramcharger or a Scout, whatever we had then. And this one young guy in his twenties didn't have any interest in water. And this is where I feel guilty, I should have taken the clue right there. I kept hauling them around, trying to gather up some more of them and then I smelled crap. He had crapped his britches, dying. A radio tech was coming through on I-8 with an air-conditioned vehicle—we didn't have a van with an air conditioner. So I put this guy into the car and said, "Get him to the port of entry and release him as soon as possible." And when they got him just over the line, he died.

That's always bugged me. Had I realized. . . . I should have took the clue right there, when he didn't have interest in water—get him help! But by the time he crapped his britches, it was already too late. That's when I realized, he's dying. I always thought I let that ol' boy down. I could have saved him had I realized that he was in such damned bad shape when he didn't have interest in water.

I had a hell of a lot of sad things, too, when we didn't get them out alive—find them dead. Everybody says, "Well, give them mouth-to-mouth respiration or something." But you knew they were already dead. With flies running in and out of their nostrils, they're dead. I don't know, we did a lot of work—I say routine. We caught a lot of aliens, we saved a lot of lives, a lot of people died down here, and we caught a lot of dope. It seemed pretty damned routine.

We made a lot of rescues down here that I did feel good about, where we got them out of here alive. We could track a bunch of aliens three days. Some of them we caught just south of Arlington, near Phoenix. One time we tracked a man and woman to Arlington, where witnesses had seen them and told us that he was a little guy and she was a fat woman. And he was carrying her! My thought at the time was that he must be a good man, and I was kind of glad we didn't catch him.

We were damned good at our work. We didn't lose very damned many. Of course there wasn't near as many coming in as there is now. And now, these agents are overwhelmed. If we caught thirty aliens in a month, we did pretty good. The way it is now, there's so damned many coming, you'd better get them real quick, 'cause there's ten more bunches right behind them.

It was starting to perk up before I left here, because the last damned day I worked, I took Mike Higgins in to sign the station property over to him, to give him temporary charge of the station, and we was coming back in a car. At the first bridge this side of the checkpoint, there was a pickup signal there, a stack of rocks beside the road indicating, "We're ready. Pick us up." I spotted that signal and stopped. There were thirty-seven under that damned bridge. That was my last day of duty at Tacna. Mike and I got thirty-seven aliens. We had to call in for a couple of vans to come and get them. We just held them under that bridge 'til they got there. So it was starting to perk up then.

My management style? I was a hard-ass. Some things I would not tolerate. I would not tolerate dishonesty or anything like that. And if the men knew their job, I didn't try to micromanage them. It seemed like I was getting all kinds of people, so I'd always find something they were good at and use their talents some way. One guy couldn't track an elephant in a snowdrift, but when we put him on the highway, man, he was dynamite; he'd bring them in. I didn't believe in that micromanagement: if you've got a good man, let him do his job.

Of course I never had, really, many personnel problems. A lot of them didn't like me, but that's normal when you're the boss—some people won't like you—that's just the way it is. And Joe McCraw probably had problems when *he* took it over, because my crew was used to the way *I* ran things, and when Joe took over, damn it, you do it the way Joe wants it; he's the boss.

A lot of things you have to think about when you're a manager. A lot of times, the guy that gets in trouble now and then is your hardest worker. The guy that never steps in dukie is probably just sitting on his ass. If you don't ever get in trouble, you're not doing nothin'! A lot of your hard-chargers will step in dukie once in a while. Bosses have to realize all that. I think the biggest compliment I ever got paid was from Mike Higgins. He didn't like me worth a damn, and after he became the PAIC in Casa Grande, the shoe was on the other foot. I saw him there one day, and he come up and said, "You know, I want to thank you for what you taught me." The shoe was on the other foot then. I thought that was a pretty damned-good compliment. I liked that.

The vehicles, in a place like Tacna, get filthy as quick as you go out. They're not on paved city streets. They come down here in the dirt and sand and mud. We had a chief that would come out raising hell with me about dirty vehicles and just kept raising hell, so finally I told the men, "All right, come in an hour early from your patrol and wash that damned vehicle before you park it." That was the important thing to that chief. He beat me down, so we washed them. And ol' Roy Kelland built us a place to wash them right next to the station. To me, it was so worthless, because the next morning they go right out in the dirt. Take a look at that damned waste of time and water.

The rest of us tried to use common sense. At the end of the *bracero* program, I kind of told the men, "If you catch an irrigator and he's irrigating one of them terraced fields, and if you can't find somebody to take charge of that water, turn the man loose and catch him later. Don't destroy the damned field or crop." We never made any deals; we were straight arrow. But in something like that, tens of thousands of dollars were at stake. I remember a farmer in Dome Valley hated us. Man, he hated the Border

Patrol. But one time he was trying to get some onions in—onion seed—and the storm clouds were rolling in. If the seeds had got wet, he'd have lost his crop. And he had nine aliens out there that I could see. I told him, called him by name, "I see what you're trying to do here, so you get that onion seed in, and day after tomorrow, you don't pay those aliens 'til I get them." He did, and he gave me *ten* aliens, too, including one I didn't see. From that day on he was a friend of Border Patrol.

I was running a good station, and the brass left me alone. The station was built up to eight men, mostly Army and Marine Corps veterans. As we gained control of the area, the crew was allowed to dwindle to four men. In 1978 I was replaced by Joe McCraw and transferred to San Luis Obispo, California.

One thing I didn't tell you, a personal secret, happened down there in Big Pass. We had a portable radio repeater for the sensor system then, and it was run by batteries, these big ol' six-volt batteries they use on electric fencing. It'd take three of them. They're six volts, and you split one to get nine volts. We were operating with no money, as usual.

The repeater was on top of Coyote Mountain. It was July 17 and usually you go down there real early in the morning while it's cool, but due to an incident, I got there late in the morning, in the heat of the day. And I found that the batteries hadn't been split by the guys in the shop. But I just put the backpack on my back and went up there. I tried to split that battery with a pocket knife, and I sort of remember cutting myself real bad and bleeding, and feeling exhausted with the heat, but that's the last thing I remember. That mountain is full of cholla cactus and rocky cliffs. Somehow I came down, but I didn't have one cholla in me, and I somehow drove out of the desert . . .

I didn't remember nothin'! Nothin', absolutely nothing. But the guys started calling on the radio, because when we had a man down here alone, we'd periodically call them on the radio to see how they're doing. That's the first I recollected being back in this world. A damned good guardian angel brought me out of this desert that day. I should have been a dead man right there.

After that, they wanted to give me disability retirement, and I didn't want that. So, they offered me a transfer to San Luis Obispo, California, where it's never hot, to do my last three years, and I retired there on my fiftieth birthday. I wanted to do my thirty years, counting military service and unused sick leave, and I did. We did our job, and we enjoyed our damn work, didn't we?

Ed Tuffly

JIM RUNYAN

James S. "Jim" Runyan worked at Tacna Station from 1981 to 1983. His Border Patrol career spanned 1978–2000, and from 2005 to 2009 he was an instructor at the Border Patrol Academy in Artesia, New Mexico.

Although I was raised around Border Patrol, it took me a long round-about way to get *in* the Border Patrol, but I finally did. I'm a third-generation sheepherder by birth, and been around the Border Patrol all my life—mostly running from them. I left the ranch, went in the Marine Corps 1968 to '72, and spent most of my time in Hawaii. I came back to the ranch for a little while and piddly-farted around. The ranch was northeast of El Paso, Texas, and midway to Roswell, New Mexico. El Paso was sixty-five miles down that dirt road then, and sixty-five miles down that dirt road to this day.

My family ran the southernmost apple farm in the United States and also raised sheep on a hundred sections or so down there at Piñon, New Mexico. As a kid growing up I knew that my Daddy would leave the house for two or three weeks ever' summer and disappear, but it wasn't 'til much later that I figured out where he went. He was going down into Mexico to find pickers and herders. Later in August, by the time the apples were ready to pick, 300, 400, sometimes 500 Mexicans would show up in the middle of the night. A group on foot or a car with two or three or six guys would drive up in the dark. Before long we'd have a regular village there. Heck, it'd take them two or three months to pick all them apples.

And we always had sheep to do. One day we were fixing to cut and mark lambs. We had maybe a couple dozen Mexicans there ready to do about four or five hundred lambs. We had eight or ten horses saddled in the corral and beans and tortillas cooking in the cook shack, when we heard a Dodge

Power Wagon coming up the road. My crew scattered up over the ridge of the hill and peeked out through the cactus and brush. Out stepped Border Patrolman Ed Bentley, a lanky guy who stood about twenty feet tall. Of all times to show up, this wasn't it.

He said, "Hello, Mr. Runyan. How you doin' today?"

I replied, "Fine, sir."

"What are you doin'?" he asked, seeing everything plain as day.

"I'm fixin' to work these lambs, sir."

"All 500 of them?"

"Yes, sir. You bet."

So, I started cutting and notching and marking, just hoping he'd leave 'fore I got tuckered out. I had to do somethin', but I could see that he was calling my bluff. And I knew those Mexicans peeking down from the ridge must be laughing themselves silly, seeing me work like a crazy man. After about 30 lambs my tongue was hanging out and my arms started to get kinks in them so bad they hurt, but he kept watching so I had to keep working. I'm covered with blood and dirt and tired as could be.

After a while he stood up and I thought he was fixing to leave, but that sorry ol' boy just asked if he could have a plate of that grub he smelled cooking in the shack.

"Sure a lotta grub for one guy," he said.

"Yeah, yeah, I get real hungry," I said, "I figure to work all week. Help yerself." I just kept digging my hole deeper, and he knew it. That ol' boy was enjoying watching me suffer.

Bit later he asks, "Mr. Runyan, you gonna leave those horses saddled in the corral?"

"No, sir, I'm plannin' to get to that right quick, soon as I finish a few more sheep." When he finally left, I was so tard that I couldn't even spit. He taught me a lesson, sure thing.

Eventually I went to school at Texas Tech, for a little while, and then got on the fire department in Lubbock, so I'd have a job. They had a Border Patrol station there in Lubbock, and I got talking to those guys. They got me lined out on it. I knew one of the agents, Don Vaughn, and talked to him one day, and he told me what form to fill out, and then how to go about taking the test. It wasn't really publicized back then—you had to find out. And I filled out that form and sent her in and took the test. About two and a half years after I took that test I finally hired on. Slow process, for sure. Finally I got in the outfit. I was twenty-eight years old when I started.

When I went for my Border Patrol board interview, they knew my family's history, and probably knew 'bout my day with the sheep. They

Jim Runyan. Photo by Bill Broyles, 2009.

knew 'bout my daddy and my uncle, Bulley Runyan. They knew my family had always hired "wets" to work our family orchards and sheep. They knew that I'd worked with aliens all my life. When I went before that hiring board, they started slow.

One of them asks, "Mr. Runyan, why do you of all people want to join Border Patrol?" I told them straight out, "Money. Pure and simple, money. I've been a farmer and rancher, and today I'm a fireman. You pay twice as much for half the hours." And, I wanted to be outdoors.

We had some other questions. Then one of them, Raymond Reeves, tries to run me off the cliff and asks, "Suppose, Mr. Runyan, suppose that we hire you, and suppose we sent you to work out of El Paso. And suppose we gave you a badge and gun and sent you over to southern New Mexico, maybe even near a little town called Piñon. And maybe we even sent you out to your daddy's ranch. And suppose you found him workin' illegal aliens. What would you do, Mr. Runyan?"

I thought a minute. It was a tough question. I took a breath and answered, "Supposin' you hired me, and supposin' you sent me to New Mexico, and if by chance I found my daddy had hired an alien or two to work on his place, I'd arrest them and my daddy. If I raise my hand and take that oath, that's what I gotta do. But know this, I'd hate all you sorry suckers to the day you die, every last one of you."

The board said, "Good answer, Mr. Runyan. Welcome to the Border Patrol."

I hadn't told my daddy that I was even thinking 'bout joining up with the Border Patrol. But when I got hired on, I called him and told him. All I heard was a long pause and then a click. He didn't speak to me for four years. When I'd visit home he wouldn't be there, but Momma and our family said Daddy kept shaking his head and saying over and over, "How could any boy of mine do that to me?!" It was four years before he called me, and then he wanted to know some answer 'bout immigration law. He never really forgave me for joining up.

I entered on duty at El Paso Station One in 1978 and stayed in El Paso until January of '81. I put in for a job out here at Tacna, Arizona, when it came open. I figured, "Well, I won't get it unless I put my name in." So I put my name in the hat. There were seven of us on the list. Five of us were out of the El Paso Sector. I was rookie of the whole list, and I got picked for the job. I was flattered.

Really I was wanting to get back to Carlsbad, New Mexico, 'cuz there was a Border Patrol station at Carlsbad, and it's close to Piñon. Tacna was a hardship station back then, which meant you could transfer out automatically after two years. I never heard of Tacna in my life. I thought, "Well hell, I can work two years anywhere." And so I came out to Tacna that January and left my wife and two little girls there in El Paso. I came out here in January and rented a little old place off Clyde and Marguerite Knott back there behind the old Chaparral Motel, and for about two and a half, three months, I slept on a pallet on the floor. It wasn't much of a place to live, but it was comfy enough. Anyway, my whole purpose for coming out here was to spend about two years and then go back to Carlsbad, and work for the Border Patrol around that area until I retired.

But the best thing that ever happened to me when I came out to Tacna was I learned that there's another world to the Border Patrol besides an urban metropolitan area like I was working in El Paso. Different world, different kind of tough. Tacna opened my eyes. I grew up with alien Mexicans all my life. That's all I knew. I spoke Spanish as a kid, first, and learned English when I went to school—a towhead with blue eyes that talked like a little Mexican boy. I thought I knew Mexicans, I really did, but I never realized the hardships those human beings put themselves through to get here. I knew they walked up to the ranch all the time when I was a kid, but I never knew how tough it was, 'til I came out here to Tacna and started chasing them. It gave me a god-awful appreciation for what those poor people went through—changed my outlook on life, just 180 degrees. I went from being fairly calloused, having worked the El Paso metro area where *everybody* wants to stick you with something sharp, U.S. citizen or illegal alike.

Tacna was the only place in my career I ever had an alien Mexican come up to me and *thank* me for catching him. We were out there at Mohawk Flat one day, August, September maybe. We got out there in the middle of that big flat chasing one old man. And he stopped after a while—he was probably a quarter mile ahead of us when he heard us—and he just dropped everything on the ground with his back to us. We just stopped. He looked back and took off a-running, just running lickety-split, out there probably another two or three hundred yards. Jim Clarida was with me in one Ramcharger, and I was in another. We looked at each other through the open windows—we couldn't run the air conditioner back in those days because the engines would overheat—and said, "Where in the hell does he think he's goin'?" That Mohawk Flat, it's thirty miles of nothin'. We just sat there. The old man stopped about four hundred yards past where he dropped all his stuff, and just fell to his knees, shaking his head, sobbing. That old man, I wish I remembered his name, was about sixty, sixty-one years old. I started my Ramcharger up and drove up there alongside of him, and got out. The old man was just sitting there crying. He got up and said, "I don't know what I was thinking." I said, "That's okay, partner. Shoot, that's all right, everybody acts a little different out here in this ol' desert. It's something that we'll all do some time or another." And he come over and gave both of us a hug and thanked us for catching him. That's the only one that ever did that in my entire career—he thanked me for catching him.

That old boy, along with a lot of others out there, gave me a renewed appreciation. I get a little emotional sometimes, thinking about it. I had never picked up a dead body in my life. Well, I take that back—when I worked on the fire department, we picked up dead bodies there, but they'd died from accidents and burns and car wrecks. But I had never . . . . You know, you hate thinking about some things. Picking up a dead body of a nineteen-year-old kid, or a sixty-, seventy-year-old man, that all they ever wanted to do was feed their family. It never dawned on me that people would be so desperate, where *I* lived, to do such a thing. It made me reach within myself to find out if I could do this job.

I came real close to quitting, I sure did, because, boy, who in the hell can do this? We didn't talk about it. We just did our job and went on. One year I remember the number 31, thirty-one dead that we picked up. Thirty-one that we actually picked up and somebody did something with.

But there were others . . . , the ones that we found and couldn't do anything with. If ol' John Phipps, sheriff of Yuma County back then, didn't have enough money in his budget, we couldn't bring in Juan Does for burial; the county couldn't handle it and wouldn't even take them. And the Mexican consulate wouldn't take them unless they had papers on them to identify them, a Forma 13 or whatever. So when we'd find just bones or bodies without identification, there was nothing official that we could do. There were times, too many times, that with a shovel and a prayer we'd have our own little funerals out there in the desert for the poor ol' boys, and then we'd have to go on about our business, just like it was nothin'. I never realized all those Border Patrol guys that worked this area did it before me and had gone through the same thing I was going through. And I thought, "You know, if they can do this, so can I."

Nobody ever told me about this. Nobody. Glen Payne had been out here for a while; Jim Clarida had been out here for several years. I knew both of them from my El Paso days. Fred Borrego was out here then, God rest his soul. He never told me anything about it nor did Mike McDowell or ol' Oscar Martinez. And Joe McCraw, who was my boss at the time, never said a word. They talked about the dead that were found, but never talked about the emotional impact. It's something that we dealt with on our own. We just kind of handled it, I guess is the best way to put it. Anyway, over time, you start to get a little calloused up over it—not in a negative sense, but in a self-preservation way. But you never forget those days. There're some things in your life, like the Kennedy assassination or 9/11, that you just can't forget. You pinpoint turning points in your life. And that's what turned me, sure did.

When I first saw Tacna, I thought, "Damn! This is a pretty good deal!" My hometown of Piñon was about a fourth the size of Tacna. I thought, "Hell! They got runnin' water here! And, they have irrigated farmland and green fields year-round." I thought, "This is gonna be a pretty good place!" And it was. It was a pretty good spot.

Neither my wife nor I came out here and looked at Tacna before I accepted the job. I came out two and a half, three months before the wife and family. After she sold the house and packed everything up, I went back home and brought her out here, and drove her into town. I said, "Well, what do you think?" She said, "Well, it's not as bad as Piñon," which is where I took her right after I got out of the Marine Corps, when we first got married. Heck, she had to haul water down there.

I said, "Well, honey, I found a place for us to live here in Tacna. We don't have to live in that old *jacalito*, that little shack where I've been staying. I found a little trailer house for you. The only thing is, hon, it doesn't have any water. There's a little water trailer there, and I've got a hitch on the back of the car. We'll pump water out of the canal and put it in the cistern." She said, "You have got to be kiddin' me." I said, "No, ma'am, that's all I could find." "Well, if that's all you could find, let's go!" It was a nice trailer. When I was gone on detail and what not, she had to hook that trailer up and go haul water to fill that cistern, so it wasn't much different than living at the ranch when we were first married.

I married a good one. She's a good gal, she sure is. Whether the men want to admit it or not, the woman is a crown that God gives to a man. That crown will only shine as much as the man of the house will polish that crown, and the better you treat it, the better it'll shine. Sometimes the Lord gives you a crown that's got some stones out of it and what not, but He gave me a crown that had a permanent shine on it, because He knew I wouldn't shine too much. She's been a blessing to me all our married life.

Summertimes in Tacna we worked 6A to 2P, 6:00 A.M. to 2:00 P.M., because of the heat. In the wintertime, we worked 7A to 3P. There were no more than two of us off duty on any day, what with vacation or sick leave. Station chief Joe McCraw rotated our days off. Most of the guys didn't go to church. I went to church every Sunday with my wife and kids, if I was off. Ol' Joe's a Baptist, and when he found that out and asked me about it one time, I said, "Yes, I go to church." "You go to the Baptist church?" "No, sir," I said, "used to go to the Methodist church, but there's not one out here, so we go to the Presbyterian church." And we did. So he gave me Sundays and Mondays off, much to the chagrin of some of the older guys around there who didn't go to church on Sundays. I didn't say anything. I took the Sundays off and went. Most of the guys here never held a grudge on it. Everybody else had their days off that they liked to have.

One or two guys would be assigned call-outs every pay period, a two-week period. And if you had call-out, the sector radio room would call you on the phone at maybe ten o'clock at night and say that so-and-so reported X-number of aliens at Aztec or Sentinel or Hyder or wherever, and you'd put your Levis and your cowboy shirt on, get in the car, drive over to the office, and get your flashlight and gun belt, grab a Ramcharger, and go. You might be out there 'til one or two o'clock in the morning, but you didn't take the next day off. You went home, changed, got your uniform on, and went back to work at six o'clock that next morning, ready for the next day—we got 'er done, whatever needed to be done. And those call-outs happened more often than not.

We were all working a regular day and then stacking four or five hours of overtime on top of it. When you'd be out there in Mohawk Flat, especially during the summertime while working them ol' trails, you're not gonna quit tracking them 'til you find the person, alive or dead. And you'd come out of the desert, and with the help of the pilots you might run the trails all the way from the border fifty or sixty miles to the interstate. If it hadn't been for the pilots, we would have had to work trails four or five days. We'd follow guys all the way from the border to Red Mountain Farm and up toward Phoenix along the rail line sixty, seventy miles from where we first saw tracks.

The emphasis when I was here was line watch. Joe McCraw set that focus. The boss always sets the tone and sets the goal. And Joe's focus was the line. He said, "Our job is to make sure as few of them die down there as possible." And, that's what we did. Sometimes we'd do a farm and ranch check up there in the valley, check the lettuce crews, the planters, and some of the old irrigators. But, our primary job was this ol' desert down here and making sure they survived. Like Joe said, "We gotta catch them or make sure they made it to the highway and got picked up. That way we know they're alive." That's one thing I really admire about that old man. He grew up in this valley, and he probably knew this ol' desert as good, if not better, than any man I've ever seen or known in my life, and he's forgotten more about it than most people will ever know. He has his own name for places, but he knows where they all are.

Ol' Joe was pretty tough. He actively participated in every trail every day, even if we had four or five trails going. If he and two guys were on one trail, and you found another trail, boom, he'd be 10-8 [radio call for "in-service"] just high-balling as fast as he could to get over on the trail and help you. Joe was a hands-on supervisor. Joe didn't care much about paperwork, but I never met a Border Patrol agent in my life who does, except for the payroll and the payroll slip—we all like that part of it. Joe hated paperwork. Jim Clarida and Glen Payne did most of the end-of-the-month reports back then. Joe had his points, and his points were "get out there in the field." He didn't tell us much, but he was training us. He didn't do it with words, but with action. Men are monkey-see, monkey-do people anyway, and we could monkey-see, monkey-do behind Joe real good.

I thought I knew how to track before I came over here. I didn't. Oh, I thought I did. I grew up on a ranch and thought I could track anything. Shoot! I didn't have a clue! I didn't know what a brushout was, no clue. Some of the Tacna guys would help you a little bit, they'd tell you what to watch out for, but you pretty much learned by watching other guys and listening to their vernacular on the radio or at the station. Sign cutting and tracking is something that you can't learn out of a book. You can get the basic understanding of it out of a book, but to learn it, you've got to do it. And the more you do it, the better you get. It prepared me for where I went later on in life.

We had a 1977 Ramcharger. There was one old van that was about a '75 Dodge three-quarter-ton long van. We had one tired sedan out here that we didn't use much. We had four fairly new Ramchargers, '81 models. And that was it. We didn't have night vision goggles, not one pair. We had an old shotgun we kept at our station, but a shotgun's kinda useless out in this desert. If you're gonna be that close to someone shooting it out with a shotgun and standing behind a creosote bush for cover, you need to have your head examined. What you do is run away and call for backup. We had a couple walkie-talkies, but walkie-talkies were useless out in this desert. I don't think anybody ever carried them. Even the radios in the old Jeeps couldn't hit the repeater, unless you directly saw Telegraph Mountain. You could talk to each other on a "local" frequency pretty good over on Mohawk Flat, but if you were down here on Coyote Wash and you were stuck bad and starting to run out of sap to dig yourself out, you could forget it. You're stuck right there until the angel comes by, and our angels were pilots, like ol' Dave Roberson, Hank Hays, and Jackie Mason. They were our angels. Those three guys always knew where to come find you.

I had worked around Border Patrol aircraft and seen them, but I'd never worked *with* them 'til Tacna. Hank Hays and Jackie Mason were the first two pilots. Dave Roberson came here right after I did. Dave—oh, God, that boy was a fast learner. Of course he was already a sign cutter, having worked at the Fort Stockton Station years ago, but he picked up that sign cutting out of an airplane as good as anybody I ever saw. I thought Hank was just the best there ever was. Jackie was pretty good. Those guys could run a trail and save you ungodly suffering in the heat. They had little or no equipment, either. They had their own little ol' homemade survival kits with probably a jug of Gatorade and a flare gun off somebody's Navy surplus life raft. But they were all out here. All they had at that time were Super Cubs, and then later on they got a little helicopter out here—one of those little ol' Loaches, little OH-6.

What's it take to make a good agent? I can answer a hundred different ways, but if I was going to boil the fat off the hog, you've got to have the "want to." If you don't have the want to, you'll never do it. You can apply that to any vocation, I guess, but it takes a special "want to" to make a *good* agent. There're a lot of agents out there, but to make an agent to work this desert takes the same "want to" that it takes an agent to want to work the highway checkpoint. Anyone can just sit there and wave their hand or just drive up and down the road making tracks in the sand. But an agent that actually looks for sign, learns how to follow it, and finds aliens or smugglers, that person has accomplished the job that they're hired to do. If you've got the "want to," you can do it.

Stamina's something that comes with time; you build up doing the job. If you've got the "want to," you can come out here and you can be as good as anyone, sure can. Ethnicity has nothing to do with it. Fred Borrego was as good a hand as anybody ever saw. Fred Borrego was the first Hispanic agent that I worked with, and he was hands above a lot of other guys I worked with because he had the want to. He taught me a lot. He was an old street cop out of Brownsville, Texas, and he worked in El Paso with me as well. He was just as good and acclimated as fast as any man I ever saw. Glen and Hank were country boys from New Mexico and had worked on them ol' ranches. Oscar Martinez was raised over at Marfa, Texas, a little small ranching community. Oscar did real good, too. People like Glen Payne and Dave Roberson and Joe McCraw dedicated the best years of their lives to this desert. I'm in total awe of those guys, I really am.

At first I was just blowing through like any other ignorant kid saying it's just a job, but somewhere along the way I decided "I'm going to do the best I can." There wasn't a philosophy involved but later on, I think it evolved into a philosophy. I didn't want anybody to suffer over something I did not do, whether it be a co-worker or an alien. I wanted to earn everything that was paid to me by the American taxpayer. Everybody has their days where they say, "Well, screw this. I'm gonna go find me a shady ironwood tree and take me a nap." And I did that a time or two when nothin' was going on. Sometimes you just get sapped out and can't drag them tires anymore. Everybody has their days where they give out a little bit, but I always wanted to earn what I was paid.

I remember how hard my ol' daddy worked for *his* money up on the ol' ranch. And I also saw some of these old Gila River valley farmers just scratching a living as hard as they could go. They had to work their butts off to pay taxes. I wasn't getting rich, but I was making a pretty good living— not as good as I wanted, but I was going to make a better one. Every fourteen or fifteen days they'd give me a little something. I don't think I ever had one day in my whole career that I felt like I didn't earn my money. I always wanted to do that, and I tried to pass that same value on to all my rookies that worked for me over the years.

Mexico City has no perspective at all on this border. They haven't worked this ol' Tacna desert. Mexico City doesn't have a clue. They *think* they do. They think what the news media tells them is the absolute gospel truth. Nobody really has a clue, unless they're down here. You have to be here, smell it, feel it, touch it. They think they know the number and the volume and the crossings, but they have no idea what these people do or why they're doing it.

Or if they do know, they don't care. Their bottom line is money. They don't have the emotional bond to their own people other than "gimme money, gimme money." They're so wrapped up in getting money to come into their country that they really don't give a hoot about the human flesh and misery that goes out of their country.

I've only met one Mexican consul in my life, a kid working out of Eagle Pass years ago, who really cared about the Mexican nationals who were coming up here. He was the only one that ever talked to them. That's when I was station senior down at Del Rio Station in Del Rio Sector. He would talk to them from his heart. He really cared, but he didn't last long. He was displaced, and another boy come in there who didn't give a hoot 'n' holler. "I don't care, just gimme this."

I've always felt—and I felt this way even before I came aboard Border Patrol when I worked for Daddy all those years, and growing up with all them aliens—I've always felt that the only people who really care about the aliens, truly care about the aliens, is them ol' guys and gals wearing the green Border Patrol uniforms. Good or bad, day or night, the only ones that really care about their welfare are Border Patrol agents. We want to pull them out of the desert. If they violate the law, we're hired to make sure they go back home and don't violate that law again. But we're also the only ones that give a hoot 'n' holler whether that girl gets hurt by this smuggler, or whether that guide that's walking across the Mohawk Flat out here walks off and leaves her. We want to save *her*, and we want to go get that so-and-so smuggler locked up.

We're the only ones that'll rescue them, not that we're supermen or self-promoting people. The agents that cared were usually the ones that were quiet, and just like the old elephant they're out there just plodding along every day, getting 'er done. These new agents, once they become emotionally attached to their job—and they will, over time—will care, too. All these kids will be emotionally attached to the Border Patrol, just like the rest of us are. And they'll develop a caring sense for those alien Mexicans down here, just like we did. When I was here, we didn't have any OTMs, nationalities other than Mexicans, walking the desert.

When we'd pull someone outta the desert, it was common to buy them a soda and sandwich. Every day. And that wasn't somethin' you bragged about—just somethin' you went out and did. Many a time I've sat under an ol' ironwood tree down there, and that ol' alien would have a little ol' *triques* bag with two or three tins of sardines in there, and they'll be swelled up in the damned heat. And the old fart'd sit there, peel that lid back, and offer you some. Well, I was not about to deny him his pleasure, and so I'd drag out my old green baloney sandwich, I'd whack off part of that ol' baloney sandwich, and I'd give him some, and we'd swap groceries. And at the same time, sitting under these old ironwood trees, we'd discuss politics of the day, his president and my president, and how neither one of us liked them. Some of them ol' *campesinos* couldn't even sign their name, all they knew was "X." But, every one of them knew a little bit about current events and civic affairs. They weren't eloquent speakers, but they all have opinions. We always had somethin' in common, we really did, to just sit and visit. That was real common. I never saw half a dozen agents that wouldn't sit there and provide groceries for an alien—it happened almost every day.

There was a lot of times we'd bring these ol' aliens out of this ol' flat in the dadgummed heat of the summer, and boy, they'd be just all dried out. They'd get their ol' core temperature up, and their ol' thermostat would be popping off. But if you don't get it down pretty quick, they ain't gonna make it and they're gonna die on ya'. Three, four, five hours later, they're gonna be dead. Old Lady Finch had a grocery store over at Tacna, with a beer cooler in back, one little bitty room, with a concrete floor just as cool and cold as it could be. Whether she was open or not, we had access to that beer cooler—not to drink beer—but I've gone in there lots of times.

We wasn't catching big groups back them—three or five was a big group. We'd take them ol' boys in there that needed it, strip them down, lay them on that concrete floor, and stack that beer around them for an hour or so. They'd get the chills pretty quick, but it'd get that core temperature down.

A lot of times we called Doc Kline. He's dead now. He was a doctor over at Wellton. We'd run one by old Doc Kline's house seven, eight, nine o'clock at night. Doc was one of those dependable guys who always helped, and he would treat them the best he could. Ol' Doc wouldn't give them IVs—he'd give them salt pills and diagnose whether or not we needed to get them to the emergency room or not, whether or not to call the ambulance. But ol' Doc never charged a dime, didn't send a bill to nobody. We had no budget to pay him anyway. That was our low-tech search and rescue back then—we did it all.

I always relied a whole lot, not on just my co-workers, but on the people that I worked around—farmers and the local folks. I met an ol' boy here named Old Man Bob Woodhouse. He's dead now. Ol' Bob taught me a lot about the Mohawk Valley, and who the honorable folks were, and who were less than honorable, and how to deal with them. Every locale has a different temperament. And I grew up in sheep country, and there were a lot of sheepherders here, too, Basque mainly. Bob taught me how to get along with these farmers. Vegetable farmers are a little bit different breed than regular ol' hay farmers, you know.

Jack Dale, the superintendent of schools at Roll, helped me a lot, too. One thing I already knew was just to be yourself and be honest. But Jack also told me some of the quirks about individual farmers, Joe Blow this, Joe Blow that. Or, "He doesn't really like this kind of attitude, or that kind of attitude." So it kind of helped me to deal with them. And he told me who blew off steam, who'd call your mama all the dirty names. Of course, I was used to that. But it helped me to know who it was, so I wouldn't be so surprised when it happened. And I got called a lot of things, and my mother got called a lot of things too, but for the most part I don't know one of them out there I didn't get along with.

I just learned to shrug it off. That's what I told all the kids that worked for me years later, "It's not a personal thing. The only thing personal to them is you're hauling out their cheap labor, and that gets to be personal. But as far as personal things between them and you, it's not a personal thing at all. If you took the uniform off and walked up to them, they wouldn't even know who you were and wouldn't be mad at you."

We didn't have any narcotics busts during my tenure at Tacna. Most everybody out here we caught were campesinos, just old farm laborers who farmed a little garden or field. I never caught a whole lot of *vaqueros* out here. There's not a whole lot of cattle ranching around here. The ones I seen crossing out here when *I* was out here were just old farm boys from down there around Los Mochis, Mazatlán, Michoacán, and every once in a while we'd get an oddball group, maybe kids out of Baja California. The only ones we'd catch were the walking boys who wanted to go get a job. We'd go over and hit the fields once in a while. Ol' Joe Mc-Craw had told us, "Make sure these people don't die. Those people are always going to work them fields up there. Make sure these people don't die." That was our big thing.

That dadgummed White Wing Ranch was just like a magnet to those aliens. If they could get there, they'd earn their grubstake and go to Phoenix and get on that airplane, and next day they'd be in North Carolina topping corn or whatever, making *good* money. That was a big magnet for them, it sure was. Most of these old boys were just ol' workin' boys. We saw a lot of *huaraches* back then. You don't see huaraches on aliens anymore. Huaraches are the first indicator that that ol' boy is dirt damn poor. He made his own, and all of us working this desert saw them boys walk across that sand out there, 130, 135 degrees, wearing homemade huaraches, and that ol' burning sand would get up underneath them things and burn their feet. The calluses on their feet would be just as tough as the sole of your shoe.

I never found a gun on one of them—homemade knives, but never a gun, not one time. Almost all them ol' boys carried somethin' that you never see anymore, called a *sacatripa*. A sacatripa is a homemade knife. They'd find a piece of metal and fashion a blade that looks like a homemade linoleum knife, and put a cow-horn handle on it. Sacatripa means "cut out the guts," where they'll take that curved blade and cut them out. That's the literal meaning of the thing. They could hurt you bad. I found some of those things as big as eight and ten inches on down to pinky-finger-sized.

And some of those ol' boys believed that they could keep snakes away at night. For sleeping they'd take sticks and old brush and lay it down in a circle around them, thinking that would keep the snakes from crawling over and getting them. The aliens walking that railroad line to Phoenix would lay down between them damned ol' rails, thinking a snake wouldn't crawl over them rails. Thank God we only had two trains a day on that line. Poor things. They'd heard the same wives' tales I had, except they were ignorant enough to put them into application. But then again, we never had any snakebites, either.

Those Mexicans took stories back to Mexico. Just like we sit around and talk about the aliens today, they sit around and talk about what the Border Patrol agents did and how the Border Patrol outfoxed them. And they sit around those old farms, those old *ejidos* down there in Mexico and talk about the coup they pulled on us. Those old stories proliferate over time, they really do. And they'd talk about how they were treated, too. You can always tell a Mexican that was treated humanely—maybe tough, but humanely and with respect—because they'll respect you. Thank God for all our predecessors. Everybody meets some hard-nosed guys to deal with, but I've learned that most all Mexican nationals that were crossing this border respected that green Border Patrol uniform, even those that ran. It was a rare occasion I ever had one try to hit me. And the ones that did, they had to suffer the consequences. And they would take that story back, too. I never wanted to demand respect because I had a badge and a gun or a patch on my shoulder. I always wanted to *earn* that respect from the alien or the rancher or farmer or citizen or my peers.

I guess the high point of my career was working this desert. The first six or eight months I was out here, I didn't think it was. But the high point in my career was where I become educated and really realized how much an ol' Mexican can suffer walking this desert just to feed a wife and kids.

In 2005 I went back to work at the Border Patrol Academy as a rehired annuitant. I'm enjoying it, I am. I teach operations classes to the trainees. Operations covers line watch, sign cutting, alien smuggling, freight train check, city patrol, and bus and taxi checks. And, the one thing that all of us guys are teaching is officer integrity. All of the recruits have integrity built in, but sometimes they just don't know how to pull it out of themselves. I'm trying to teach these kids how *they* are responsible for how clean the Border Patrol stays. And if there's a dirty apple in there, then *you*—not the yahoo from Vegas, or so-and-so from Salt Lake—but *you* have to get the bad apple out. So-and-so in Salt Lake doesn't know what that bad apple is until it gets rotten and starts stinking. You don't want it to get to that point. When it starts getting sour, you want it out of there, so it doesn't ruin the rest of the apples. And that, I think, can do more for promoting good publicity for the agency and esprit de corps for the rookies than anything else in the world. It'll get the public off your back and *alongside* of you.

As a trainee in El Paso, before I ever took my ten-month exam, I turned a guy in. All my supervisors said, "Are you sure you want to sign this thing?"

I said, "Here!" They threatened to fire me over it—that closed little shop of the Border Patrol back then, the El Paso Sector. "It's in there, I signed it, and it's on your desk." They never did anything with it, and later on the guy ended up in the federal pen anyway, but he needed it. He was a really, *really* bad guy. Ex-Marine, Bronze Star winner, Vietnam vet, but he was a scumbag. With my recruits, I try to teach them about these Mexicans—"You're going to be dealing with a lot of hard-nosed people, but you don't hit nobody unless he hits you. You don't take that gun, that badge, and beat on somebody just 'cause you got the power to do it. This is not Gestapo-land. Use the old Golden Rule."

We tried real hard to be fair. Our policy when you caught a farm worker—as a matter of fact, it was a written policy—was you *would* go to the boss or payroll guy to get their money for them. You couldn't make that farmer pay that alien, but you could encourage him with other ways, personally, to do that. The official way was to report him to the Department of Labor. Well, that's not going to happen—just another bureaucratic bunch of bull. What we *would* do is say, "Well, partner, if you don't want to pay this guy, that's fine. I can't hold a gun to your head and make you squirt money at him. But what I can guarantee you is I will be here every day, and I'll make sure that you're the one with that shovel in your hand, and *you're* the one irrigating, 'cause there ain't nobody else going to irrigate on this place but you." Real quick they'd usually find the money that they owed. I've met only a few farmers that didn't want to pay their aliens; more often than not they'd pay them what they owed them.

Alien attitudes have changed. They used to think about the consequences of what they were doing, and they did it anyway, because they had needs that they had to meet. The campesinos have depleted themselves over the years, having come back and forth up here. We don't see a campesino culture like we saw just twenty years ago. You'll still get the occasional poor kid from some little village out in the boondocks, do-wah-diddy, or Tlaxcala, but you won't see the groups of working people anymore. What we're seeing now is an urban culture coming up here illegally. Nowadays it's all city folks wearing Nikes and Tommy Hilfiger T-shirts. God, where do they get this stuff? They know nothing of what farm life was.

And Border Patrol is changing. When I first joined up all the old seniors and journeymen were workin' guys coming off farms. They'd come off a little ol' farm, or their granddaddy had a farm. We'd sometimes get a few Yankees and city boys coming in, but most of the guys were farm kids. That's all changing, too.

I left Tacna in May of '83. I went to Tucson on a lateral promotion and stayed there eighteen months. Then I went to Del Rio, Texas, as a trainee Border Patrol pilot. I flew there for about four years. That was the best job I've ever had in my life. Of course, I thought every job was the best job I ever had. Flying was sure fun. When I got out here to Tacna, I watched these guys and the way they worked, and I developed a real love for it. And boy, how they saved me a lot of heartache and suffering, and aliens, too. I'd always wanted to do that. And, it paid a lot more, too, and that helped.

I started flying because my dad had a little ol' Tri-Pacer back at the ranch when I was a kid. My cousin Sonny Runyan had a Cub; so did my Uncle Frank. I flew a little bit as a little boy there, probably seven, eight, ten hours. But I got kind of a taste for it. I had my private pilot's license when I hired on with Border Patrol. I finished my commercial license when I started building hours at Tacna and finished my commercial, my instrument ticket, my multi-engine ticket, and my certified instructor while I was in Tucson. I did all that in eighteen months. To come up with all the money, I hocked my wife and both my girls, but we got 'er done!

In the Marine Corps, I was an F-4 Phantom mechanic at Kaneohe Bay Marine Corps Air Station, Hawaii. Then I became an F-4 crew chief—"plane captain," the Marine Corps calls it—with my name stenciled on the plane cabin. One day my boss, a colonel in charge of the squadron, called and asked me if I wanted to go ride in an F-4. And I said, "Oh, man!" So I got to ride five sorties in the back seat of an F-4 and one time got to go Mach 1. I really got bitten by the flying bug. I also had a part-time job, working at the base flying club. They paid me $2.50 an hour to work on the airplane, cash, although I could trade that for flying lessons. I wasn't getting paid a lot back then, so I usually took the money.

While I was in Del Rio, I flew for about four years and reached the top of the food chain, as far as pay goes. I was a young buck, and I was wanting to hurry up and get 'er done, and I ended up getting the patrol-agent-in-charge job out of Brackettville, Texas, back in 1988. I stayed there for six and a half years. Then a job came open at Del Rio Station—same type job but a bigger station. The bigger the station, the more responsibility, and the more responsibility, the better the pay. So, they put me over at Del Rio, where I ran the station for six years.

I never received a personal commendation in my entire Border Patrol career. That shocks a lot of people. You always have kids working for you who ask why they're not written up for outstanding this thing or that. I said, "Partner, I don't have one in the lot." One of my bosses asked me, "How'd you get where you're at without an award or outstanding rating somewhere in your career?" I told him, "God took a liking to me." A "thank you" and a paycheck every two weeks is all I ever aspired to. I did get an outstanding rating a couple of years before I retired, but it was after my supervisor asked, "You've never had one?" So he wrote me up for one, and I said, "I don't want it. It's useless. I'm retiring in twenty-four months, so it doesn't help me a rat's fanny." I was never heartbroken because I did not get a commendation. That may be a little surprising to some, but I never got a personal award in my entire career. My personal award for my entire life was doing my job. Simple as that.

Some of us old guys sit around the campfire talking about the new agents and say, "Well, heck, they're not doin' near as good as *I* did." Well, that's all bull. They really are as good, they truly are. Those old-timers said the same thing about me when *I* was a trainee. "Damn that Runyan, he's gonna screw up *my* Border Patrol!" The Border Patrol evolves, just like everything else does.

Americans really need to start caring and need to understand that it takes a special human being to put on that green suit. These kids are hanging themselves out, trying to protect America's borders. They're willing to drive around out here at night by themselves, or walk down the alley at night alone, both of them are equally as dangerous. It's a dangerous job standing on that borderline, waiting by the river at El Paso, or driving up and down the Camino Diablo from High Tanks over to Tule Well, looking for a track at two in the morning, not knowing what's a quarter mile up the road. Or bumping into some cocaine smuggler from Mexico, guarded by the Mexican Army or a sniper with a big ol' German night-sight on a .50 calibre—it'd blow their damned head off. These kids are hanging it out every day, every day of the world. Some of them don't even realize it, just like I didn't when I started. Many don't yet have a sense of country, but they will. Americans need to really understand it takes a special breed of person to do this, and they ought to be thankful that there're still young men and women willing to protect our borders, so we don't lose our country.

Tacna got into my blood and ever' February since 1988, I've come back to camp out with those *compadres* that I knew back then, Glen Payne, Hank Hays, Jim Clarida, Howard Aitken, and others. We call it Campo de Ratones, camp of the desert rats, and I'm awfully proud—grateful, really—to have known and worked with those ol' boys.

JACKIE MASON

*Now enjoying retirement in Florida, Jack G. "Jackie"
Mason served in the U.S. Border Patrol from 1974 to
1994 and was a pilot in Yuma Sector from 1978 to 1988.*

When I joined Border Patrol I was flying for a company that
was fighting forest fires in Arizona, and after the fire season ended, they let
me go. So I went down to Phoenix, was walking around, and happened to
pass by a Civil Service office. I walked in, looked around, and saw a picture
of a Border Patrol pilot flying a Super Cub, and he was working with two
ground units. And I thought, "Well, I could do that! I'd enjoy that." But,
the problem was, I didn't realize it was going to take me five years after
joining the Border Patrol before I was selected as a pilot. Nevertheless,
I enjoyed working as a ground agent. My first duty station was in Indio,
California, and the time passed quickly working at this location. We did
just about everything there: farm and ranch check, traffic, train and bus
check, and city patrol. That was time well spent, and I got a knack, a feel,
for what a pilot should do by working with the sector pilots out of El Centro, and I enjoyed that.

At the same time I had my own little airplane and was building up hours
so I could put in for the pilot's position. I had a little Cessna 120. Several
agents used that plane to build up hours after I finished with it. I loaned
it to them. My uncle and I grew up talking airplanes. He is six years older
than me, and we always loved flying. We used to bicycle out to the St.
Louis Lambert Airfield, stand on the side of the runway, and watch planes
take off and land. We were enthused about flying and both of us made
careers out of flying. His son is an American Airlines pilot, so we all were
airplane enthusiasts. We loved it.

When a Yuma Sector pilot job came open, I was the only person that put in for it, so I got the job. It was thrilling to get that job, but in November of '78 I was the only pilot there! I showed up and really didn't have anyone to work with, although Carl Ott and John Jennings from the El Centro Sector would come over once a month and work with me. They tried to get me up to speed. Mostly I was on my own and worked by myself. Since there hadn't been another pilot there for about two years, the agents didn't know how to work with the airplane and didn't *want* to. They didn't know how much of a benefit it could be. At first the agents would hardly talk to me, but by the time that I left, they were calling for help as soon as I went airborne.

We flew Super Cubs during the day, and eventually they brought in the OH-6 helicopter, which we flew at night. Later we had a Hughes 500, which is the civilian version of the OH-6. The OH-6s were a little underpowered, but eventually they upgraded those things to a bigger engine, and it was a fine aircraft with the C-20 engine in it. The Super Cub was Nine-Zero-Lima. N6590L was the complete number. Pilot trainee Lester Haynie was killed in this aircraft after colliding with power lines west of Yuma on July 14, 1985. The next Super Cub was 4331Z. And then eventually we got Four-Seven-Yankee. The Border Patrol cross-trained me as a helicopter pilot in 1982 and sent me up to San Jose, California. I was there about two weeks, got forty hours in. Then after that, they sent Dave Roberson and me over to San Diego for transitional training in the OH-6s.

At Yuma, most of the aliens were just passing through. They're coming across the border and passing through Yuma, so you don't catch them at work—you catch them crossing, with the exception of Blythe and Tacna Station. About once a month we'd go up to Blythe and work that farm area, and also the Aguila area for farm and ranch check. We'd work citrus groves, farms, and ranches in the Tacna area. White Wing Ranch was one of them. In Yuma we worked the farms and ranches about once a month. You keep them honest a little bit, thin them out a little bit. The main station at Yuma didn't work many smuggling loads—it was basically a line watch station, and we worked everything coming off the line.

When I was in Indio, I used to fly down to Yuma quite often, so I was fairly familiar with Yuma, and I liked it. It was a smaller town, which I liked. The temperature was not much different—it was hot both places. People were friendly and houses were cheap, so I liked Yuma. And the flying, you know, you couldn't ask for any better flying. Very seldom were we grounded due to the weather.

Jackie Mason. Photo by Bill Broyles, 1983.

In '78 we were using one hangar on the northwest side of the airport right off Runway 1-7. We only had one airplane at the time. Paul Burch had his operation there, and Paul worked on the Border Patrol aircraft, before the accident. A Navy pilot flying an A-4 Skyhawk started to take off, but he hit some runway lights, so he ejected. The airplane just kept going about ten feet off the ground and hit Paul Burch's hangar. I was in the hangar at the time. In fact, I had just been talking to Paul Burch, before I went in to talk with his parts man in the office. The jet went right through the hangar, beside the office. It went in one side and out the other side and just exploded in one big pop. And it killed Paul Burch. He'd gone to the back of the building to turn on the air compressor. The jet caught him back there, killed him. That was a pretty close call for me, because usually I would walk back there talking with Paul. This time I didn't.

That was really unfortunate. Paul did great work for us. He was very friendly. I think he was about sixty-seven years old, and for a guy his age, I never saw anyone who had so much energy. During the weekends he was building a retirement cabin. When I came in on a Sunday to refuel, ol' Paul would be waiting for me. He'd take me out for coffee. I really liked him, liked talking to him, and he really knew aviation. He really was a good maintenance guy. He had worked in aircraft factories during World War II.

What was the flight routine in Yuma? For the daylight hours, two pilots would take off early in the morning. One of us would work the side west of Yuma, and the other pilot would go east and work the Tacna area. As soon as he took off, the Yuma pilot would immediately turn northbound and pick up the railroad tracks and start following those railroad tracks and work the train yards in Yuma. Then he would continue on out and search the sidings: Dune Siding, Cactus Siding, and sometimes go as far as Glamis. A lot of times, once you got airborne, immediately one of the agents would be calling you, "C'mon over and help me. I've got a trail going." So you would help him, or if it was kind of slow, you'd go out and check the railroad sidings or some drag roads on the west side. But usually an agent had something for you to do immediately when you took off. If nothing was going on, you'd go somewhere else and make something happen. It wouldn't take long to get on a group that had crossed during the night.

And the pilot who flew out to Tacna would fly south immediately after takeoff and usually work the drag road along the border, and fly right on out to the Tacna area. If he saw some groups that had crossed, he'd make a note of them. If he could land, he would figure out the sign for each group, and then he'd call the Tacna agents to tell them what he had. Once the pilot and ground units joined forces, we would leapfrog the trail.

That was about our daily routine. We usually got in about four or five in the afternoon, after taking off at sunrise. We always took our lunch. We stopped to refuel out at Tacna where we had a fuel tank at that old World War II field by Randy January's jojoba farm. It was a nice little gravel strip. To save time, we'd have our lunch while we were refueling.

When you were checking the trains, you could also look in those wheat cars. On each end they had little holes, and aliens used to climb up in those holes, and you could spot them in there. We followed the train, and we let our ground units know. The trains wouldn't stop for us all the time, so I'd call up El Centro pilots and say, "Hey, there's a train coming your way, and this is what I found." A lot of times the train would stop, though, to let a train going the opposite direction pass by, and that'd give us a chance to get the aliens off the train.

Getting on and off moving trains checking for illegals is pretty dangerous. I know! I worked trains for over four and a half years while in Indio. But I can't remember any agents being killed, but it is a fairly dangerous job. When I transferred up to Havre, Montana, and there were some days I couldn't fly because of the weather, I started to go down and check some trains, and boy, the railroad frowned upon it. They did have their train detectives checking, but they didn't want anybody but their people on those trains. It's a dangerous deal, checking trains.

By the time I left Yuma we had other pilots. Hank Hays arrived about a year after I came on board at Yuma. And a year or two after that, we had Dave Roberson, and then Hank was promoted to supervisor at Tucson, so it was just Dave and me for several years. And then Colonel Child came on board as a pilot and then Lester Haynie. Lester transferred from Tucson as an agent to the position of pilot trainee. Walt Jones also became a pilot before I left Yuma.

Les crashed. He hit that power line wire out there on the north side of Dune Siding with his main gear. He hit them, and then he bounced down through the wires, and the plane landed upside down. The ground unit he was working with had left and no one saw this happen. When the plane landed upside down, apparently Les was still alive, but it bent his head down to his chest, and they said he suffocated. The plane never caught on fire; the power lines weren't turned on at the time. It's just too bad someone wasn't there to see that happen. Les was still a trainee pilot and he shouldn't have been down that low. But we all did it. He was warned; we asked him not to. He was just short of getting his hours as a trainee pilot and getting ready to put in for a pilot's position.

Within a day or two of the time that Lester hit the power lines at Dunes Siding and was killed, a large group crossed the border illegally and apparently headed in the direction of Mohawk Pass. Dave was out of state on vacation; Colonel and I were tied up with paperwork, assisting the National Transportation Safety Board, driving staff to the crash site, and retrieving the damaged airplane. So, there were no pilots checking the lower drag in the Tacna area. The group got into serious trouble about eight miles south of the interstate, resulting in two women and three children dying. Joe McCraw was able to find four out of the five—one woman was still missing. Joe called me about the third day and informed me what was going on and that he sure would like to find her. I flew to Tacna and, with Joe acting as observer, we began flying a search pattern around the area where the other bodies were found. Joe was the first to spot her body barely visible under some brush. In the back of my mind I have always thought that if we had not been occupied with Lester's accident we would have continued to check the lower drag and we would have been able to track this group down before they got into trouble. Maybe not. Anyway, when I think of the day Lester died, I also think about the other five who died within a few days of his death.

The usual altitude for Super Cubs when you were tracking depended on the light and how the tracks would show up. I would say fifty to seventy-five feet, sometimes one hundred feet. And if you needed to go lower, you sometimes would. If we needed to go higher to see the tracks better, we'd go higher. I was working with one of the Tacna agents, a good friend, and he got mad at me. We'd been on a trail, he and I, and we'd worked the trail all the way up to the interstate, or just short of the interstate, where it looked like they were picked up, so we never caught these aliens. But he got mad at me because I'd gotten up higher, and he told me so. He said, "What are you doin' way up there?!" I said, "I can see the tracks up here. What difference does it make how high I am, if I can stay on the tracks?"

Our air speed was right around fifty-five to sixty miles an hour. I thought you'd have to go fifty-five miles an hour at first, but I got so I could track across the ground pretty good at sixty. Sixty added a little more safety. The stall buzzer speed was set right around fifty-five, so that's one reason I boosted it up a little—I got tired of listening to the stall horn. We did have a switch we could turn it off. But I figured if I was gonna turn that thing off, I wanted to go a little faster.

Hank Hays was a good pilot and very hard worker. We had a good time. We caught a lot of aliens. In fact, when he first showed up, he got on a trail out east of Yuma, and to tell you the truth, I kept looking at these trails and thought they were old. Hank got on this trail, and by golly he caught a group of about twenty to twenty-five. Come to find out, these people were dragging a big old blanket behind them, and it made the tracks look older. So that's the last time we were fooled. Hank caught onto that little trick. I enjoyed working with him. He just wouldn't quit a trail. As long as the ground units would stay on a trail, Hank would work with them. So would I.

I enjoyed flying with Dave, too. He was a good, hard worker. He loved to work that Tacna area. Once he got onto that Tacna area I could hardly get over there. He loved that desert out there. I enjoyed working with him. We'd get together every afternoon just before we went home and have a cup of coffee and talk over the day's experiences. If we learned anything or if we found a little landing strip anywhere, we'd inform each other. For example, if I was going to be working the east side, and he was going to be off the next day, he'd tell me what sign he had found and where it was located. It was good working with Dave.

We had to turn in our apprehensions for the month, so we'd keep score amongst ourselves, just for kicks, but never did we claim, say, 300 on our own paperwork. We'd lump it as 300 for all the pilots, because we caught different numbers in different areas. We never tried to get any bragging rights there.

We could fly 100 hours a month, but rules said we couldn't fly over 100 hours. That's a fairly good amount of hours to fly a month, out there in that heat. If you did fly over 100 hours, you'd get a call from the chief pilot, and he'd have a little talk with you. And you'd better not do it too many times, or you would get grounded.

Rescues were the problem. I got one of those telephone calls one day because I had exceeded my 100 by many hours, but for a couple days I was the only pilot, and I flew some ten-hour days, which put me over. On most chases in the Tacna area, if you didn't catch them, they might die on you. We're just not gonna all of a sudden say, "I've got my hours in, so I gotta go home, guys." Nobody ever mentioned a maximum on the number of hours per day. I don't know if there is now, but it was never brought up. It was always that monthly total. And I tell you what, I've flown some days that I felt good in the airplane, but when I landed and got out of the airplane, I felt the ground rocking back and forth like I was a sailor. But as long as I was in the airplane, I felt good.

It's tedious flying, so you have to concentrate on what you're doing. It wasn't boring. You were always looking. Either you were on a trail, or you were looking for somebody. And you were listening. You were listening to anything that went on. Some agent might all of a sudden be in trouble and you might have to go help him. Or an agent might call you. So you really couldn't daydream up there. And you were always looking for something out of the ordinary. If I got a little drowsy in the heat of the day, I'd just land and walk around for a few minutes.

If things got slow on the west side, I'd pick up on some tracks that an agent told me had made it to the train, but I'd walk out the siding and sometimes I'd find the tracks going *over* the siding and walk it out about a half a mile. Forty percent of the time, I'd find the illegals out there sleeping, waiting for a night train. In the Tacna area, we'd land and walk a ways to check on sign and figure out who you were trailing. That kept you awake. Especially out in the Tacna area, you'd better not daydream too much, because you had those military jets flying around doing *their* exercises. At that time, 200 feet AGL was ours—from ground level up to 200 feet. Anything over that belonged to the military, but they got down on ground level from time to time. So you'd better be watching out for those boys. I've had them come right alongside of me. I don't know if they saw me, or they were just playing with me.

One time I was heading down to the lower drag in a Super Cub. I followed the interstate out east and went over the mountains. All of a sudden I found one of those Cobra helicopters beside me, which I thought was kind of odd. And then here comes one of those jets. That Cobra was trying to hide behind me, and these jets were making passes on it. They had some kind of a maneuver going. And I tell you, that's a little scary. I landed as soon as I could find me a little strip to set down, and I watched the show. The Cobra pilot was trying to throw that jet off, but they'd just make their pass, circle around, and here they'd come again.

Once we got the helicopter, we started working at night. And at that time I think we had three pilots. So we would have two pilots work the day shift, and then the third pilot would work the helicopter. We worked four weeks on days and then two weeks on nights. That was a good routine, because by the time you finished up with two weeks on nights flying that helicopter, you were pretty exhausted. It's a little easier flying daytime. That helicopter keeps you pretty busy at night.

We got observers from the Yuma Station to assist the pilot in spotting aliens. The observer operated a powerful spotlight and his job was to search out people trying to hide from us. Some of the agents were not worth a damn due to airsickness; some just couldn't concentrate due to flying so close to the ground at night. But most of them were terrific. If an agent wasn't working out, you hated to send him back to the station so you just worked with him. I had one fellow who was airsick the whole two weeks he flew with me, but he wouldn't give up. In my case anyway, if the observer wasn't working out, that just meant that I had to do more work. I had a spotlight, also, that I could use on my own. But most of those agents picked it up very quickly which really made it easy for me. We were too short-handed to have two pilots in an aircraft; besides, Dave and I liked to be in command of the aircraft so we didn't like flying with each other for long periods. Both of us liked to work with an agent. It gave us another chance to interact with the personnel on the ground.

We saved many lives working the desert around Tacna and Yuma. I wish we could have saved all of them, but there's just no way. Some of it was just plain luck when we saved a life. I remember one rescue in particular. An alien had made it up to the interstate, turned himself in, and said that two buddies were still down in the desert. So we started backtracking, working from the interstate southward. It was a windy day and the tracks were being blown out, and the agents were having a hard time keeping on the tracks, and I was flying a line that I thought was the direction this guy had come from. We'd worked all afternoon, and it was getting late. I happened to fly over a small tree among a lot of bushes and trees. There were clothes spread all over that tree. The people had seen me flying back and forth, so they threw bright clothes up there so I could see them. It turned out to be a group of I forget how many men and women, but it was just blind luck that I came across them. They weren't going any farther. They were exhausted and had given up. They were out of water. That was one highlight that kind of amazed me. It was just blind luck that we found them. We never did find the original two that we went after.

The El Salvadoran group of twenty-six in the dunes group was a memorable search. A Marine helicopter pilot spotted them in the military firing range and reported them to the Border Patrol. I was the first one for the Border Patrol to spot two of them. That group had split up into several bunches, and I spotted two guys perhaps eight miles south of the interstate. As I was circling, one guy was staggering, so on the loud speaker I told him to sit down, and I landed. The closest place I could get was about a mile. Dave was working his airplane south of me, still trying to catch up with the group at that time. We informed the agents in Yuma to head out our way. I grabbed a water jug and finally caught up with them. One guy was "out of it" and fainted, so I poured water on him. Then he sat straight up, looked at me, and went back down. I tried to give him a little water, but he wouldn't take any. The other guy got his fill of water. I took a shirt and placed it over the face of the guy who had passed out. I dragged him to a bush so he could be in the shade, and I put the shirt over the bush to give him more shade. I walked back to the airplane so I could guide our agents in there, and when I got back to where these two aliens were, the other guy had taken the shirt that I'd put over the bush for his friend and was shading *himself* with it. Some buddy! The fellow that passed out didn't survive. We looked for the rest of that group, but those two were the only ones I found. Dave and Colonel worked that group the next day and found the rest of them.

When we found a dead body out there, especially if he hadn't been dead that long, you'd go home that night and feel kind of bad about that. It kind of upset you. We wouldn't give up if we were after somebody. I'd fly until the agent said, "Okay, Jackie, we're not gonna get this guy. He's already made it out." Or we'd fly 'til it got dark. Sometimes we got outfoxed, and someone would make it to the mountains or to one of the watering holes, but we'd look again the next day. And sometimes you'd find him down in the desert, to his ill fate. But that just happens.

A low point in my career was when Lester hit the power lines at Dune Siding. That was a pretty dark period. My goodness, that was terrible. He was from Tucson and had several kids. It was a bad time. And after I transferred out of Yuma, about a year later Dave died, and that was pretty bad. Dave and I had worked together for many years. That was pretty hard to take.

I'll tell you another low point, also. There were two young kids, and one of the boys was traveling with his mother about four or five miles south of the Mohawk Pass. They decided to cross over the mountain, but when the mother got almost to the top—I'd say she was within fifty yards—she stopped. She couldn't make it anymore, climbing that mountain. She sat under a bush and told the boys to go ahead and get some help. And they did. They turned themselves in, flagged down somebody on the interstate who called the Border Patrol. We took off and found where they crossed the mountain, but she wasn't there—she went on over that mountain. And it was just hard rocks on the east side of that mountain, and we never did pick up her, her tracks, the body, or anything. We're pretty sure that she didn't make it out. That was such a bad feeling. The boys were around fifteen.

I miss flying for the Border Patrol. Number one, I just miss flying. I wish I could fly again. I wish I had the money to do whatever I wanted with aircraft. But what really I miss is working with the agents. They were the best!

To become a good Border Patrol pilot I think you have to love flying, and you have to love working with the agents. You have to be able to track. And for survival, you'd better be able to fly. I think you have to be dedicated. When I think about it now, you have to be a little insane. My goodness, working out there in that heat, day after day?! How did we do it?

But it was fun. I enjoyed it, and believed in what I was doing. That's the main thing, I think—I believed in my work. And the more you got into it, the more dedicated you became—especially over in Tacna. You realized, especially in summertime, that if you didn't get these guys that day, they might not make it out. So we worked as hard as we could to catch those folks before they ran out of water.

I'd like the public to know that the pilots and also the agents I worked with were a very dedicated bunch, and we worked long and hard hours, and mostly in extreme temperatures. We did the best we could do, and we did it day after day, and year after year. One thing we all had in common, we loved to work outdoors. And I think that that's why we loved it. I like walking across the desert from time to time. When Dave Roberson showed up, boy, he was gonna put his time in at Yuma and then head back to Texas as soon as he could. I told him, "Dave, I don't think you will ever go back to Texas, as a pilot, anyway, because I think you're gonna like it here. You're gonna like the flying, and you're gonna like the area." It turned out to be true. He loved that desert. He loved walking in that desert.

Besides doing Border Patrol work, we'd help out the other agencies as much as we could. I can remember some guys from L.A. had robbed a grocery store in Yuma, and I was sitting just on the other side of the Gila Mountains. There's a little airstrip on the north side of the highway. I was setting there having a cup of coffee with Glen Payne, one of the Tacna agents, and the call went out to the checkpoint giving the description of the car that was involved in the robbery. About five minutes later the checkpoint said that they'd just waved that car through. So I got airborne and started down the interstate, and immediately there's that car right in front of me. Glen Payne was right behind me on the interstate. And then a couple of other agents from Tacna fell in line. I think probably Highway Patrol was involved, too. We got the robbers up at Tacna, pulled them over, and they were apprehended. They didn't try to bail out and run, not with the plane circling over them and about four ground units around them. They decided to give up. They must have been surprised. They had escaped in town and then got caught in the middle of nowhere. It's amazing somebody would try to do a robbery there in Yuma when there's nowhere to go.

And some of our work didn't involve aliens or criminals. We found a boy who had gone missing out in the sand dunes south of Glamis. He was riding one of those four-wheelers with his dad, and the boy had a flat tire. So the dad told the boy to wait there, and took off to get the tire fixed. He left the boy there. And when he returned, he couldn't find his boy. He got all mixed up. I had just come on duty and was working the evening shift, flying the helicopter. So my observer and I took off and started working the sand dunes. We worked almost until I was gonna have to go refuel before we finally found him. He was unharmed, just scared and thirsty. And his dad was pretty scared, too. You never knew what was gonna be happening from day to day. It was a pretty exciting job.

And we had a holiday candy drop. When I first started flying, I was checking the borderline out near a little Mexican community about twenty miles east of Yuma. I'd fly that line, checking for sign, and as I flew by this one particular building, I'd notice the bottom portion of this building didn't have any siding on it. I could see little feet in there, school kids in a semi-open classroom. They realized that it was a Border Patrol plane, and every time I flew by them, they'd all come out of there and wave. So come Christmastime, I got some little packets of candy, and I'd go over there and I'd drop some candy to the kids. And then when Hank came aboard, he did the same thing. And then of course Dave did it, too. The kids got a kick out of watching that plane go by every day. Eventually that little town dried up, and we noticed one day there was just nobody there. We never got any static about doing that. I don't even know if the chiefs knew about it. I never said anything, and I don't know if Hank ever said anything. There we were, invading Mexico with candy!

HANK HAYS

Richard E. "Hank" Hays lives in New Mexico and works as a helicopter cowboy. He was in the U.S. Border Patrol from 1970 to 1999 and at Yuma Sector Air Operations from 1979 to 1982 and from 1990 to 1997.

I joined Border Patrol looking for a good job. I couldn't afford to be a cowboy, couldn't make a living at it. I was married and thought about applying to the New Mexico State Police. I was living on a ranch, working in a mine, and working on the ranch up between Lordsburg and Silver City, New Mexico. The Border Patrol was there every few days looking for aliens, so I got to talking to some of the agents. One of them, Greg Whipple, I'd known for a long time, and he ended up a Border Patrol pilot. That's what got me interested in Border Patrol.

I became a pilot to get off the ground. Yuma was the only place I could find a patrol pilot's job. At that time, the Border Patrol required a commercial instrument rating and 1,500 hours. So I started flying while I was an agent at Lordsburg, and got my private pilot license, and then went for my commercial and my instrument ratings, and kept flying until I got the 1,500 hours. It took a while and it cost a lot of money. Nowadays they've got to have 250 hours to get in a training program. Back then, it was quite a deal. I flew with the El Paso Sector pilots quite a bit, and I got pointers from all of them. But the one I flew with the most was probably Clarence Townsend. When I got my 1,500 hours, I started applying for jobs. Buck Brandemuehl, the new chief at Yuma, knew me from El Paso, so he picked me.

When I came out to Yuma, they had no supervisory pilot. Jackie Mason had been here two months when I got here, and he hadn't had an airplane until the week before I got here, because it was in the shop being rebuilt.

So we kind of started off together, the two of us did. We managed to get a second airplane not too long after Jackie and I started. And then David Roberson showed up nearly two years later. We still just had two aircraft, but with days off, there was just one day a week where one of us had to go work in the vehicle. The rest of the time we had something to fly. We had two Super Cubs at the time: Three-One-Zulu [N4331-Z] and Nine-Zero-Lima [N6590-L].

In 1982 I transferred to Tucson and took a supervisory job in Tucson. The chiefs would get their heads together and kind of see who they wanted to pick for some job, and they recruited me for Tucson. I would have probably stayed in Yuma for a long time, but they needed a supervisor at Tucson, and so they kind of coerced me. I didn't have to do it, but I had some people pushing me, "You need to put in for that." I didn't stay in Tucson but a year and a half, before I went to El Paso flight operations as an assistant chief. Ed Kennedy was the chief at El Paso when I got there. Kennedy had talked me into taking the job at El Paso. I stayed with him for a while, and that was becoming so political that I got tired of it, so I went over to the El Paso Sector as the sector pilot. And then when Kennedy left, I went back over as the chief pilot at El Paso flight operations.

I got crossways with one boss when he took over Border Patrol, because he wanted to use air ops for a pawn to force the chiefs to do what he wanted them to do. He told me, "If you don't do so and so, I'll just move all your pilots and aircraft." We said, "Nah, we ain't doin' that." And I got crossways with him. In fact, he detailed me to Washington, D.C., for an unspecified duration, so I would become a team player. And I told him, "You ain't got enough time left in your career or enough money in your detail budget to keep me up there to be a team player on *your* team, because that ain't gonna happen." That really smoked him.

And then when David Roberson got killed in Yuma, Johnny Williams called that morning to tell me. I walked into the boss's office and said, "I'll be going to Yuma." He said, "You ain't goin' nowhere." And I said, "We'll see about that." And I went to Yuma. That guy was ultrapolitical, and he didn't last long up there. It was the whole bureaucratic thing. It was just a mess. My guess is it's much more of a mess now because there're so many more of them up there. I don't deal well with politics. Of course, we've always had the political-type chiefs, too, always looking out for themselves first. So what can you say? That's how they made their careers.

Yuma was all Super Cubs the first time I was here, and then it was nearly all helicopter operations my second tour of seven years. At El Paso and Tucson we had Cessnas, Pipers, and helicopters, so we kind of rotated.

Hank Hays. Photo by Bill Broyles, 2006.

You flew a Cessna one day, a Piper the next, and a helicopter the next, and depending on what aircraft you had kind of dictated what area you worked and what you did. At Yuma it was pretty much the same thing every day: somebody would go cut the east desert, and somebody would go cut the west desert.

As long as you're there to support those agents on the ground, it's a great job. It took a while to get rid of some of the hassles that had been stirred up, and to make some of the older pilots see that we needed to do check rides every six months and keep a record, so everybody's on board. And the safety issues, I thought we did real good with them, because we got a lot of safety training and got everybody into the Airborne Law Enforcement Association, which really focuses on law enforcement aircraft safety.

I thought it went really well over there, but it was kind of like we, myself and all the pilots, were against headquarters, because it was like pulling teeth to get those people to do anything. We had been flying Super Cubs low level for years working trails. But after Dave Roberson's crash in a Christen Husky, the bureaucrats were scared to death of Christen Industries, makers of the Christen Husky aircraft, and Senator Alan Simpson, from Christen's home state. That Husky was a bad airplane. And it went so far as for us to have a conference call with the guy that ran the aircraft company in Afton, Wyoming, Senator Alan Simpson, our headquarters people, and myself. And when *that* came about, I asked Senator Simpson, "Have the people at Christen Industries told you about the characteristics of the Husky when it encounters wake turbulence?" And he said, "No, I don't believe they have." And I said, "Maybe they ought to be telling you what it does." We didn't know what happened to David, but I had a good idea. The test pilot for the Husky told me they had duplicated what happened.

Then when Charlie Chandler had his accident in a Husky, I went to the intensive care unit at Tucson Medical Center because he wanted to see me. The doctor came out and said, "Are you Hank Hays?" "Yes, sir." "You've got *five* minutes." And I went in and Charlie told me, "I hit my own wake, and it was completely uncontrollable." So we grounded all the Huskies. Then Christen Industries said, "Oh, you're ruining our reputation!" I said, "Well, you're ruining our pilots!" And I wanted to ground all the Huskies, but our headquarters, to not tick somebody off, just grounded all the fixed wings. I told Senator Simpson, "This airplane has some inherent problems. It's a design flaw. It's not the way we're operating it." But what did headquarters do? They said, "No more low-level flights in the fixed-wing airplanes, even Super Cubs," and they completely wiped out an operation that had been productive for many years.

Grounding all the fixed wings from sign-cutting at low level never needed to happen. It was just absolutely absurd. In fact, the deputy at headquarters ordered me to put the Huskies back in the air. He said, "You put out a memo *now* putting those airplanes back in the air." And I said, "Nope, *you* put out the memo with *your* name on it—ol' Hank ain't doin' it." And he threatened me with disciplinary action, and I said, "Hop to it. You do whatever you think you need to do. But I will not do that, because I'm not gonna kill another pilot." And it didn't happen. It was just hassle all the time with that bunch up there.

When I first went to work for headquarters, Buck Brandemuehl was up there and it was fine. Buck left, and Hugh Brian took over, and he was great, no problems. Hugh selected me for the Chief Pilot job. But the minute the politico came in and all the professionals left, it just fell apart. The leadership at headquarters makes a big difference.

I wanted to get rid of the Huskies right now. And then they said, "No, we're going to put a flight restriction on *everything*, on all the fixed-wing aircraft: you can't fly them below 500 feet." I said, "Well, you're messin' up, but if that's what you're gonna do, do it. I'm going to Yuma." And they said, "Well, you can't do that. You'd have to take a reduction in pay." I said, "You hide in the grass and watch."

So I called Gene Corder, chief at Yuma, and told him I wanted a pilot's job, and he said, "Well, you ain't gettin' one. I've got a pilot supervisor's job open. If you're comin' out here, you're takin' *that*." I said, "I don't want it." He said, "Well, then I guess that's the end of this conversation." I said, "Well, if you put it that way, I'll take it." He said, "Send me your paperwork. With all the experience and training you've had, they would hang me out to dry if I took you as a pilot and didn't bring you out here as a supervisor." "Okay, Gene, whatever." And this is a really good bunch of guys here at Yuma—still is. I had Howard Aitken, Colonel Child, Walt Jones, then we got Joe Dunn as a trainee. Yuma is a good operation. I was fed up with that other bunch.

What made the operation at Yuma better to work with than other places was the work ethic. The guys were eager to fly. At some places, you have to tell them to fly, otherwise they all want to hang around the hangar. I've heard supervisors telling their pilots, "You know, if an alien walks in here, I'll catch him for y'all. Why don't y'all go on and fly today." You didn't have to make these Yuma guys go fly. And the weather's decent for flying, but it is a lot of other places, too. There're places where the guys want the money, but they don't want to fly the aircraft. And if they've got a supervisor that lets them get by with that, it just gets worse.

We had a good unit here in Yuma when I was working, and they had a really good unit in Del Rio. Those guys flew a lot of hours and did a lot of work. I always told staff that they needed to pay these pilots agent wages and then pay them extra for flying—that would get them off their tails and out there flying to make a little money. When they give them that GS-12 rating and all they had to do to earn it was sit in the hangar, a whole lot of them sat in the hangar. If they'd have been making the same wages that the guys on the ground were making, they'd have been out there putting some time on those airplanes. That was never a problem in Yuma. And I never saw it as a problem in Del Rio, but most other places, there was a lot of hangar flyin'. It varied, too, depending on who the sector chief was, not just the supervisory pilot, and how much they demanded or didn't demand.

When I was at El Paso I was called in a number of times for flying *too* much. And I wasn't going over the 100-hour-a-month limit. I asked the supervisor, "What's the problem with how much I'm flying?" "Well, you're making these other guys look bad." "Well, maybe these other guys ought to get off their duff and go fly." There were three of us there that flew 90–100 hours a month, and three more there that flew 20–30 hours a month. And they do that a lot of places. But it seems like Yuma's always had a bunch of guys that would go fly. And a lot of that's driven by what needs to be done. You're not going to go out and fly only four hours on a trail if you know somebody's going to die in the desert. You're going to go fly 'til you find them, or until it gets too dark to look.

My favorite airplane to fly is the Piper Super Cub. But my favorite air-*craft* would be a Huey. For a while we had a special Huey at Yuma. That was an amazing aircraft. And not all Hueys are that way. That one was special, because it had that electronic-controlled engine in it, which gave it four hours of fuel range and lots of power. You could pick up lots of people with it: and we did, we evacuated quite a few groups from the desert with it, not having to wait for a ground unit. Load them in the back and go. We actually used it for search and rescue and worked trails with it. You gotta have a little technique to work a trail with it, so that you don't blow all the sign away, but I just liked to fly the thing.

Joe Dunn and I found a van down here on the lower drag road one morning and followed the occupants. They were going towards Tule Well afoot, because the van broke down. And they were out of water, writing s.o.s. in the sand. We picked them up, I told Joe, "Load seven of them and we'll go to Wellton Station, then come back and get the other seven." Some were protesting at being left behind, so I said, "Okay, load all four-teen of them. Load them all, and we'll see if we've got enough power to pick up." Joe Dunn was calling out power as I was pulling pitch, and we were off the ground and flying at 72 percent. We hauled them all out in one load. The Huey was neat to have.

That little OH-6 is the best aircraft the Border Patrol ever had, but they're just so antiquated that you can't get parts for them, and they served their useful life. The last one was built in 1967. So we needed something else. They're buying A-Stars now, and those are really good machines, but I don't know how the guys like them, because I've flown one very little.

Now I'm flying a little Robinson helicopter and rounding up cattle with it. I cowboyed as a kid up until I got in the Border Patrol. When I retired and moved back to Deming, I met a ranch family there in New Mexico that has probably the biggest family-owned cattle ranch in New Mexico, 475,000 acres. I went to work for them in September of 1999, and I've enjoyed it. The owner asked me one time, "Are you having fun?" I said, "William, I wouldn't be here if I wasn't havin' fun. I don't *have* to have this job." But I do a lot more than fly down there. I pretty much ranch-hand the rest of the time. I guess you go back to your roots. That's what I've done.

Glen Payne, who became station chief at Wellton, and I went to high school together, though we weren't in the same class. There's been some other people from Silver City since then that have gone to Border Patrol, but not that I knew very well. Glen and I were buddies, kind of ran in the same circle and all that there in high school.

I believe more in leadership than I do bossing. I don't like bosses, so I didn't want to be a boss. I'm not going to ask somebody to do something that I won't go do myself. I'm a puller, not a pusher. "Y'all come on. Lead, follow, or get the hell out of the way."

This bunch of pilots at Yuma was really bummed out, all of us were, when David Roberson got killed, and they weren't flying as much when I got back there. I said, "We all miss him, but it's time to really get back in the groove." And they did. They snapped right to and we started working. And then when I said, "Well, we're going to do some helicopter night operations," they responded reluctantly. I said, "I'm gonna do the first two weeks." I got an observer from the station, and we were just knocking them dead. I mean, the aliens weren't used to being harassed at night with a helicopter. And I thought, "Well, instead of doing two weeks, I'll just do a full month of it." But before my month was up, Colonel and Howard were asking, "Hey, when's *our* turn? *We* want to do that!"

I've always believed that it was easier to get somebody to do something like that if you show them it was going to work, than it is to tell them. If I'd have slammed my hand on the desk and said, "You guys are gonna fly at night!" you can imagine how unenthusiastic they would have been about flying at night. It got to the point where we were all asking, "Hey, when's my turn?"

I had some people who were really good examples through my career. I had some bosses, and I had some leaders, and there's a big difference. John Neal was my first leader. He was the senior at Lordsburg. He was one of those same kind of people. Bill Gibson was a leader. Mark Haynes was definitely a leader. I really enjoyed working for Mark. I was in a supervisory position when I worked for Mark. He was helpful. I'd go down to the office and I'd say, "Well, I've got to call El Paso," or call this or that to get something that we needed. He'd say, "You want to go fly? I'll take care of that for you." He just made it so easy to get along.

One time at Yuma, we got a new assistant chief. Every year they assigned us to an assistant chief who had an area responsibility, and they rotated every year on the thirty-first of March. I'd been working for Mark Haynes for a year, and just before the first of April, a new list came out with all the assistant chiefs' names and areas of responsibility. Now I was working for another guy. The first month I worked for this guy, we had thirty-two calls to assist other agencies: Imperial County sheriff, Yuma County sheriff, Yuma Police Department, and Arizona Department of Public Safety. We always had some calls from them, but thirty-two was a fairly high number.

I turned my report in and the new assistant chief looked at it and said, "This has got to stop! You guys are here to work for the Border Patrol, not all these other agencies." And I told him, "We all live in the community, and we need to help these other cops as much as we can, because they help us a lot." He said, "I'm gonna put a stop to this. I don't want you doing this." I said, "I'll tell you what I need, if you're gonna do that. I need it in writing, because I'm not going to walk across the street to Sheriff Ralph Ogden's office and tell him not to call me anymore. Somebody else is gonna have to take the heat for that." He said, "Okay, you'll get it."

So I went on, and the next day when I got in from flying, the mechanic said, "The Chief wants to see you." And I said, "Well, I'll call him." And he said, "No, he wants to *see* you." "Oh, okay, I'll go down there." And Jim Switzer was the chief then. I went down and knocked on his door. "C'mon in." I walked in. "Close the door." I said, "Oh, okay." I closed the door. He dug around on his desk a little bit, and he pulled out this assistant chief chart with the areas of responsibility, and shoved it across his desk, and said, "I made some changes on this. I wanted to show it to you." I said, "Oh?" I picked it up and looked at it.

I figured when I went down there, he was going to give me the memo telling me not to take calls from the other agencies anymore. I picked it up and looked at it, and he said, "I've moved you back under Mark Haynes. You have a problem with that?" I said, "No, sir, I really don't. Mark and I can work real well together." And we did. The other guy didn't get his way. Obviously he hit the Chief with a memo for a signature, and the Chief probably said, "Nah, you go back and sit down, and I'll take care of this. You won't have to deal with Air Ops anymore." So we continued to do the other agency thing, and I thought it paid great dividends. You just can't not work with other law enforcement agencies. Where this guy was coming from, I don't know. I guess he needed to change something to show he was in charge.

In the Wellton-Yuma area the most important thing Border Patrol does is search and rescue. I think they get recognized enough for it, but the general population doesn't know the risks that these guys take to save these people out here. If pilots or agents come out here and crack one up, we're gonna find them, but it may be too late, because this old desert is hard. And I don't think there's a real appreciation for how much risk that they're taking to come out here and save lives and work these trails. I think it's been a real professional bunch of guys over the years.

You go through some pretty rough times when you lose buddies like Les Haynie and David Roberson. I lost one in El Paso who I was pretty close to, Louie Stahl. One of my classmates at Lordsburg in '74, Lee Bounds, got killed. So you kind of get some bonds there that people don't understand who haven't been in law enforcement and haven't done what you've done.

Les was still on trainee status. He was just *almost* to a pilot's job. He was just short of his 1,500 hours. And Dave knew that Les was flying low level and he wasn't supposed to until he made pilot, and all that stuff, but he was plenty competent controlling the aircraft and all, so he was just kind of letting him go work. He went out there and drove into a wire. The crash didn't kill him. When he hit upside down, it knocked him out, and he suffocated. So if there'd been a ground unit there with him, I don't think he'd have had that severe of injuries. I think he'd have made it if there'd been somebody there to get him out of the airplane. It just wasn't to be. He clipped that top wire, and it came down on the other wires, and then bounced off of them and went upside down, according to the investigation. I didn't come out for that one. I didn't come for David's either, since I was in Washington on disciplinary detail. Those times were pretty rough times. Kinda gotta wade through them, but the Border Patrol family really sticks together when something like that happens.

When we got Joe Dunn as a trainee, he told me one time, "I hope I can learn to fly one of these things as good as *you* do." And I said, "Nah, Joe, that's the wrong way to look at this." "What do you mean?" And I said, "If you don't fly *better* than I fly, I didn't do my job, because you've got guys like Colonel and Howard to fly with, too. You take something good home from everybody, and you should be a better pilot than any of us." I think he probably is. His boss says he's really good, and he was already pretty good before I left.

And then when you've got a bunch of guys that are willing to teach the younger ones, they *should* be better. They should be able to do it quicker and easier. I enjoyed the training part of it. You get kind of spoiled, flying by yourself and doing what you want to do, but you gotta pass it on. And I had the same opportunities when *I* started flying. Those El Paso pilots, for a while there I flew with a different guy every day. And then I'd fly some — a day by myself, and a day with one of them. They all showed me how to do something in a different way, and you kind of pick the one that works good for you, and you go on with it. And then there's a few that you fly with that you learn how *not* to do things, and that's always good too! "Boy, I wouldn't do *that*!" and "I'll never do it again!" and "Don't do it with me in the aircraft." Clarence Townsend gave me some advice when I started flying. He said, "Always fly a little bit scared." I don't think I fly scared, but you've really got to pay attention, because low level is not forgiving.

The weather can be tricky certain times of year with airplanes. It's not so bad with the helicopters, but the desert air is so heavy that wake turbulence is a problem. And if you do a real tight turn back through where you just flew, you can definitely crunch one—even a Super Cub. I had a Super Cub on its back up here at the interstate where the Wellton-Mohawk Canal comes under the interstate one morning. That was the only trail I ever quit before I really got started. Joe McCraw was there, and he had these tracks. I came in there, did a turn around there to get them lined out, and hit my own wake, and the airplane went upside down and I scared myself pretty bad. When I hit that wake, I was right over those wires there, probably sixty, seventy feet. And when I came out of it, I was right over those paloverdes at about two feet. I mean, I came real close to hitting the ground. I don't know whether he saw me go upside down or not; he was out looking at sign. It took full power and all that old Cub had to pull out of it. When I got it leveled back out, I said, "Joe, I just scared myself, I'm going home." He said, "Okay, Hank." So I just went to Yuma, parked it, propped my feet up, and drank a Coke. That's probably the worst I ever scared myself, but it was a real eye-opener.

John L'Hullier and I were in a crash the first of September, 1972, and it was a year later that Fritz Karl and John Blue got killed at Tacna. Our crash was traumatic! The Patrol Agent in Charge from Lordsburg, Bennie Dunlap, and I, were going to El Paso in a sedan to turn in end-of-month reports and pick up a new pursuit sedan. We stopped at the truck stop in Deming for breakfast, and met the PAIC and pilot John L'Hullier for breakfast there. Benny had brought *his* end-of-month report from the Lordsburg Station, and there were reports to be picked up at Columbus.

John said, "Hank can go with me. We'll take you guys' reports, go get those at Columbus, and we'll just take them to El Paso, and you won't have to drive down there." And they thought that was a good idea, so I got in the back seat. We flew down to Columbus and got the reports, and we were almost to El Paso when the El Paso farm and ranch check unit in the upper valley called us for some air support. They were checking some crews. John asked me, "You got time to go up there and help those guys?" "Sure, I've got all day, whatever you want to do." We went up there, made one turn around that field, and planted the plane. We went into a real tight turn to avoid some wires, and the airplane stalled and went on its back. John ended up with a medical retirement, and I ended up with a lot of plate and wire in my head. We did both survive, but it was a really close call.

We stalled in a real tight turn on a wingtip, and when the bottom wing stalled, the airplane flipped back this way and went inverted. And he lowered the nose and tried to roll it back upright to get some airspeed; when the wings came back around, we were maybe ten feet from impact. The first thing that hit the ground was the prop spinner. We were in such a steep angle that the main gear didn't even contact the ground 'til after the prop did. It folded the wings forward, and my seat belt broke where it was welded into the airframe, and I smashed John's seat into the instrument panel. It really messed us up.

We had ground units right there, and they carried us out of the field. I can recall only some of it. John was fairly heavy, so the farmer went and tore a door off a storage shed, and they laid John on it to carry him out of the field. A big guy named Mike Waters carried me out in his arms. They laid us there on the pavement. Louie Castaneda was on radio at dispatch. Virgil Franks was the senior there that day, and he called dispatch in El Paso and said, "Louie, we got an airplane down, we need an ambulance." He said, "Is it a service aircraft?" "That's affirmative. It's L'Hullier and Hays from Lordsburg." And Louie went on the all-channel button and told everybody to hold their radio calls in order to keep it clear for emergency radio traffic only. He had El Paso, Anthony, and Las Cruces ambulances en route. He dispatched all three of them. They picked us up and took us to El Paso to the hospital and patched us up.

I didn't stay off work but about six weeks, and then I just had to go back and sit around the office, because they had my mouth wired shut for my broken jaw and stuff. I lost down to 115 pounds. I answered the phone and sat around the office and processed wets. I couldn't do much. And John *tried* to go back to work and couldn't. So he finally took a medical retirement. That was my only crash, but it was one experience too many. I thought maybe I'd better learn to fly myself. I was tired of riding with those crazy Border Patrol pilots.

I came close to shooting my first person on duty during that fiasco. A little nurse's aide at Providence Hospital in El Paso tried to take my pistol away from me. I was in and out of consciousness. I was losing lots of blood, but it was going into my stomach, so they didn't realize how much I was bleeding from my innards. She came in there and tried to take my gun belt and gun away from me, and all I could remember was my training at the academy: "Don't let them take your gun." And I just about capped her. Mike Waters stepped in the door and hollered, "Hank! Don't shoot!" And I didn't pull the trigger; she nearly fainted. Mike came over and said, "Hank, how about letting me take your gun and your badge out to the office and lock them up?" "Oh, okay, Mike." Gosh, that would have been horrible. The little gal was just trying to get me prepped so they could work on me, but she was after my gun is all I knew, and she was fixing to get the business end of it. I felt bad about it later, but I wouldn't have had a clue.

From high-speed chases on the highway with Arizona DPS to working these trails in the desert, the chases have been too numerous to mention. I did 220 incident reports in the last seven years I was at Yuma.

Joe Dunn and I caught a trail of Russians who would have certainly died by the time they got to Big Pass drag road. A Mexican smuggler had taken their money and given them a map that he tore out of a State Farm road atlas with some marks on it. They didn't have a clue how far it was. Two of them could speak very little English, and the others couldn't speak *any*. And I told Joe when we got on the trail, "This is not Mexicans," because they were discarding hair spray bottles and alarm clocks and magazines and stuff. We never stopped and looked at any of the stuff. The next day, Howard came out and recovered some of it, and got an alarm clock with Russian numerals on it. But we were busy pushing the trail. And then we got to a point where they spent the night, and they broke a bunch of limbs off a paloverde and made them a kind of a pallet to lay on. When we caught up with them, they were all waving, trying to get our attention. Instead of being buried under a bush, hiding, they were out in the open, trying to get us flagged down. I got out and asked a blond-headed guy. "Where are you from?" And he said, "Roosha!" That's about all he could tell me.

Agent Reggie Felker was about six-foot-seven, real good guy, hard-working guy, and *huge*. He was working that day, and we tricked him into doing the paperwork. We radioed him and said, "We've got a group in Little Pass, would you come pick them up?" When we saw his dust coming, we jumped in the helicopter and left. We told them, "That guy's comin' to get you. We're goin'." When he got there and figured out it wasn't a group of Mexicans, he called, "You've got to help process these people!" "Nope. It says in the administrative manual that pilots don't process aliens."

I guess we didn't realize what the air traffic controllers at Yuma Marine Corps airbase thought of us. One time I landed on Runway 8, turned off at the first intersection, and went back to the 1-7 intersection and asked for a clearance across the runway to go to where we parked over at Burch Aircraft. I kind of turned, looked out the windshield of the Cub, and there was a Bonanza on short final approach, landing gear down and all that. I just held short of the runway, even though they'd already cleared me to cross. About that time, this panicked voice come on the radio, "Three-One-Zulu, hold short! hold short!" I was just setting there. The Bonanza landed. If I'd pulled out on the runway, he'd have hit me. It was some doctor; they're not known for flying skills. The little controller that had cleared me to park came back on. He keyed his mic to tell me to go on across the runway, and the tower chief was standing behind him, ripping him a new one. The words I heard were, "If that hadn't been a Border Patrol aircraft, you would have had an accident on your hands!"

Actually, I'd rather fly down there with the military pilots than with the civilian pilots. They've got more discipline and they're better trained. Our Border Patrol airspace from the ground to 200 feet wasn't always ground to 200. Sometimes the military pilots were down at 50 feet, and they're pretty fast movers, so you gotta watch them. But it wasn't bad out here, really. They tried to violate me one time. You know what the elevation is at Buck Peak? Maybe twenty-five hundred feet. I was out here taking Dennis Segura, on staff at Cabeza Prieta National Wildlife Refuge, to Buck Peak to install a radio repeater up there. I had my ground-to-200-feet clearance, when dispatch called and said, "Air traffic control's tryin' to get ahold of you." So I switched over to their frequency and called them. They said "Six-Two-Quebec? We've got you in violation of your clearance." "Oh? How so?" "Well, we're showin' you at 2,500 feet," or whatever it was up there. I said, "I was of the understanding that my clearance was ground to 200 feet AGL, above ground level." "That's correct, and we're showing you at 2,000 and something." I said, "Well, I'm settin' on the ground right now. I've still got 200 feet above me that's mine." One of their F-16s had locked onto me with his radar, and was getting my transponder readout on my altitude and called it in. I said, "I saw your guy go by. I don't think he saw me, but here I am sittin' on Buck Peak, so I don't think I'm in violation of being above 200 feet." They decided they wouldn't violate me when they found out I was sitting on the ground.

Then Colonel Child, our pilot, and I went on a Mexican incursion. I think it was Mexican soldiers, but it could have been cops, who came into the U.S. down here east of border boundary marker 198, and stopped a civilian range employee who was out reading sound meters for an environmental assessment. And the Mexicans came across the line and stopped this guy with M-16s. He was in a panic. He called the base on his cell phone, and they called us to go down there. And Colonel and I jumped in the helicopter and started down there. And I called the departure control and told them we were entering the restricted airspace. The little controller said, "Negative! Six-Two-Quebec, you can't go in there, the range is hot!" And I called him back and said, "I ain't askin', I'm tellin' ya'. We're entering 2301-West." The new controller didn't know what the deal was.

Colonel looked at me like, "Are we gonna get in trouble with this?" I said, "You don't worry about it. I'll take care of this. Let's go!" And we went buzzing down there, and by the time we got there, the guy was still there, really shook up, but the Mexicans had gone back south. So we turned around and come back out. When we got clear of the range, I called approach control, "Border Patrol Six-Two-Quebec clear of the range." And the supervisor in there came on and said, "Hey, Hank, sorry about the mix up awhile ago." I tell you, the handling that the Marines give the Border Patrol pilots at Yuma is like nowhere else. They were really, really good to us.

One morning I returned to the airport in a dust storm and the airport was closed. A Sky West commuter airliner and several other flights were holding, stacked up at Bard V-O-R, waiting for the storm to clear. And the base was recovering their jets. I called in three miles north. I was already in the airport traffic area. "Tower, Three-One-Zulu's inbound 1-7." "Three-One-Zulu, cleared to land." And this Sky West airline pilot comes on and says, "What are you doing letting *him* in when we're out here holding?!" The controller came right back and said, "We are recovering our own aircraft." And that was the end of that conversation.

I really had a good career. There were a few years here and there that weren't too enjoyable, but overall it was really a good career, the interesting administration and the duties that I had. When I was chief pilot in El Paso, it was just one political hassle after another one. That's why I went back to Yuma the *second* time in 1990. The turnover at headquarters and the bureaucratic shuffle up there was troublesome. When I used to go up there to meetings, some of them would ask me, "How are things in the field?" because I would make the rounds to all the field operations. And I said, "Well, you know, the field continues to operate in spite of this place." And that was not what they liked to hear, but it was true. It seemed like everything that the field tried to do enforcement-wise was blocked by some little bureaucrat in headquarters, for whatever political motive they had up there. I think they're still having that today, the same thing. They've got so many little politicians up there, wanting to get their agenda done, that the actual enforcement is not the priority. They tell the media that it is, but that's not happening.

Many of them are furthering their own personal agendas, and getting more pay grades for themselves. Enforcement is the furthest thing from their mind, and most of them don't have a clue what needs to be done in the field. When I came in the Border Patrol in 1970, it took on the average three minutes to do the paperwork on one alien. And now it takes about three *hours* to write one up. That's how the politicians are controlling how many we can catch. They have us so loaded with paperwork that if the agents catch one, their shift is over, and in effect it keeps them out of the field. With all the automated fingerprint and photography stuff they've got, and computers, it's taking them three hours to process somebody. It's ridiculous. And they've got equipment like we never saw, and they've got personnel like we never saw, and they *still* can't control it. It's just a mess. Office staff could handle some of those chores. Or they could do a rehired annuitant program for alien processing, and use retired agents, if they wanted to, until they got some civilians trained up to do it.

My whole take on it is they don't *want* us to control the border. I've even had a U.S. congressman tell me that it's not going to happen. He says the administration is afraid that if we close Mexico out, that China will move in down there, and they'll be right on our doorstep. That's his take on it. I had an eye-to-eye, heart-to-heart with the guy. He said if you think they're going to close this border, it ain't gonna happen. But all you hear on the media is we've got 10 million Border Patrol agents down there, and they're going to close it down. There ain't no way, because the politicians are going to keep them from working. And people are going to keep dying. We've bagged lots of bodies out here.

I walked in the control tower at Tucson International Airport one day, and Arizona Senator Dennis DeConcini was sitting there. He got up and glad-handed me, patting me on the back and all. "What's goin' on, on the border?" I said, "You see that Hughes 500 settin' out there, they're pumpin' fuel in?" "Yeah." I said, "Well, go hop in that sucker and I'll take you and show you what's goin' on." Boy, there was no way he was gonna load up in a helicopter with me. That was the end of *that* conversation.

I really enjoyed the whole thing. I've got no regrets that I retired, but I've sure got no regrets that I joined the Border Patrol. And I look at the mess now, and I think, "Boy, if I had to put up with what the guys are putting up with, I'd probably be disgruntled." But they don't know any better, so more power to them.

JOE McCRAW

Joe McCraw served in the U.S. Border Patrol from 1968 to 1988 and was patrol agent in charge at Tacna Station from 1978 to 1988. He still lives in the lower Gila River valley, not far from Tacna and Wellton, where he grew up.

If they offered me my job back, I'd start tomorrow. But they've got too many young ones out there who can do it. I got in the Border Patrol and never had any regrets. I loved it. The only regret I've got is they said at fifty-five I had to quit, mandatory retirement. That torqued my butt. If I could, I'd still be working for the Border Patrol. I'd be there tomorrow at roll call.

From the time I was six years old, I was raised in the valley right down here about two miles, and I lived in Wellton until I went in the Border Patrol in 1968. I came here in 1939. My granddad and my stepdad farmed over here on about 160 acres. My stepdad farmed up until, oh, '58—then we lost it all, lost every bit of it. He got the mining bug and sunk a bunch of money into uranium over here in the hills. He had claims of a pretty good thing, then some manganese and stuff up in Death Valley, but he lost his butt. One day he said, "Well, son, it's root, hog, or die." And I said, "What are you talking about?" "I have $14.40 in my pocket and a wife and three kids." That's when things got rough for a while.

When my stepdad told me that, I went to work on the farm. I got a job with a farmer here, who ran sheep. He had them on alfalfa in the summertime, cut hay, and I got a job with him cutting hay at 90¢ an hour. Turns out he was smarter than I was, because he made me foreman at a flat $300 a month. Three months later I figured it out that if I'd have worked by the hour, I'd have got better than $480 a month! Oh, that man worked me! He

Joe McCraw, left, with Mark Haynes and Glen Payne. Photo by Bill Broyles, 2008.

worked me harder than my stepdad ever did, and I thought my stepdad was bad.

I went in the Border Patrol in 1968, ninety-first session in the academy. We were the first class to go through Los Fresnos, and it was right after a hurricane hit it. The blooming buildings had roofs caved in and windows busted. We couldn't get up on the third floor, 'cause it was in such bad shape. I think there were forty-eight of us in the class. I took two semesters of Spanish in high school, but by the time I got in the Border Patrol, I'd forgotten all of it, except maybe a few numbers, that's about all. I went over to the academy and learned it there. I never was real fluent.

My first duty station was Calexico. I was there 'til '75, when I made supervisor at El Centro. When I came to Tacna only Mike Higgins and Bob Rogers were here. I came out here and walked in the office and they were sitting, had their feet up on the desk, and I walked in and said, "Ten-hut!" real loud, and they jumped. Both of them come clear out of their chairs and stood up straight. I kind of grinned at them, I said, "At ease." Why I did it, I don't know, but I don't think Higgins ever liked me after that. He's the only guy I ever had working for me that told me he hated my guts. And he told me that before he left. And I asked, "Why?" I guess I spent the next two years trying to figure that out, why he hated my guts.

And the only thing I could come up with was he wanted the job as station chief and he thought he had it cornered—he didn't even bother to put in for the job, because he'd set there for over ninety days in charge of the station. But they didn't give it to him, they gave it to me.

And another thing burned him. I went into McElhaney's feed lot. He told me there wasn't no need to go to McElhaney's, they weren't hiring aliens. Shoot, when you drove by McElhaney's, you *knew* they were hiring aliens. So I had him make a morning raid. I came on up there after they'd started, figured I'd let them handle it, with about five men. Mike told me, "We went all through here, we can't find anyone." I looked at him, I said, "Let's go look again." And I went in there, we came out with twenty. He didn't like that. But then later on, after he got down to Casa Grande, he seemed to warm up to me a little bit. I saw him a couple of years before he died and talked to him—pretty friendly, a lot more than he used to be.

I had a class with Ed Tuffly at a school that they sent us to. He was a nice guy. I had a lot of fun talking to him. Ed was at Tacna back when I was working on the farm. We were using aliens to pick cotton, but I never had much contact with Ed then. I'd see him working trails across farm-land when I was out stubbing cotton and stuff like that. You'd see him going through, but he never came on the farm. I used to get up on the cotton wagon and holler "La Migra!" I had one old guy by the name of Andreas. I'll never forget him. He'd chase me around the cotton wagon for half an hour, trying to catch me to whup my butt. I had to finally tell him I wouldn't do that no more. He'd be out there picking away, and I'd holler, "La Migra!" and then "pop, pop, pop, boom!" right down, like a bunch of quail. I thought it was funny, but they didn't seem to think so—a seventeen-year-old kid doing that to them.

Our emphasis of the station when I came to Tacna was farm and ranch check and the border. When we had enough men, we worked both. We'd have a farm and ranch crew out working and another crew down on the border. When there were just three or four of us, we couldn't do it all. We worked on the border for a while, and come up and worked on the farm. The most agents I ever had was nine, somethin' like that. I only had two when I took over the station. It wasn't long after that they sent us some boys out of El Paso: Glen Payne and Robert somebody. And, we had Borrego and May.

My management philosophy at the station was treat everybody that worked for me like I'd like to be treated. And I treated the illegals like I'd want to be treated. When I saw an illegal, I'd take them if I could. If I couldn't catch him, or if he was on a farm and I couldn't get ahold of the owner, I've been known to leave him, and tell the alien to come see me. I had one old boy who told his boss, "I gotta go to the station. Take me to the station. Jefe said I had to come up." "Jefe," he called me. So, the farmer brought him up and said, "He was just about to have a fit to get up here. He was afraid that you was gonna get mean with him." I said, "I've never been mean with a guy in my life." He turned himself in. But I left him. That's one of the few I left. I worked them when I was a kid, worked *with* them when I got older. They're just like anybody else, I think—they're just trying to make a living.

Most of the Tacna guys never had problems with them. El Paso and Nogales, Calexico and Yuma had some problems with them, with the *pachucos* that live right on the border. But you get a guy from down in the interior, he's a completely different Mexican than up here on the border. He's got a better attitude. You go up to Riverside or Las Vegas on detail, and they're running like rabbits—you gotta chase them. Down here on the border, they see you, and they just sit there and wait. They know we're gonna get them. And if you treat them right, they don't give you no static. All the time I was in the patrol, I never got in a fight.

The traffic at Tacna would go up and down mostly. In spring it usually started up and it'd increase. Then during the summer, it was always very steady. Accomplishments I was proud of at the Tacna Station? We had the most apprehensions for one day in the entire sector while I was there, and we had the most for one month. We also had the least for one day, and the least for one month. We got down to zero apprehensions for almost a month, and we finally caught two one December.

The change came in 1986 when they changed that immigration law. And if they'd left that law alone, we wouldn't have the problem we've got today. You'd go down and work your butt off and wouldn't find any tracks. And then they changed that law and required search warrants to enter farms or ranches. We got the first search warrant *ever* going into a building on a farm, while I was there, too. Mike Obregon and I trailed them in there and got a couple out of a shack. I knew the family, but they said, "No, get a search warrant." I said, "Okay." We just sat on the place while we got a search warrant. By the time we got the search warrant, though, the two aliens were coming out.

The biggest challenge we faced was overcoming these farmers. Some of them resented the fact that before 1986 we'd come on the place and go in and check for the aliens and stuff. Some of them would get pretty irate, cuss you out and everything else. We just had to stand there and take it and say, "Look, I don't blame you a bit. I'd probably be the same way you are.

But I have a job to do. You're paying my wages. If you have a man working for you, you expect him to do a day's work for his wages, don't you?" That usually would calm them down, when they get to thinking about that. But that's what we were doing, working for the government. The government's the people, you know.

The station got recognition for rescuing twenty-five aliens south of Dateland. We lost two, who died, but we got the rest of them out. One of them didn't think he was gonna come outta there, so he had cut his own throat. One of our pilots, David Roberson, had picked his track up, and I went down, got on the track, and found him under that tree. I asked the other guys why they let him do that, and they said, "We were gonna die anyway. If he wants to die his way, it's his privilege." He'd taken somethin' and cut a hole in his throat, just missed his jugular vein and cut into his esophagus. When I first saw him, he was under a paloverde tree, and I drove up there beside it, and I said, "Well, howdy." He came crawling out from under the tree with a big hole in his neck. I gave him water, and he had to hold that hole so he could get water down in his stomach. I didn't think he'd make it out, but the chopper from the Marine base came by and picked him up. Oscar Martinez went with him to the hospital in the chopper, and *Oscar* didn't think the man would survive, but he did. The whole station got a commendation over that. Actually, we got a $100 award each, but by the time they took taxes out, we got $80. I bought a new pair of boots.

One thing that still bothers me is a child I was trailing at Calexico when I first joined the patrol. Keith Riley, that was his name. He was with a church group down there around Easter, and they were having a picnic and Easter egg hunt. He told his brother and another kid that he was gonna go climb that mountain—Mt. Signal down there. The kid was six years old—six or nine or somethin' like that. He disappeared, and when they got to looking for him, they couldn't find him. They got ready to go home, and one of the kids told his mother that he'd said he was going up that hill. They called the Border Patrol out—we were in class up at El Centro, and we searched. I was a probie at the time. And we went down, and actually I saw . . .

After I learned how to track, I know what I saw, and even then I knew that I'd seen the track of that kid. I told Fred D'Albini that I saw the track, what I *thought* was a track. It was just really a scuff mark, where the kid had slipped going up out of a dry wash, but I couldn't find more sign going one way or the other. And then they flew a guy by the name of Carpenter, who was in my class, and a couple other guys up on top of Mt. Signal.

Carpenter says to this day he'd swear up and down he saw the boy's track up there. But when he tried to tell them that, nobody would believe him, either. We were both probies, so nobody would listen. Some folks think probies don't have sense enough to pour water out of a boot. The pilot had been flying around that hill with a loudspeaker telling him, "Sit down and be still. We'll get to you."

They found the kid's body the next day. He had gone up over the top of that hill, and came down on the east side of Mt. Signal, on the Mexican side. The Mexicans didn't want us going in there, because it was Mexico; they were the ones searching on the east side. Finally they found him up there. Apparently he'd been sleeping on a ledge during the night and rolled off the ledge, landed on his head, and it killed him. They said his clothes were piled up in a neat little pile. And he was just laying in his shorts when they found him. That bothered me for a long time, too, after I finally figured out what actually I had seen.

When I was at Calexico, there was a little rivalry between El Centro and Calexico, and even with Yuma. But none of them liked a probie catching their aliens. I wasn't supposed to do that. One day I was just driving around in a sedan, nothin' to do, killing time, when I heard El Centro working this trail. I went sneaking in there on a canal, and caught this guy out from under a tree. Neal Novak come up there and said, "Joe! You're supposed to leave my aliens alone! I'll catch my wets."

And after I made supervisor in El Centro, I was out there in them dunes one morning, *nothin'* going on. So I went over the bridge, and that was Yuma's territory. I cut some tracks taking off down under there. I headed out. I called El Centro and told them that I was working the trail and they needed to call Yuma, because the aliens were going in Yuma's area. Pretty soon a pilot showed up, and he was flying around wanting to know who in the world I was. He couldn't get me on my radio, because I was talking on El Centro, and he didn't want to talk to me on *that* channel. When I got back in later that day, Chief Henry Felchlin called me into the office and said, "Joe, leave Yuma's area alone. We've got enough to do over here."

I've been in lots of rescues. One really convinced my younger boy to get in the patrol. He was with me after I got permission for him to ride with me a few times. We were down there at that wildlife water tank in the Mohawk Mountains, north of Game Tank. Aliens went there all the time. We had got word that there was a group down there, and we went looking for them. We were working the trail, and we found a couple, but we didn't find any around the tank. They were gone from there. My son was riding with me, and he spotted something up on the side of the hill when we were coming into the pass. He saw something white up there, and he said, "There's a bighorn sheep, Dad." I turned and looked and said, "I don't think that's a sheep. I think that's an alien up there." A guy had gone way up the darned hill, a couple or three hundred feet, under a huge boulder. My boy and I got up to him, and he said, "I'd really given up. I said my prayers, I saw my brother and my mother go by. I don't know whether they're dead or not, but they were headed towards the tank up there. I haven't been able to find the tank. I crawled under here, and this was where I was gonna die. And then I saw you guys." After that, young Joe was real strong on going to the patrol.

I don't know where DART, the Desert Area Rescue Team, began. I never heard about it until it was formed. We didn't really appreciate it. One time they called me up and told me they were coming. I said, "There's some aliens down near Rat Gap." The pilot had talked about two. And so we sent the DART crew down to the east of the Mohawks, and sent them on down toward that road that went way on down to Papago Well. We sent them down there, and they brought out two out of a group of twenty-five. When they got those two, they turned around and came home. They'd had all they wanted of that rough country. We had to go get the other twenty-three.

Fred D'Albini was the last of the great sign cutters. And he was one of the best sign cutters I ever saw. He was good. Calexico had good sign trackers down there. Stroop was an awful good one. Sam Dunn was good. Neal Novak was one of the best supervisors and sign cutters I know of. Ol' Tom Carnes was better than most—just so much better it wasn't even funny. Carnes would be at home and not even supposed to be out there, and we'd be on the chase, and here the peckerwood would be, right out there with you. He'd just show up. One night I followed a load and called in to say they got picked up down there on the border road. And if I was a betting man, I'd have bet money on that one.

Carnes came out there and he was fiddling around, and he said, "Joe, go up to 98 and Cole Road and cut there and tell me what you see." "All right." I thought I was wasting time. I got up there, and lo and behold, here are those guys' tracks. I called him and I said, "I got their sign up here. Looks like they got picked up." He said, "How many times did they get picked up, Joe?" I cut the rest of the night—no orders or anything—but I cut the rest of the night, looking for them boogers. I worked clear to El Centro, I never found another sign on them. They got picked up at the second place. But man, I'd have sworn on that first one. They were in a ditch, and they come out of the ditch and out onto the blacktop in a nice neat bunch. Oh, I "knew" they'd got picked up. That was one of the times I learnt somethin'. It's kind of hard to get things in my head, but I do learn once in a while. Carnes was good.

To become a good sign cutter, a guy's got to have a lot of curiosity, a lot of patience, and the willingness to stick with it. Anybody can learn how to sign cut. I can tell you all there is to know about it, and others probably can, too, in thirty, forty minutes. And I mean, that's *everything*. From then on, it's up to the individual.

I'll never forget ol' Rod Bryant out of El Centro. When I made supervisor, he thought he should have had the job. And for a long time, he and I were at odds. But anyway, I went out one night in the sand dunes. I had a small unit, and because we had to work traffic check *and* sign cut, I'd run out to the west side and cut that myself. If I didn't have anything, I'd head for the east side. And if I didn't have *anybody* working, I'd just cut both sides myself. And I was always ending up with trails.

Rod would tell me, "No, nobody's crossed." One night I'd cut my sign and got tired of fiddlin' over there, so I came over and thought, "I'm gonna see how they did." So, I got out and I did me a nice brush-out and left all kinds of sign. I'd have sworn anybody could see that except a blind man. I got in my vehicle, and I bumped on. They come around, and every one of them made the rotation back around to me. And I'd ask, "Did you guys see anything on the drag road?" And they all said, "No, it's clean." I said, "Well, come on, follow me," and took them all down there. I drove up, and I stopped. I said, "Do you see anything on that drag road?" Ol' Rod said, "Nah, there ain't nothin' here!" And I said, "Okay, come here a minute."

And I got him out of his vehicle, and I got him around where he could see my headlights looking on the ground, sign cut, right? And I said, "Now do you see anything?" "No." I said, "Get a little lower and closer and take a *good* look." He said, "Oh. Yeah, I saw that, but I didn't think that was anything. I thought that was the wind." And I said, "We're gonna have training right now." So I made them take their blamed shoes off, walk across the road barefooted, on their heels, on their toes, had them do it with their boots on, and I had them brush out and everything. For a while ol' Rod stayed mad at me, but from then on he didn't miss any tracks. He finally got over that before I left that station. He finally got straightened out and was all fun again.

One chief I worked for, Felchlin at El Centro, I liked. I got crossways with him, too, sometimes, but I liked him better than most. He's a good square man. He didn't mind if you did something wrong. He'd tell you about it. If you improved, great. If you didn't improve, he'd talk to you about it again. Gene Corder, at Yuma, I liked him, too. But I got crossways with him one day in the office. I walked in there and he says, "How's it goin', Joe?" And I says, "Oh, I'm still kickin' against the pricks." He took it wrong. I thought sure he'd know what I was talking about. Paul in the Bible said that he was still kicking against the pricks of his conscience. And that's what I was referring to, but he thought I had called him a prick. After I said it, I thought, "That's a heck of a thing to say to some guy." But I thought, "No, he's Southern Baptist, he'll know what that means." Lily, my wife, she liked to kill me for saying it.

I always said somethin' screwy. When some guy asks me how I am, I'll say "terrible," or something like that, you know. "Oh? What's wrong?" I'd say, "Nothin', just normal." I'd say anything to get him to talk a little more. My pet peeve is going through a checkpoint where they ask me a stupid question that requires "yes" or "no." That's the silliest thing you can do on a checkpoint. You gotta ask them something that makes them say more than one yes or no. I always told my men that. I can't go telling these guys now—they get a little ticked at the old goat, standing out there talking to them.

I like the desert, any part of it. And it's interesting. For example, those elephant trees. I found them when I was at the college. I'd run across them and I couldn't figure out what they were, and I got to talking to this teacher of the zoology class I was in. I asked her what they were, but she couldn't figure it out. I told her they have a real strong turpentine smell. She asked a University of Arizona professor and he told her, "Why, that's the elephant tree." They kick every leaf off in the summertime and they'll have a little seed on them in June. The biggest one I know of is right down here in the north end of the Copper Mountains. There's one down there that is as tall as a mulberry tree. And the base of it is humongous. That's the biggest elephant tree I ever saw. I found it one year quail hunting, before I went in the Border Patrol.

In the old days, if you turned on the Jeep's air conditioner, the blamed engine would overheat. And I told every man working for me, "Now, don't use your air conditioner when you're workin' a trail, because you gotta get in and out. Getting into cold, then gettin' out in the heat, you're gonna end up with the flu or a cold or somethin'. It's better on your body if you keep it one temperature, even if it's hot." On the freeway to town, I turned the air conditioner on, but when I got out in the field, it was a different story. For me, it worked better.

The others guys all drank cold water, and I drank warm water. I put half a bag of ice in my two-and-a-half-gallon Gott jug, and that'd last me for four or five days, 'til it got *too* hot to drink. And I had a coffee thermos. Back then I'd drink anywhere from a quart to three quarts a day, but now I'm down to two cups a day. The doctor told me I was nuts. I had a physical and the form asked "Do you drink coffee?" I marked "yes." The next question, "How many cups? One? Two? Three? Four? Five? Or more?" I put "or more." He says, "How many do you drink?!" I says, "Well, it varies between a quart and three quarts." He looked at me, he said, "You're crazy! You can't drink that much coffee!" I did. I drank a lot of coffee in the patrol.

I put in for other stations *before* I got over here to Tacna, but once I got here, I wanted to stay. It had taken me ten years to get out of California and back to God's country. I mighta got something, but my paperwork wasn't all that great according to my supervisors. I went through a class on writing papers for the government. They gave us a story and said, "Now write a memo to this woman telling them you're sorry such-and-such happened." I set there and I thought about it, and I thought, "Well, all right." So I wrote my little story. The instructor got it and he read that to the whole class, said that was the best memo he had ever seen a government official write. And he said, "He puts the facts, and he don't state anything but facts, and he puts it in such a way it can't make anybody mad. They enjoy readin' it." But my supervisors wanted big, long words, and make a long thing about something simple. I don't like to do that. And this guy was teaching the class, trying to get them to change it, and they couldn't find anything to change in my report. I didn't get it back—he kept it to show to people and say, "*Here's* the way you're supposed to do it."

I loved the Patrol, just the fun of it all. And the pay was good, better than any job I had in my life. Best job I ever had. Some people said I was working too hard out here, but I was just having fun. And it was fun when I was tracking. That's hunting to me, and I love to hunt. The thrill is tracking 'em up before they die. It's a rough ol' way to go—run outta water in this desert.

COLONEL R. CHILD

*After serving in the Border Patrol from 1976 to 2002 and
at Yuma Station from 1976 to 2000, Colonel Child now
teaches at the Border Patrol Academy in Artesia, New
Mexico.*

I'm a pilot, and I was broken in by Dave Roberson. He epito-
mizes, to me, what being a Border Patrol pilot means. One of the things
that he told me when I got on as a junior or new pilot under him was, "Remember that ground agents can catch aliens without you, but you can't do
a thing without them." And his whole mindset was towards helping Border
Patrol agents. I think there's a great tendency for some pilots to want to
run the show and do pilot stuff. They forget their days on the ground. I was
a ground agent for seven years and Dave was for twelve years or so. If you
get a lot of that ground time, it's harder to forget where you come from
and what you're up there for. And a lot of guys now come in and do their
minimum time on the ground. In the future there may not be any minimum time, and they'll go right to the air corps and do pilot stuff. That'd
definitely be a mistake.

It sounds like the Marine Corps philosophy of you're a Marine first and
a pilot second. And that's always been the Border Patrol philosophy: you're
a Border Patrol agent first, and you're a pilot second. For the most part,
you never really get away from the agent mentality—at least if you are a
good pilot, you stay in that agent mentality. Right from the git-go, you go
to the academy and they teach you the duty of a Border Patrol agent is to
detect and prevent entries, and to apprehend violators. And so you come
back from the academy, and you go, "My job is to catch them. Let's go get
them!"

Colonel Child. Photo by David J. Griffin, 2009.

But, administratively everything seems to stand in your way. Early on I learned that the people who never step in shit were the people who never do anything. And if you don't do anything, everybody's happy because you don't get in any trouble. And it's real hard to be productive and not get into scrapes and have things turn left on you. Those of us whose attitude was "go out and catch as much as you can, and get as much done as you can," sometimes didn't sit well with the administrators who just wanted things to go along smoothly, who wanted to look good in front of everybody, and who didn't want anything to ever go wrong. But there were a lot of people along the way, like Dave Roberson, who managed to walk that fine line between keeping the administration happy, and yet still, when out in the field, he just went like gangbusters. He was just awesome out in the field.

I did the vast majority of my time, twenty-four years, in Yuma. In 1999 I transferred over to Tucson on detail for some big operation. I was here for two months, permanent nights, and they said, "What we want you to do is fly up and down the border at Nogales, at altitude, with the lights on. Fly back and forth, and have the lights on, and by your presence aliens'll know that we're here, and they won't enter." One of the pilots who'd been here for a period of time said, "If you adopt a 5,000-foot floor, never go below 5,000 feet, you won't have any trouble, you won't hit anything." So I show up to work there, knowing that what I've been assigned to do is fly back and forth along the border with the lights on at 5,000 feet. I looked around and saw all these ground agents running around chasing stuff. And I thought, "I can't do this from 5,000 feet." So about halfway through the first shift on the first night, I took my helicopter down into the canyons, helping these ground guys knock down groups. And I immediately developed an unwarranted reputation for doing nothing more than I had been doing all along in Yuma: getting down low and catching aliens.

Traditionally the work in Yuma was fabulous. As an agent, I had very little traffic check; it was almost all line watch or farm and ranch check in those days. It was just all sign cutting. You'd go to a briefing in the morning and you'd sit through five minutes of folderol with the administration, and they'd give you the keys to a truck, and they'd say, "Don't get hurt, don't break anything, and go catch aliens." The attitude in those days was, "If you're not driving at least a hundred miles, then you're being lazy." That suited me great, because I'm all about getting around the desert, learning the area, tracking, and catching aliens.

As the years went by, I got in on the end of an era, and they got into more technology. I watched them try ideas that we'd already tried and knew didn't work, but somebody new had come along, "Well, let's try *that*." On the simple end of things, take the tire drags for example. Before I came along, they had tried chain link, iron rail, and boards bolted together, before someone started using worn-out tires. The old-timers said, "That's the hot ticket for pulling a drag." Then, as I got older, I saw others come along and say, "Let's try chain, and we'll weight it down with wood." And they did all those things, but a few months would go by and we'd be back to dragging tires again.

On the complicated end of things, we're spending millions of dollars on unmanned aerial vehicles (UAVs) to fly around and look for aliens, when we've already established that we can't work at 12,000 feet. They may catch a few things, but for the money spent, we can do much better. But the UAVs *look* good. It's like our Aerostat balloon, which is another tender subject. You go to the vast majority of the public and crow, "Look what we've got!" and they swoon, "Ooh!" But agents down on the ground look at the big money being spent and what little it's accomplishing and think, "If they'd cough up a few of those dollars for extra vehicles for us or just stuff that we need to do our job, we'd sure be more effective." Even with advanced equipment, you still need somebody on the ground to make the contact with aliens and put them in the van. You've still got to go *mano a mano*.

Dave Roberson's accident in a Husky, followed by Charlie Chandler's, is what prompted the shift to helicopters. The service wasn't willing to follow up and say, "There's a problem." They simply said, "It must be our pilots, so we'll just get out of the fixed-wing business." I don't think they should have dropped the issue with the aircraft. But then I don't think the move to helicopters was a bad move, either. It *tremendously* improved the safety buffer.

Hank Hays was the chief pilot at that time and kind of was responsible for the Husky purchases. And after Charlie's accident, when it was clear that there was a problem, Hank was the one responsible for getting us back *out* of the Huskies, too. He was not—to his credit—one to say, "We've got scads of them. If I made a decision, it's got to be right, and we'll stick by it." He saw that something was not right, and he got us out of those aircraft. I always thought a lot of Hank because of that.

The era of the Super Cub kind of ended about 1989. We wound down out of a fixed-wing arena. That *really* changed things for the better, though we required a much larger budget to operate a helicopter operation. I was thinking this morning about all the old-time Border Patrol pilots who were Super Cub pilots. And of course there's not a better aircraft made for that. But I was a young fellow when I was doing that, and that allows you certain liberties. I used to just scare the shit out of myself on a regular basis. And when I got older and started flying a helicopter, that didn't happen as often. I looked back and thought, "You know, that's *crazy!*"

Dave and I had the opportunity to sit and talk about these things over breakfast many times. While working the railroad sidings, you'd think you'd see something, and come back around and look under a tree or a bush or something, and hit your own wake turbulence, and at thirty to fifty feet, the plane tries to roll over on its back. And you go full rudder, full aileron, and all that does is hold it from rolling over while it goes down and down and down, until right about treetop level, it pops out of it. You always thought, "I just *know* this is gonna come out. Close to the ground, where that wake dissipates, it's gonna pop out of this," then pop! it would. On you'd go. Helicopters don't have wake turbulence. They have their own set of problems, but they just dramatically increase the safety factor.

There have been crashes with helicopters. There have been some fatals. I'm thinking of one over in Texas: Louis Stahl hit a wire. There've been some other non-fatal injuries from wire strikes and engine failures from various reasons. And some other aircraft destroyed where nobody was hurt. But again, if you look at the operation from the early '80s, where we had sixty, seventy pilots, flying only day shift, only Super Cubs, and the numbers of hours that they flew. And then you compare that to today. The high number of pilots and the number of hours that they're flying is phenomenal today compared to the accidents recorded. Accidents per hour is really low now.

Our OH-6s are older. I used to get a kick out of that, because I woke up one of these young Border Patrol agent-observers when I explained to him that the aircraft he was riding in was made before he was born. Everything on a helicopter is "time life." Every piece has a serial number on it: gear boxes, rotor blades, right down to the tail boom itself—everything but the chassis is good for so many hours, and it's kept in a log book. When that component reaches so many hours, it comes off, and a new one goes on. Say it's a 1968 helicopter with 15,000 hours on it. In reality, all the components are just what you should be flying. On paper it looks ancient, but the parts are new. The only problem that creates is the supply chain and parts can be hard to get. The OH-6 is a fabulous aircraft, crash worthy. The problems that they've had have not been from the fact that they're old.

The OH-6 is my favorite aircraft, absolutely. It's *highly* maneuverable and very tolerant of the type of flying that I like to do. I'm fairly aggressive in my flying. In the instances that they have crashed, it's an extremely crash-worthy aircraft. The rescue guys from Vietnam used to say, "If we go in for Huey crashes, we go in looking for bodies. If we go in for an OH-6 crash, we're looking for survivors." The aircraft has that reputation.

The chief pilot who gave me my check-ride for my job originally hit the nail right on the head. He said, "Flying's got to be secondary, so that you don't have to think about it." You've got to wear the aircraft. And that's one of the reasons for the high pilot-time qualification to get a job, because they want people who are comfortable enough with the flying that it takes care of itself. It's reactionary, and you're more or less, after a time, just unaware of it. When you don't think about the flying, then the communication, the tracking, and all that becomes what you actually focus on, and the flying just takes care of itself.

During those seven years as an agent on the ground, I found the desert east of San Luis was the easiest sign cutting. We'd track from a vehicle. I'd get on a trail, after cutting the drag road, and follow it, and lose it. That went on a bunch of times. One night, I remember I had a spotlight hung out the window, and I was driving along, following these tracks, and all of a sudden there were shoes. I thought, "Oh! I caught one!" And so you kind of learned to track there.

I didn't know Yuma pilot Jim Landon well, but one time when I was still a ground agent, he called me out to the sand dunes and said, "I think maybe I've got something here. I've got a trail in the sand dunes, and it goes up to this tree, and I don't see it any more, and I'd appreciate it if you'd take a look at this." And I drove out there, and got his aliens out of the tree for him. It wasn't until later, when I became a pilot, and I'd follow trails through the sand dunes, that I saw how patently obvious a trail ends. There's no mistaking it, he *knew* they were in that tree. But I always reflected on the way that he handled it. He didn't say, "Come out here and get this group I got under the tree." He was very nice about it. "You know, I've got a trail here, and it doesn't go any farther, and I think maybe I've got something. And I'd really appreciate it if you'd come." That's my recollection of Jim. He was a great big fella—I don't know how he ever fit in that Cub. As far as I'm concerned, if a guy flew a Super Cub that many years in the Border Patrol and walked away, retired afterward, he was good. You either get good, or you get gone, one way or another. You quit, or you get run off, or . . .

As a young pilot, I put people on more than one cow trail before I learned to recognize cows and horses from people prints. I learned a lot from Dave. But that was a golden opportunity, those seven years working on the ground in Yuma. That was certainly the bedrock of my sign-cutting experience. We had trails coming out of El Sahuaro, a truck stop in Sonora, that would go up through the desert to the north side of the interstate and beyond Dateland—that's a hundred miles or better. I've worked some of those trails several days and caught the aliens way up north of Dateland. I don't think agents have time to mess with that kind of stuff these days. They catch what they can catch right here and now, and if they were to follow something like that, they would be letting others get away in the process.

I remember working a group of six through Little Pass and they ran up into those hills. It's rocky ol' ground. And we got five of them straight away. And there was probably half a dozen of us walking around. Of course, there's no sign up in those rocks. We hollered and yelled, and we had the guys we had caught hollering and yelling. We knew we were missing one. Finally I kicked around and kicked a rock over and found where this guy had pulled a bunch of rocks on top of himself. We jerked him out of there. I asked him—and remember that we're talking the middle of summer—

"Do you have any water with you?" "No." "Do you mean to tell me you were going to hide here and let us drive off and leave you? You were going to stay hidden?" "Sí." "And you don't have any water?" "No." "What were you going to do?!" "I don't know." I'm at a loss, speechless, but I've seen that lots of times.

As long as you rescued aliens, it was great. But reaching women and kids out there too late sure got old. And, it didn't take much of it to get old. More of that went on than should have. There was a group of El Salvadorans in the Mohawk Dunes: a mother and three kids, and a guy who went on to the White Wing Ranch. I didn't get there in time. The three kids were about 200 yards apart. It's one thing when you've got a guy who strikes off across the desert of his own volition, more or less knowing the risk that he's taking. And it's another thing when he's got a woman with him, but she was at least a grown-up and can make up her own mind about that sort of thing, even if she's dragged along. But kids . . . they have no say. They are absolutely, completely innocent victims. That one was particularly bad.

What percent get caught crossing that country? You need to look at the day-by-day basis and the overall basis. Because whenever you talk apprehensions, you can say, "It's likely that a hundred people entered during this twenty-four-hour period, and we caught sixty of them. So forty got away. Of those sixty, they'll make up forty of tomorrow's one hundred that enter. And a percentage of those will get away. So after the second, third, or fourth try, ultimately they get away. So your overall apprehension is not nearly as high as your daily apprehension rate. And of course there's no way of measuring that. In some cases I've seen the same guy pass the write-up table three, four, five days in a row, and then you never saw him again. Am I supposed to believe that after the fifth time he gave up and went back home to the interior? No.

And yet I know I've caught other people, they've said, "This was too much of a hassle, I'm going back home," and I have every reason to believe they did give up. But if they want to come in, they're going to risk being caught. And of course each time they get caught, they learn, "I'm not going to do *that* again." In the case of Yuma, you catch them off of a device, they know, "I crossed that head gate last time, and *bang!* The helicopter showed up, and the agents showed up. I think maybe I'll go around that head gate this time." So, I don't have any real idea of the apprehension rate.

Our desert was dangerous. Countless times I'd say as I threw them in the back of the truck, "You know, there's a drinking fountain in the park in the town of San Luis, and the penalty for getting caught there is the same as it is for getting caught here. Don't come back through the desert." They think their chances of getting away are better in the open desert, but they aren't. When we work that area, we try to dissuade them. More are getting away now than used to, just because there are more of them.

One day, we were on the east side of the Mohawks. We'd gone through Rat Gap. It's miserable tracking out in there. We'd had one rescue out of it, and we backtracked, found where the group had split, and we were working it north. I was flying the line in a Cub, and I got way ahead of these agents eight or ten miles. Not far south of the highway, I saw an old boy under a tree. He didn't even stand up; he was just kind of waving his wrist. "Okay, guys, I got him. Come on up." And so they beat eight, ten miles across that desert, caught up to the guy, called me on the radio and said, "This ain't the one. We don't know where he came from. We've never seen his tracks before." We didn't know who he was, where he came from, if he was a solo from the beginning, or if he was from a group we didn't know about. It was just his lucky day, because we didn't even know he existed. So the agents had to turn around and bounce all the way back down to where they came from to get back on the original trail.

I often wonder how many people are out here. Periodically I'd land near some metal corrals out there in one of those passes in the Bryan Mountains. Howard Aitken and I were out poking around one day and landed there to look at those corrals. There was a fresh set of five or six tracks going through there. "That's *got to* be alien traffic." And yet, their tracks were nowhere on the line.

As a young border patrol agent working at night, I had pulled up near an irrigation canal and the river, shut off my truck, and was drinking a cup of coffee in the moonlight. I saw aliens running across the levee road in front of me. This is a sweet deal! So I waited until they all disappeared. I gave them about thirty, forty seconds, hit the starter, turned on the headlights, and whipped up there. They were all hunkered down. I grabbed all the bodies, stuck them in the back of the truck, and thought, "Okay, now I'll go run out the sign where they came in," but I couldn't find it. I don't know where they came in. I could never find it. So there was an instance where if I hadn't been sitting there watching them, they'd have been gone into the valley. So we only sample what's going on. There's a percentage of entries that we're completely unaware of. I've seen that enough times to know.

Some of them are better at eluding us than others. Some disguise their tracks better. Some of them are better-paid coyotes. In this case, it was a blanket that they threw down and walked on. Then they picked the blanket up after the last alien went by, and there was nothin' there. So we have just a sampling of apprehensions and entries.

Over the years I don't think the behavior or the tenor of the aliens changed. I think if you took a cross section of humanity, you've got a percentage of pretty good folks, and a percentage of really rotten people. I think if you took any group, if you went "white, Oriental, Mexican, low class, upper class, rich, poor, educated, not," I think the cut would be the same when you talk the moral ground. I've arrested people that I can look at and know that they'd stick a shiv between my ribs and sleep just fine that night. And others were as honest as could be. I've dealt with good people and crummy ones, and I don't see particularly a change: there's still good ones and there's still crummy ones.

Right before I got a pilot's job I worked a group up out of the east desert into the groves, and I worked them up through the groves into one where they were picking. I found three of them. I looked up on a ladder and saw one shoe that I'd been looking for. "C'mon down." I grabbed that guy, threw a set of cuffs on him, and found the others. I said, "Okay, let's go." They said, "We only get paid for a full box. We don't get paid for a partial, and we've been working here since early this morning. Why don't you let us finish so we can get paid?" And I thought, I'm almost done with this, so I took the handcuffs back off of them and said, "I'll be here at three o'clock. You be sitting out in front of the grove waiting for me." And I left. At three o'clock those three boys were sitting in the front of the grove waiting for me. I loaded them in the truck, wrote them up, and gave them a ride back to the border at San Luis and let them go right away. Why should I make them spend a night in the tank?

Some of the Yuma pilots had a tradition of the candy drop at Christmastime. There were three or four *ejidos* or orphanages on the south side of the line, out east of San Luis. We'd get all our wives together, and they'd bag up little bags of candy at Christmastime. Sometimes we'd put in little plastic toys or whatever. Then, whoever was working on Christmas Day would fly out to these orphanages on the south side of the fence, mind you, and drop out bags of Christmas treats. As far as I know, Jackie and Dave started the tradition, but it may have gone back further than that. It dried up when the ejidos were abandoned. We enjoyed that candy drop.

I did make a couple other flights into Mexico. Headquarters got me to give a ride to Ben Davidian, the Western Regional Commissioner at the time. He lasted only a short time, but he was *great*. They said, "We want you to give this guy a tour." So I picked him up in Wellton and I flew him down south through the desert, showed him our drag roads, and showed him a skull that was sitting out there in a flat. I asked, "Do you want to see where all the entries in this area come from?" And he said, "Sure." So we flew down to El Sahuaro, and I went around the south edge of the High Tank Mountains. There's a little café, El Saguaro. That's where these aliens get off the bus. We hooked around the end of the mountains, came back up, and flew him back down the line and into the airport. He said, "That was wonderful! That was fantastic. I really appreciate that. That was great."

A couple of weeks later, some guy from Washington, D.C., showed up and Davidian asked for me to fly him. "I want you to give him the exact same ride you gave me. Show him the skull, show him El Saguaro, show him everything just exactly the way you did it for me." "Okay." I picked the guy up at the Wellton Station, flew him south through Big Pass, showed him the skull, went down, hit El Sahuaro, came back up, picked up the line, and the guy said, "Is that the border?" "Yeah." "Well, does that mean we were just south of the border?" "Yeah. You wanted to see the truck stop, didn't you?" He got real quiet. I flew him on in, and a day later I found myself standing in front of the chief arguing my case.

But, there was another instance that got more notoriety. That was the one down there by a little Indian village southwest of Sells, Arizona, near Menagers Dam. I was working a group in the Baboquivari Mountains, and the guys were just catching up to the mules with the dope, when on aircraft frequency 121.5, I heard, "I've had an engine failure, I'm goin' down." And I thought, "Gee, these radios are line of sight. This guy's had an engine failure. He's going down and I can hear him, so he's out here in this desert someplace close by."

He went down about six miles south of the border. I got the coordinates for him, and on the way, I ascertained he had no water or survival equipment. There were two people on board. In summertime that area south of Sells is not very hospitable—and there's not much out there. You can walk for a long way and not cross any ranches or wells. I had water on board, so I grabbed a load of fuel and started heading his way. Not too long before I got to him, foop!—that was the border that just went by. "How do I deal with this?" I thought, "Well, the high moral ground is to go help this guy." So I did. Goodness, we had F-16s flying high cover for us.

I landed on the ground, gave them water, and picked them up. Actually, I flew back north to a little place east of Lukeville with my observer, dropped him off, went back and got the first of those two guys, and brought him back. I dropped him off with my observer, went back, got the second one, brought him back, landed, shut down, and waited for Customs. In the meantime, DPS [Arizona Department of Public Safety helicopter] shows up. He lands alongside me in Mexico, and we talk. "Well, guess you've got this all under control. Really nothing we can do to help you." Because it was all over the aircraft radio—even airliners were involved on the emergency frequency.

So DPS leaves, and then Customs shows up, but they're out there to the north of us, in an orbit. Finally they land in one of their A-Star helicopters. I thought, "What is going on here? Why don't they come pick these guys up? Get this show on the road here! I'm tired of waiting, I'll just fly you up to where they're at." So I loaded the first guy up, fired it up, took off, went north, realized the road I had gone north of and landed was *not* the border like I thought it was. *They* were down there at the border. So I went across there, landed, gave them the first guy. I went back and got the second.

So now it's really out of the bag, because they're watching me come and go across the border, and it was just really hard to deny that one. I got my observer, went back and landed next to Customs. "You want to talk to me or anything?" "No, no, no. Have a nice day. We'll take care of these guys." So I went on back to base and did my memo. The DPS pilot evidently got a huge amount of trouble for that. He had a moving map display GPS and "failed" to notice that *he'd* gone on the other side of the border. I think he took a letter of reprimand out of the deal. Customs came down and met with the people and took them away, processed them, gave them a ride to the airport and let them go, because they were fine.

But evidently the Mexican authorities caught wind of something, and so they went through the Mexican consulate in Washington, D.C., to the Immigration Service, back down to the chief patrol agent in Tucson, who was in a meeting at the time and was asked, "What's this about your aircraft rescuing people in Mexico?"

I received a reprimand and nearly lost a commendation they were planning for me. The commendation was for my part in that *huge* rescue that took place over on the end of the Mohawk Drag. A group of twenty-five or something went down. There were more rescues than fatals out of that one. So on one hand they were saying, "Good job for rescuing *these* people, but, oh, you shouldn't be rescuing United States citizens."

In retrospect, I really didn't handle it quite right. What I should have done is called on the radio and said, "Please advise the chief that I'm on my way into Mexico to make this rescue." What I didn't want to do was say, "They've gone down in Mexico, can I go get them?" because that inevitably results in a "Wait a minute, don't do anything, we'll get back with you . . . we'll get back with you . . . we'll get back with you." I didn't want to play that game. So instead, I thought, "I'll just do this on the QT." When I got back and it was all over, I wrote a memo saying, "I did this." I gave it to my supervisor who went on vacation the following day, so the memo didn't get turned in and the chief got blindsided from above. In retrospect, I probably should have said on the air, "Call the chief and tell him I'm doing this." That was a learning experience for me.

Today I would not handle it quite the same way, but I would definitely do it again. It's the high moral ground. I couldn't very well leave those guys, *knowing* that they didn't have any water, knowing that even if they were uninjured from their forced landing, things could have gone awry any one of a number of ways for them. That was the right thing to do. I try to do the right thing. I just don't always find the right way to do it.

Something was pointed out to me early in my career that I was sensing but couldn't put my finger on: if you're a carpenter and you go to work, at the end of the day you can turn around, look at what you built, and say, "That's what I did today." At the end of the week, you can look back and say, "There's the house that I built," and move on to the next project. In immigration or law enforcement in general, you work all day, and you come home, and you've got nothing to show for it. There's nothing tangible. In fact, you can't even really share it with anybody. You don't have anything to show for your day's work. That's one of the reasons there's a huge divorce rate in the law enforcement community, because only other people in that job can relate to what you're doing. You can't come home and tell somebody. It's like talking about the dark side of the moon, so it creates rifts. You're doing a politically controversial thing. You catch the same person over and over again until they finally get away. You can't look at job satisfaction in terms of what you're accomplishing. You can ask yourself, "Do they need to be caught? Are they really good for the economy? Are they good for the country, or are they bad for the country?" Those are political arguments with no right answer. So is what I'm doing good, or is it wasted?

So I discovered that working a good trail was very satisfying. I could have been just as happy to walk up and say to an alien, "Tag! You're it!" and let him walk away again. It's over at that point. Whether we arrest him or we deport him, he comes back tomorrow. It's all the same. The only thing that mattered to me was this trail. You lose some, and you catch some, but it became all about the chase. Over the years there were some agents who you'd rather work with. You could say, "So-and-so's working Andrade today. When I work with him, good things happen." Some folks liked to cut sign as much as I did, and their goals were the same. We don't really care if they go back or not, we just care about finding a trail and getting on it. Towards the end of my career I was kind of catering to the schedule of who was working where. It was all about the trail.

One Easter my wife had gotten all her kids a passel of these little, live chicks. I don't know how many of them there were, a dozen of them maybe. Howard Aitken had stopped by the house for some reason, and it was discovered that the chicks had made the great escape. Howard and I followed that trail of chickens down the alley behind the houses a couple of blocks away, through somebody's yard and out into the street. We followed these chickens all around the neighborhood, and finally came up with them.

I really found my niche when I started flying. Things were not going real well for me up to that point. I had supervisors who referred to me as "Problem Child." But I was learning the skills that I needed. If I'd been on a regular police force, I might have become a detective. I liked putting together "how did it happen?" I would love to do aircraft accident investigation, but I'm not sure that I had it together enough when I was younger to have done that. The gift that I have is flying. From the time I learned tracking, I thought, "This is a blast!" Combining that with flying was perfect.

Checklist: How to Fly Again Tomorrow

1. Make sure your life insurance is up to date.
2. Never maneuver while you're emotionally involved.
3. Whenever possible, work with the wires at your back.
4. Always work downslope.
5. Never commit to a course of action without an alternative.
6. Always keep a little "sacrificial" altitude.
7. Listen carefully and pay heed to your little inner voice.
8. Always, always, always, fly the aircraft first.

COLONEL CHILD, NOVEMBER 2006

Apparently, I have a fairly aggressive flying style. The windows in the roof of the helicopter or an airplane are for me to keep track of my target while I'm in a turn. I have no trouble doing that, so long as I'm uninvolved emotionally. But as soon as I find myself going, "He can't flip me off like that and get away with it!" Or, "He can't run back into Mexico! That's not fair!" Once those emotions well up, that's when my close calls happen. I get emotional and start whipping an aircraft around, and then things don't go well. All of my really close calls have been like that. So long as I'm detached, I can do the same maneuvers, the same thing, and they just come out better, safer. I did hit a wire in a helicopter one night, causing $80,000 worth of damage. I know that wire. I knew that wire from the day I started as a Border Patrol agent, but for one brief moment I just didn't realize that's where I was. That's the only serious damage I've done.

I'm proud that people on the ground liked having me come out and work with them. Not many better things could be said about me than the people that I supported *liked* having me come to work with them. You hear of other pilots who show up in an area and the ground agents change radio frequencies. Agents always told me that as long as I'm on the chase, they'll stay with it, and that's a huge compliment.

I've been privileged to work with some exceptional people. There're still some of them over there in Yuma and Wellton. There's a young fellow there at Wellton named Matthew Sutton—when you work with Matt, you make things happen. You knew something good was going to happen when you worked with Matt. And Joe McCraw, there's one of those crotchety old farts. I don't think that man ever had anything nice to say to me. But if I could handpick somebody to trail with, he'd be out there. I just don't think he liked pilots, but the man was good out in the desert. So was Glen Payne. I almost cried when they made him chief at Wellton and he quit coming out in the field. That guy was awesome. I'd do it all over again. Absolutely. You bet. It was everything I ever wanted.

GLEN PAYNE

After growing up in Silver City, New Mexico, Glen Payne served in the Border Patrol from 1976 to 2003 and at the Tacna-Wellton Station from 1979 to 2003. Currently he is an instructor at the Border Patrol Academy.

The Tacna-Wellton Station was the best-kept secret in the Border Patrol, and then all of a sudden it somehow got recognized. We've had a lot of interesting things happen down there. We even had the attorney general visit us once, and that was a real big deal. We enjoyed that, with Janet Reno. She was a very personable lady. It's just a really great place to have worked. I can't say enough good things about it, because I just really loved it, and had such a good time doing it.

Originally, I came to Tacna for the two-year hardship rotation. It was a hardship station. After spending two years here, you could rotate to a station of your choice. My intention was to spend two years at Tacna, and then transfer to Deming, New Mexico, which was a hard station to get into at that time. It was closer to home. My wife was from Hatch, New Mexico—it's forty-five miles northeast from Deming. And I was from Silver City, which is forty-five miles north of Deming. That put us, really, halfway between our parents.

But I never put in for Deming. After my first two years here at Tacna, I was enjoying what I was doing and didn't want to leave. The sign cutting was a big thing at Tacna. I had not done much sign cutting at El Paso, but when I got to Tacna, I learned quite a bit working with Joe McCraw and the guys, Jim Clarida and John Elton. They were good sign cutters. I really enjoyed it, and I got pretty good at it too. When you get good at something, of course, you enjoy it even a little more.

Glen Payne. Photo by Bill Broyles, 2006.

I always liked being outside, and Border Patrol got me outside. It kept me in a "hunt mode," because I just love to hunt, though I don't hunt now—I don't know why—but I rarely go out and do any of that. I rarely go out and shoot my guns. I do have a grandson now, and he's getting at that age where he's ready to go out and shoot, learn some gun safety and that sort of thing. I doubt if he'll be a Border Patrolman. I don't know that Border Patrol is what I would *want* him to be nowadays. If he could be in Border Patrol at Wellton, Arizona, and do sign cut, and the things that I did, I would say go for it. But if he's going to have to go to El Paso or Chula Vista or a big urban station like that, I don't think that I would encourage him. It was good when I was there, but everybody tells me that I retired at the most opportune time. Things have really changed since, and it's not near as much fun. Everything now is really, really political. It's just really hard to get your job done and stay out of trouble, the way things are now.

And the UDAs, undocumented aliens, have turned into a different group of people than we dealt with. Most of them that we dealt with in the early days at Tacna were the working class. Very rarely did you have a problem with any of those people. They were polite to me, and of course I was polite with them, and did my job. It was kind of like, "I'll do my job today, and if I see you tomorrow, I'll do it tomorrow." They accepted that. It was all okay. And the working class I was talking about would be like the farm workers, lemon pickers, the cotton stompers, and melon pickers.

As time went on, we ran into people that were being smuggled to the interior states and who didn't intend to work on farms. It was just a whole different class of people. They were belligerent; they wanted something for nothing. If we arrested one, the first thing he wanted was water and then a soda, and then food, and then "Let's go to the restaurant." It was always "Give me something." And then we ran into a lot more that wanted to escape from being arrested. When they would try to escape, of course we had to prevent that. Consequently, you'd get into a tussle with them every now and then—not every time, but on occasion we'd have to subdue one. And it could be in the middle of twenty-five others. Fortunately, all twenty-five of them didn't jump on you at the same time.

One *did* steal my truck once, for a short period of time. This was back in the early 1980s. I had arrested four aliens at Roll, and we had a group trail up the railroad tracks toward Phoenix, so I followed it all the way up to the Horn cotton gin, where I saw a bunch of people working in a cotton field there. It appeared that they probably were illegal, so I talked to them. Sure enough, of seven in the field five were illegal. I already had four back in the truck. It was hot out, so I had left the motor running with the air conditioner on. As I was bringing the five from the field, one of them got way out in front of us there, and just walked up to the back of the truck, one of those old Dodge Ramchargers with a big tailgate that lifted up when you hit the button. That's what he did. When it opened, one guy that I had arrested at Roll bailed out, ran around, got in the driver's seat, and took off with the truck. I got on my walkie-talkie, telling him to stop but he wouldn't do it. So I shot the right front tire off of it. He decided that he couldn't drive on a flat tire and get away, so he stopped probably three-quarters of a mile down the road, got out, and started running.

I had too many people in tow to chase this guy. I got the ones I was bringing from the field to the road there and told them to sit down while I changed the tire. I just told them to sit right there, and that's what they did. I don't know if it had anything to do with the smoking gun in my hand or not. I went on up the road, changed the tire, and came back to get them. After you think about it, it's kind of funny, but boy, I was serious at the time. Another agent and I then looked for tracks on that guy that ran. I trailed him to the road there, and evidently somebody had stopped and given him a ride, so he got completely away. I quit looking for him in January 2003 when I retired. Fortunately I never shot anybody, never had to. As far as I know, nobody ever shot at *me*. That's pretty good for twenty-eight years.

We did have lots of rescues. Some you remember the most. We got to looking for one fellow over around Rat Gap. Dave Roberson was flying with us, working with us then. We had tracks all over the place out there where this guy had wandered around and set things on fire trying to make a signal fire. He had really been trying to get somebody's attention. After about a day and a half looking for him, we finally located him around Rat Gap. He was there in just his jockey shorts and a straw hat—that's all he had on. When I finally got around to where he was at, he just dropped down to his knees and called me his salvation. That was one that you remember. That was one of the good ones.

I remember lots and lots of bad ones, too, where you found nothing but death out there. The worst was when we found women and little children, about five and seven years old. That's probably the worst day of my life right there. It was on a Sunday, and we had cut them across the Big Pass Drag. They were headed for Mohawk Pass on the interstate. Whenever we saw those little bitty tracks, we knew that we had something of urgency here and that we had to find them. It worked out that they were deceased by the time we got there. They were the El Salvadorans. Before they got to the dunes we found a woman and two kids. And then we found another woman in the dunes later on. It was an all-day thing, and it worked into the night and then into the following day before we found her. I don't remember if it was three or if it was just two women now, but it was too many. And one of the two adult males that was in the group had walked on to White Wing Ranch near Horn. The other had walked to the Owl Station on Highway 80, near Mohawk Pass, and after he recovered enough to where he could walk, he had flagged down a highway patrolman and told them that he had left some people in the desert. We had been working it for hours before Highway Patrol gave us that information.

That event helped to get DART going. Because of the rescues, not necessarily *that* particular rescue, Benny Burns came up with this idea to start some kind of rescue program. DART was Desert Area Rescue Team. I want to say it was kicked off around 1982 or '83. We would have agents from the Yuma Station come out and learn our area, in the event that we needed assistance in tracking. Yuma Station sent out its better trackers to familiarize themselves with the Tacna area and how we worked. They did do some good. Sector didn't really have the resources to be doing something like that, because if we pulled those agents in from Yuma, then their areas were uncovered, and you just "rob Peter to pay Paul." But you could justify leaving this area uncovered in order to bring out somebody for a rescue.

One Sunday I was the only one on duty. Jackie Mason was flying, and we were working trails all over that desert. About four o'clock that afternoon, he decided that we weren't getting any closer, and he was going to the house. So he headed his airplane towards Yuma. I was coming through Little Pass, and that's thirty-five miles south of Tacna. I was coming through there in an old Ramcharger, and I hit a bump in the road. When I hit that bump, my truck stalled. I tried to start it, and it wouldn't do anything. So I got out and moved my battery cables around a little bit to see if I could get a little better contact, but all it would do is grind one time, "rrrrraar," and that was it. I tried my radio, and it was dead. I got ahold of Jackie on my walkie-talkie. He was just fixing to land at the airport in Yuma, but he was still high enough that he could hear me on that walkie-talkie. He climbed back up, and we talked for a minute there, and he said he'd help. He landed the Super Cub, went and got his car, went over to the Border Patrol garage, got me a battery, took it back to the airport, put it in the airplane, flew it out to me, and landed right there within a half-mile of where I was. I met him and took the battery off his shoulder and carried it the rest of the way, about a half-mile. That was a heavy old battery after a while. He saved my bacon that day. We had plenty of long days like that.

I was the agent in charge at Wellton for a while. As an agent and as station chief, I liked to get things done. I tried to always remember where I had come from and where all these guys under me were going and what they were going through. I tried to treat them the way that I wanted to be treated when I was in their position, and still get things done. My philosophy was "Let's get the job done, and enjoy it if we can."

I tried to lead by example mostly and be as honest and fair as I could with everybody, whether it be the chief patrol agent or the people in the headquarters or the regional office or my agents. I never wanted to forget where I came from and how I wanted to be treated when I was coming up through the ranks. Doing things that way probably rubbed off on a lot of the people that I worked with or that worked for me. Maybe it helped to get things done. I don't know that there's anybody that enjoyed doing border patrol any more than I did, and I hope it showed with those that

I worked with. I probably was the longest-serving agent at the Wellton or Tacna Station, because I was there for twenty-five years, roughly, from 1979 to 2003.

The biggest change I saw was in personnel. When I first got here, we had seven agents. We had just gone to star numbers, and Joe McCraw was PAIC, and he was 501. I was the last guy in alphabetical order out there, and I was 507. And then when I retired in 2003, there were about seventy-five on the books, plus we had about twenty-five at the academy at the time. And we had lots and lots of trainees with us. That's the biggest change right there, outside the numbers of arrests that we made. It seemed like each year it would grow in numbers. I think that we got more agents because of the sheer numbers of aliens we caught.

Sign cutting is still important. The first thing you need for good sign cutting is to have good light. Whether you're looking into the sun or in the backside of a flashlight, you've got to have good lighting to be able to find tracks. You've got to get some experience with knowing how to hide a track, what to look for, and where to look. You can't look on hard surfaces and find much. You have to be a good judge of soils, and be able to look at a spot out there and say, "Well, that looks like it may have a little dust on the top of it there, or we could see a track if it were there." Walking across the flats out there, the desert will get real rocky, but if you get in the right light, that dust will be knocked off in certain areas, and you'll be able to see the tracks all the way across. I think experience is the biggest thing, but then lighting comes right behind that. Knowledge of where they're headed helps a lot, too. If they're looking at a certain thing out there, guiding on a bright light or a mountaintop, you need to be able to pick that up and work from that end of it as well. You have to be able to communicate with anybody that you're working with, and kind of guide them in on where you think the sign might be out in front of you, leapfrog it either with aircraft or with a ground unit. You had to be able to work with somebody.

Who was the better tracker, Joe McCraw or me? Me. I had a lot more experience. It took me a long while, a year or so, to be able to get on a trail with Joe and beat him to the arrest. Initially, every time we'd get on a trail, we'd tell Joe where the aliens were headed, and he'd get out there in front and he'd catch them. First thing you know, he's on the radio saying, "They're in custody." Finally I was able to do that, too. I could get out in front of Joe and say, "They're in custody." That makes you feel good when you can do that.

GEORGE BOONE

George Boone joined the Border Patrol in 1987 and is currently stationed at Boulevard, California. He worked at Wellton Station from 1991 to 1996.

I was born in Europe and raised by my grandparents in a small village in the Carpathian Alps of Romania. My American name comes from George Bono, with the Bono, or Bunu, being my grandfather's nickname. It meant "kind" or "bueno." Romanians have small stout mountain horses. They don't ride much, but they pack them and use them to pull wagons. My grandparents had horses, and that is how I got the horse bug. They always had a couple of mares and raised colts. As a child, I used to ride the mares. By the time I started working for the Border Patrol I had enough money to afford to keep horses. I slowly got back into it, sometimes in unexpected ways.

The desert where I patrolled south of Wellton is wide open country, and it's federal land off-limits to grazing cattle or horses. There's not much vegetation there, just little ironwood trees and a few cactus. Sometimes smugglers think they can sneak past us with loads of dope on horseback.

I left the station early one December morning in 1993 to cut sign in the desert after a winter storm. We had unusual ground fog, and the pilots said they probably wouldn't fly. We had eighty miles of border to search for sign, and I knew I wasn't going to be able to search it all for sign, because the lower drag road had just too much mud and water on it. So, I went to the middle drag road which is halfway between Mexico and the interstate. I was driving slowly looking for footprints when one of our helicopter pilots, Colonel Child, came on the radio.

He said, "Hey, George, I've got sign of three horses southbound about ten miles east of you. I'm going to push this sign south and see if I can

George Boone. Photo by Bill Broyles, 2009.

catch up with them. Why don't you get on the sign and push it north and see where they are coming from?"

I headed over and found the tracks. He called back shortly to report finding a dead horse. Apparently one of the horses, a four- to five-year-old sorrel, couldn't walk any more, so they tied him up to an ironwood tree instead of turning him loose. The horse died fighting. It had pawed a big hole in the ground, and was left just hanging there, dead. That's the first one that Colonel found. Grimly he kept pushing the tracks of two horses still farther south. Only one horse and two smugglers returned to Mexico. As we unraveled the tracks, we eventually found out that this was one of four horses used by smugglers, who came across in the middle of the night. They crossed at Los Vidrios and rode sixty miles to the interstate, where they planned to drop the dope for somebody else to pick up, while they rode back south and escaped into Mexico. Their horses got exhausted, so they didn't quite make it to the interstate, and they all got lost in the fog. We followed their tracks over many miles of ground.

Driving north on the three sets of horse prints, I was startled to see a fourth set of horse prints. The fourth horse kind of veered off from the three. It looked like the horse couldn't walk any more, so they turned him loose. He was too exhausted and couldn't keep up. He was trying to follow the other three by smell, but a side wind was blowing him off course. I saw what looked like a big doughnut worn into the sand where this horse would go down to rest and couldn't get back up. Its legs must have been stove up from walking about a hundred miles nonstop, so he struggled in a circle and eventually got back on its feet. You could see the toe prints digging in, like a drunk person bracing himself. Then a hundred yards later, there'd be another doughnut and then another doughnut and another. I was afraid to look too far ahead. Sure enough, I found him dead on the ground, with cuts and bruises all over its body. I looked him in the mouth and like the other horses found, he was only four and a half years old, with a lousy Mexican shoeing job on his feet.

So I returned to push the three horses. After refueling at Wellton, Colonel came back to help me and we leapfrogged through the sand dunes. I'd stay on the sign and give him a direction of travel and he'd cut half a mile to a mile in front of me. Then he would stay on the sign and I would cut ahead. He was in a helicopter; I was in a four-by. We pushed the tracks like that for five or ten miles and suddenly he said, "Hey, George, I'm going down right here." He didn't say why, but I knew he had found something. I expected another dead horse or a human body.

Eventually I found my way to where he had landed. There were bundles of pot everywhere, big bundles, small bundles right where they had dropped them. It totaled over six hundred pounds. I took the spare tire out of the back of the Bronco, put it in the passenger seat, and we packed as much as we could into the back. The load was all the way from the security screen to the back window, and we still had some left, so Colonel had to take several big bundles in the helicopter.

As we were sitting there, I couldn't help telling him, "I told you so." In the past, now and again, I would see horse sign coming across the border. There are some Mexican ranchers on the south side doing subsistence ranching, barely surviving. They were pushing their cattle into the Cabeza Prieta Wildlife Refuge, grazing protected land. I always resented that because we're trying to protect the saguaros and wildlife habitat where these cattle intruded. But now and again I would see tracks of one or two riders, or a rider and a dog, up to fifteen miles from the cows. I used to tell Colonel, "What are these guys doing? They're not sightseeing." I thought they must be scouting for the smugglers. Colonel thought they were just chasing cows. These bundles were proof that they were not chasing cows. I believe that was Colonel's biggest dope find. So, we were happy. We had to take the dope back to the station, take the "trophy" pictures, do one I-44 form, and then we turned the dope and case over to DEA.

As he had been flying, Colonel also found two saddles, jackets, and other stuff that the smugglers left half the way down to the Mexican border. Colonel had already found where the two smugglers escaped into Mexico with one horse. Months later we found out from some people from the south side that they killed that one, too. So, we had the dope, and two saddles. Of the four horses, two were found dead, one was in Mexico, and one was missing. The next day I was off duty, but I knew the pilots were going to follow that sign again and find out if there were any other horses or people involved. We knew that there was one missing horse. I said, "If you guys find him, give me a call. Don't shoot him."

Sure enough, the next day at about ten, the radio dispatcher called me at home and said, "Hey, George, they found the horse. They want to know if you want to go and get it." I jumped at the chance. The pilot and a ground agent named Buster Hummel reported that the horse was in the middle of nowhere at a spot called the Point of the Pintas. So, I hooked up my horse trailer and hurried thirty miles down the rough, sandy Papago Road. The terrain was so sandy that I had to leave the trailer and drive the last bit in four-wheel drive.

I started seeing the desperate doughnut tracks of the last, surviving horse. He was doing the same thing as the others. He, too, was within an inch of his life. I was dizzy with rage when I finally spotted him. He was pitiful. The horse was probably about two hundred fifty pounds underweight, the skin on him was taut like a drum, and his upper lip was gone. All the fat, all the moisture in his body was gone. By then he was about three days and a hundred miles from when they had entered the country. In that time and distance the horses had gotten no water and no food, but had carried heavy loads without pack saddles. The smugglers used regular blankets tied with baling wire, so the horses' bodies were all cut up.

I had hay and I had water in my truck, so I gave him a bucket of water and he slurped it all up. I gave him a second one and he drank that, too. He wanted to drink himself to death, so I stopped. I had some hay and offered him a bite of it. He held it in his mouth and big tears rolled down his face. I thought, "What in the hell is going on?" I opened his mouth and I looked. He was about four and a half years old like the others, the dead ones. He had big, bloody cuts through his gums and around his lower jaw. I made the connection right away to a bridle we found that had baling wire on it.

Then I realized what the smugglers were doing: they had baling wire in the horses' mouths to jerk them along and make them walk that extra mile. It was pathetic.

Before Buster left we called the livestock inspector like we're supposed to do, and the guy said, "Shoot him." I thought, "No way. We're going to give this horse a chance. Let's see what's going to happen." I tried to walk him to the trailer, which I could barely see in the distance. I led him holding my bridle reins out the window of my pick-up. I drove slowly, and let him rest frequently. But the more he rested, the more stove up he got. His front legs were swollen to twice their normal size from the effort. And his toes, although shod, were worn in about an inch through the hoof and through the iron from just dragging his feet. I figured he wasn't going anywhere, so I dropped the rope and headed back to the trailer for a sandwich and a drink, and to let him rest. As I drove away I looked in the rearview mirror, and I saw him struggle again. He wanted to follow. That's when I thought, "He's fighting and going to make it." He was trying really hard but barely able to drag his feet. When I got him to the trailer, I had to pick his feet up one by one to get him in the trailer. I didn't know if he'd ever been in a trailer before or not.

I took him home and tied him up short to a hitching post. I was afraid he was going to go down—if he did, I couldn't get him back up on his feet again—but he never did. The next day the horse's fever went up to a hundred and five. My veterinarian finally showed up, as did the livestock inspector. They looked him over and said, "No, he's a goner." Great quantities of gray shit oozed down his back legs; he had no sphincter control at all. He moved in slow motion. I took off his shoes and doctored him as much as I could. Chunks of skin just flaked off of his sides where the cinches and baling twine had rubbed the skin like somebody had burned him with a torch.

I had antibiotics, but I wanted to find out where the infection was coming from, that big fever, and I did find it. It was on his spine. It was right on his withers where the mane ends. I started poking around with my pocket knife and I took out a blister about as big as a tennis ball right above his spine. A cup of pus came out of it. I cleaned it all up, put the garden hose in it, washed it, and poured in hydrogen peroxide to boil all that stuff out. Then I covered the mess with two maxi pads and duct tape, and I blanketed him to keep him warm. After this and seven days of antibiotics, he started coming back slowly.

The livestock inspector was a nice young man. I told him the story and that I'd like to keep the horse if possible. He said, "Let me see what I can do." He sent the state vet. She came over and took blood samples from the horse to make sure it didn't have brucellosis out of Mexico. In another week or two she reported that the results were negative. Everything was fine with the horse. She filled out some forms to register the horse in my name in the state of Arizona, so that it could legally belong to me. I had to pay her five dollars for the fee, and that's how I got to calling him "my five-dollar horse."

The horse took about a year to fully recover. He and I worked together for over twelve years. He turned out to be the best horse I ever rode. I always bragged on him at all the events where I would go. Other riders had fancy horses, but my horse and I would compete with them at the cowboy rendezvous, and I would brag on "my five-dollar horse" that I rode with a fifteen-hundred-dollar saddle.

I named him Colonel, after Colonel Child, our pilot who found him. That horse and I went to the bottom of the Grand Canyon several times and all over the High Sierras of California. I usually ride one horse and pack one or two on my pack trips. I rode him to the highest point you can ride a horse in the state of California, 13,200 feet over Forrester Pass. He would go any place and do whatever you asked him to. He had such a good disposition, although it took a while. He was a little wild at first. You couldn't touch his back feet and you couldn't touch his head, because he had been so abused. When you think about it, those horses saved the smugglers' lives because otherwise they would have got stranded in the desert themselves, but they had no mercy, absolutely none.

Later we did get another load that had the same markings on the bales of marijuana. Some of it had markings of the Mexican military. It apparently had been seized by the Mexican military, and they were putting it back on the market. There was all kinds of mischief. We didn't ever find the full story, and I don't think DEA ever did. The smugglers tried to get several loads like that across the desert, but they didn't use horses again; they used vehicles and quads.

I started with the Border Patrol in 1987. After a series of jobs in the states of Alaska and Washington, I took an exam for the U.S. Border Patrol, although I didn't really know what the Border Patrol did. I thought the Border Patrol were the people you showed your driver's license to when you go to Canada to buy beer. About a year later, they called me and asked, "Do you want a job in Yuma, Arizona?" I had no idea where Yuma was, so I looked it up in the Rand-McNally Atlas and figured that it had to be a wonderful place because it is right on the Colorado River. When I first saw Yuma, I was stunned. I thought, "This is not God's country. There's nothing here." It was dry and brown, nothing like the evergreen forests of Washington. For the first couple of years I desperately tried to get a transfer to the northern border, but none were available. The desert grows on you, and eventually I got to like it so much that I'm not going anywhere. This is home.

My best of times were working this desert. I really like it. I've been to every water tank and every waterhole known to people here and climbed to the top of every mountain range. I got to learn the plants and all the animals. When you learn about them, you find out that this desert is not empty. There's actually a lot of interest, but you have to spend the time to watch the seasons go by and see how things flow. Things flow slowly here. If you don't take your time, you're not going to see it.

I had the time of my career working at Tacna and Wellton. It was wonderful. Fifty-mile chases, groups, and dope. It was not very, very busy, but just busy enough to where we pretty much caught everything that came across. It was very satisfying at that time. I stayed in Wellton until 1996, and the only reason I left and went to San Diego was that there were no promotions at Wellton. I promoted to a senior-agent position at Campo, San Diego Sector.

Within a year I got lucky enough to be accepted for the mounted unit up there. I got paid to ride a horse and chase the bad guys at night. We rode government-issue horses. That was really nice. I did that for four years, and then I promoted to supervisor in Boulevard and within a year went back to the horses as a supervisor and did another year riding the horses as a supervisor. I got involved with training people, training horses, and buying horses. We worked and appeared at all sorts of public functions, and the Border Patrol even sent me to Ottawa, where I trained with the Royal Canadian Mounted Police, the Mounties.

There've been a lot of good changes in Border Patrol and some bad changes lately. Because we're hiring so many new agents so fast, we're losing the experience of the older guys. I've been involved in some of the oral hiring boards for new agents, and some days we would interview five or six candidates and none of them would pass. But, we're still getting quite a few good people. The Border Patrol used to hire more people like Glen Payne and me, outdoor types and farm kids who were not intimidated by the outdoors. Now we get a lot of young people from big cities. Some of them have never driven a car, never had a driver's license, and never camped out overnight. They can't tell cattle tracks from horse tracks.

George Boone

It takes a year, at least, just to learn your way around this desert and to feel comfortable in it. Learning is so much easier with somebody who already knows it. Some of the new guys are not involved—they don't have class parties like we used to, they don't have "choir practices" like we used to, and they don't know each other's families. When I joined, we knew each other. Everybody knew everybody else. We visited, socialized, and worked well together. Now I don't even know everybody at my station by name, and that's pretty sad. Many of the agents are very, very young and they don't have experience in other jobs or the military, like many of my generation had. And we're losing people at a lot faster rate than we used to. At my station we're probably losing about one a month. They're not retiring—these are young guys just quitting or transferring. Now fewer see the Border Patrol as a career—they're better educated and are using the Border Patrol as a stepping stone. They don't really want to be there and they imagine they have better things to do.

It is rewarding to see some of these young agents actually catching on, having a good time, and doing a good job. For some the work ethic has to be taught. Recruits have to see it. It helps if they like to work outdoors, and you've got to like to hunt. You've got to develop the determination, the patience to stay with it. Patience always pays. If you move too fast, you're not going to succeed in sign cutting and working the desert. The only way for recruits to learn is to do it and to get that bug. It's very rewarding to follow a trail and eventually catch up to a group. And in this desert in summertime, many times a group is in trouble, and catching them is really a rescue.

Agents are not going to solve the illegal immigration problem. The Border Patrol does nothing but minimize the damage. We need some kind of a political solution, such as employer sanctions. That's the only thing that's going to stop the magnet. If that would happen then mostly bad guys would try to cross, and we could seriously concentrate on that. Without employer sanctions, this will never change. The magnet is here. Aliens are going to try to come here, although a lot of the people that we catch are not the people that I used to see working in the fields. Increasingly, they're all going to the big cities and trying to get on some kind of government aid. They've learned the system.

Technology has made the job a little easier, but not necessarily faster. The time it takes to process and do the paperwork I don't think has changed much. When I came in we had nothing but manual typewriters and now, of course, everything is computerized. It used to take me about two hours to do an A-file (alien file), and it takes me about two hours to do an A-file today.

The Border Patrol has never been good at public relations. For the longest time, they've just kind of tried to keep the media and the public at arm's length. I think that was a bad idea. I wish the public knew that we're very dedicated professional people who are working our butts off. It's hard to get the message across, because a lot of people really don't know what the Border Patrol does. Border Patrol should publish some of those stats and let people know the millions that we arrest, the unbelievable amount of drugs that we seize, and all the violence we see. If all the violent incidents were published, people would be scared, really.

I love tracking. In Yuma County a deputy sheriff stopped a guy for DUI about 10 p.m. somewhere in the Gila River valley. Her back-up was in Yuma, an hour away. When she got the drunk out of the truck, he pushed her over and ran through an irrigation canal and out into the farm fields. When I arrived on scene, I could see his wet, muddy footprints on the other side of the canal, so I started jogging through the fields pushing his sign until my partner got there. We pushed him five or six miles into the river bottom, and we lost him in cattails and brush fifteen feet high. We were right on the levee. By then three or four deputies arrived along with two or three of our guys. I said quietly, "I have a plan. Why don't you all just get out of here and wait a few miles up the road. Just go."

So, they all got into their vehicles and left. I stayed behind and sat down on the ground, turned my radio off, and just sat still in the dark. Within five minutes, the suspect started moving in the river bottom. When he moved, I moved, and when he stopped, I stopped. I got within fifteen or twenty feet of him without him ever knowing I was there. I hit my radio's squelch button to signal my partner, Buster, to come in.

He came in full blast, with all lights on, and we rushed the suspect. We handcuffed him tight and dragged him back to the levee. We called the sheriffs back, and they were really happy, but they wanted to know how we tracked this guy. They all knew that we were really good at tracking, but they wanted to know what sign we followed in that river bottom. Of course we never told them that good tracking is not just about following footprints.

George Boone

HOWARD AITKEN

Howard Aitken joined the Border Patrol in 1980 and is now head of Customs and Border Protection Air Operations at Yuma, Arizona. He has worked in Yuma since 1986 and plans to retire on 11-11-11.

Flying for the Border Patrol is the most fun you can have with your pants on. It's dangerous, it's challenging, it's fun, and it's a great job. It's the greatest job in the Border Patrol. The only reason I took a supervisor's slot was so that we can maintain what we have here at Yuma, as far as how things are managed. Otherwise, I'd still be a line pilot. It's the most fun I ever had. The self-satisfaction of saving people and catching aliens is enormous. Now our mission includes preventing terrorists and weapons of mass destruction from entering the United States. We're still all in the Border Patrol. We'd rather be out there sign cutting and catching aliens.

There've been so many rescues and body recoveries that they all just careen together, but a couple stick in my mind. We spent two days tracking a pregnant female and finally found her just north of Game Tank. Her husband, who was the guide, abandoned her and another guy because they couldn't keep up, and then those two separated. When we found her the next day, I'd spent 12.7 hours in the air that first day and then six hours the next day when we found her. She was seven months pregnant, and when I found her, she had already taken all her clothes off and had begun to dig holes with her hands. I got her watered down and dressed. Jerry Scott arrived in a ground unit and got some more water in her. Then I air evac'ed her out to Dateland, where an ambulance took her to the hospital. She and the unborn baby survived. But her husband left her behind. The guy who got separated? We found his bones two years later.

Then there was a family that I picked up coming through Woodcutter's

Canyon. It was nighttime. It was a father, mother, and kids, and the smallest kid was maybe two or three years old, and they had five kids, all stepped up. None of them were in real bad shape, but they were thirsty, tired, had blisters, and were scared. We got them all watered down, and I asked the father, "What are you doing, bringing your kids through?! Why are you doing it?" "Gotta find a job." "You just endangered your kids, and you're gonna come back and try again?!" "Oh yeah, I'm gonna try again." I said, "Well, do it through San Luis or someplace else, don't come through this country." We never saw them again.

There have been times I've just been flying along, and look down at a tree and see a body that's been there for weeks or months, but nobody knew. One we found in the Butler Mountains wasn't more than a mile from help, but he had no idea. His sign was completely gone, so we had no idea if he was coming in or going back, or what. He just laid down under a tree and died in summer. I just happened to be looking for another group and ran across him.

On one chase some crossers were headed west from Little Pass instead of north. They had no clue where they were going. They got off the bus in Mexico hours earlier and somebody gave them a little map and a compass and said, "Here, this is how you get into the United States."

        I came on duty in 1980 and went to the academy right away. I started the pilot training program in June 1988 after getting hired on as a trainee pilot. I had gained my prior flight experience from a Border Patrol pilot, Colonel Child. I had bought an airplane and started flying that to get up to the 250 hours. Then I flew as a trainee pilot for a year and eight months, before getting hired on as a journeyman pilot.

My father, Harry Aitken, is a retired Border Patrol pilot. Growing up I loved to fly with him, but I never had an inclination to learn to fly. I didn't even want to be a Border Patrol pilot until I got in the Border Patrol. I worked the ground for eight years and decided, "*That's* what I want to do!" But I did join the Border Patrol because Dad kind of forced me. I had long hair, down to my back. I wasn't into drugs or anything, but I was partying and wasting my days, so he sat me down and made me fill out the Border Patrol application.

I have a rotor-wing rating and a fixed-wing rating. I fly every aircraft we have, which includes the Huey, the A-Star, Super Cub, Cessna 182, and the OH-6s. I'm *still* trying to fly all of them. My favorite plane to fly right now is the A-Star. It's a Cadillac. It's all hydraulic, it's got air condition-

Howard Aitken. Photo by Bill Broyles, 2005.

ing, and it's fast and pretty maneuverable. The tail rotor sits pretty high and protected, so you don't worry about getting brush in it. It's not a real good sign-cutting aircraft, but for whatever else—going places, transporting VIPs, whatever—it's a very stable aircraft. It's got good visibility, and it's got a lot of power. You can put four or five people in it. When I first started, we had Super Cubs, a Cessna 182, and one helicopter that Dave Roberson and Jackie Mason flew, sometimes on night shift. Slowly, now we're up to seven helicopters and two fixed-wing, because helicopters are so much better for sign cutting and tracking.

Our OH-6s were built in the Vietnam War era. They were built for the Vietnam War, and they had a life span of 500 hours at that time. They're kind of a like a Yugo car: they were built to be thrown away. We've got one with 17,000 hours on it, and I've got another one that's over 12,000 hours, and they're still going. Our oldest one is a 1965 model, and our youngest one is a '68 model. And then our Huey is a 1972, and it's the same way. The government was going to refurbish the Hueys.

We'll replace the OH-6. I was on the technical committee to select new helicopters. The one we came up with was the EC-120, made by Eurocopter, as the replacement sign-cutter. It will be kept lightweight. It's going to be for day shift only, with a light on it, in case you get caught out. The A-Star will be our night ship. Weather? The helicopter can handle pretty high winds. We have very, very few unflyable weather days. I think in fiscal year 2005 we had one day that we couldn't fly because of the weather.

When the Border Patrol started flying helicopters in the late 1970s, it was probably the smartest thing they ever did. The Super Cub was always fun, but we lost way too many pilots. And you look at the safety record from then on, we've lost *one* helicopter pilot since we've started flying helicopters. In all the rest of the accidents I investigated, everybody walked away.

We'll have fixed planes for high-altitude surveillance. We call Chad Smith the "Super Cub pilot" because he was trained just in fixed wing. He does real well spotting drive-throughs. He'll be up there at 8,000 feet where nobody can see him or hear him, and he'll sit there with a pair of binoculars, and watch. And once the vehicle comes in, he'll follow it into town. We're all required to be instrument certified, and if we have a special operation that needs an airplane, we'll follow vehicles at night.

I want to do thirty years of federal government service and then quit. So I'll be age fifty-three when it happens. My dad had thirty-three years including his military time. But I've got him beat in flight hours, because right now I've got over 11,000 hours, and he ended up with just over 10,000 hours. He never got the chance to fly helicopters, which came in just after he retired.

On October 1, 2005, our biggest change happened. We became "Customs and Border Protection, Air and Marine," the new organization they created. We pilots are now called "air interdiction agents." From the time I came in and started flying in 1988, we've seen a lot of changes, because we were getting better equipment, more equipment, and safer equipment. We've got better night vision goggles now than the Coast Guard has. With all the safety equipment that they give us, and money and fuel to fly, we have unlimited flight time. Before 2005, I remember lean years when we couldn't fly because there was no fuel—we couldn't afford it. And now parts are no problem, either. If we have a helicopter that needs a starter or generator or something, it gets shipped overnight and we have it the next day. And the number of mechanics has increased; I've got four here now—three permanent and one contract mechanic.

We're still limited on the number of hours we can fly each month, for safety reasons. It's 100 hours per month, no more than 1,000 hours per year. A hundred hours a month is a lot of flight time, especially with low-level tracking and working under night vision goggles. For night flight, you're given training on how to avoid vertigo, so you really don't get it. The night vision goggles (NVGs) open up the whole world. You can see anything and everything. The observer sometimes gets a little ill, though, because he's looking at the ground and sometimes gets vertigo. We're still using agent observers. We've instituted a new program now where we detail them here for a year. It takes a pilot and an observer about a week to learn how to work together. And some observers are better than others. We've had some of them here that just take to it like ducks to water. They pick up on it and are really good at spotting aliens and the like. Then we've others that it takes a while, if they get it at all. Those are the ones we send back; we keep the good ones.

And, not all of the pilots take to this type of work. Some of them just don't get it. I had one here who wasn't able to grasp what the job was. It takes a minimum of two years flying out in the desert to learn sign-cutting by aircraft—even if you've done it on the ground. Tracking by air is a rewarding challenge, because the aliens try so many different tricks to hide or confuse their sign. They put foam on the bottom of their shoes, then walk across that desert out there, and think they leave absolutely no track. They try carpet squares, walking backwards, walking on their hands across drags, dumping sand in their tracks. I've got a twelve-foot extension ladder at my house that they tried. They laid it across the drag road and walked on it, but we saw two ladder marks on either side of the road. They can't hide all of their tracks, however hard they try. It's a good feeling when you catch them.

The sheriff's office and we have always had real good relationships, because we assist them. Being the only flying law enforcement unit in the area, we assist anybody and everybody that wants our help. We never say "no," whether it's locating lost people or dead bodies, chasing felony suspects, or covering warrant searches. We assist the sheriff's department, the Yuma Police Department (YPD), the Arizona Department of Public Safety (DPS), FBI, and DEA. We do a lot of photo flights for everybody; if they're going to do a warrant search on a house, we'll go out and take pictures of it first. We do a lot of photography for crime scenes and fly the evidence technician from YPD. Occasionally even the Cocopah Tribal Police will request assistance.

Sometimes we directly apprehend a group. We'll be trailing a group and find it without a ground unit nearby, so we land and make them sit down while we wait for transport. If transport is too far away, or it's too deep in the Cabeza Prieta Wilderness Area, then we actually haul them out in the helicopter. Because our sector includes the Goldwater Range, a training area for Marine Corps and Air Force pilots, we're always battling military aircraft. They're training to go into combat; we're out there to stop illegal aliens from entering the range so the Marines don't have to shut down the training range. Occasionally you get a hotdog military pilot who isn't supposed to go below seven hundred feet buzz you, fly under you, or fly at your same altitude. We work below five hundred feet.

I was working with Colonel Child, and he was circling just this side of the Copper Mountains. One Harrier flew below him and one Harrier above, and they sandwiched him. The military helicopter pilots think they own the place. I was working a group one day by Coyote Wash, and I landed to look for tracks when a Cobra landed behind me. Its pilot comes screaming out of his Cobra, and he's *mad*. He's mad at me for being out there at the same time that *he's* out there. I said, "Hey, I'm doin' my job. I have clearance to be out here." "This isn't safe," blah, blah. "What isn't safe here? I'm following this foot sign." "How long are you gonna be here?" "'Til I catch them." "Well, how long's that gonna be?" "I don't know. You're trainin' for a war. Do you think things are gonna be nice and neat over there?!" Over there you've got to deal with civilians. Here it's *very* controlled.

We don't have any trouble finding people who want to do this job. I do have trouble finding people who want to come to Yuma, but once they're here, I usually keep them. I've got one pilot, Joe Cochran, who did thirteen years with the Marine Corps, flying Search and Rescue missions right here in Yuma. I met him at an air show and conned him into joining the Border Patrol. He quit the Marine Corps after thirteen years, before his thirty-seventh birthday, and joined the Border Patrol to fly. All he wanted to do is fly. Now we have some female pilots. San Diego's got one, Elizabeth Ebisuzaki, and we have another one here in Yuma, Barbie Moorhouse.

We still go out and track, and save people. My management style is laid-back. I'm not a micromanager, but I keep an eye on things. If I can see problems building up, I talk to people and I listen, and I ask them how they're doing. We try to socialize beyond the office and get our families together. I get involved with my employees, but I'm not a micromanager. If I see something that's not right, something unsafe, I will bring it to their attention right away. When I'm not here, they make their decisions on their own. I know of micromanagers that are supervisors in other places—you can blow yourself up working for them. I just don't do that here.

I used to be able to say I was probably one of the best sign cutters. I can't say that nowadays. What I can say is, I've saved lives. They thought we were just apprehending them, but we were saving their lives. Deaths—the dead bodies I have found number over a hundred. How many people have I saved over the twenty-six years? Thousands. There's a phenomenon that few people realize when you've saved their life, because they don't know how close they were to dying. They're not grateful because they don't know it, and some of them you can never convince them of the fact.

MARK HAYNES

Mark Haynes served in the Border Patrol from 1978 to 2002 and was in charge of Wellton Station from 1989 to 1991 before going to Yuma Sector as an assistant chief. Currently he is active with the Arizona Historical Society and manages property in Yuma.

My folks were born and raised in Gadsden, Arizona, and they were always within a stone's throw of the border. My father said when he was a kid in the 1930s, there were uniformed cavalry riding that border. They would be in squad formations, a dozen of them or so, and it seemed like all those horses were in the same lope, in step. I've seen photos of a whole battalion of cavalry in formation, all the men standing up on their saddles on horseback, so I know the cavalry was well trained.

We'd been familiar with the Border Patrol. I used to see the agents around Gadsden, getting lunch at the Farmhouse Café, or picking up their jeeps or International Scouts at Estes Malone's Richfield Oil Station. There was a gasoline shortage in the early seventies, and they would park their patrol vehicles at the service station in Gadsden. A van would bring the agents from Yuma. They'd fill up with gas and go to the border from there. I used to hunt and fish on the Colorado River, which is the international border, so I was always tracking up the smooth drag roads made by the agents pulling tires behind their jeeps.

I always intended to go into law enforcement. I got a BS at Arizona State University and attended law school for two years. Law clerking for attorneys during the summers convinced me I didn't want or need to be a lawyer. Then I saw an announcement in the paper that they were hiring Border Patrol agents, so I signed up to take the test. I completed the oral and physical exams in 1977 and got a letter to report to my hometown of

Mark Haynes. Photo by Bill Broyles, 2005.

Yuma, Arizona, on April 10, 1978. At the time it was not considered policy to send people back to their hometowns, so I was lucky.

When I began at Yuma and while we recruits waited for our uniforms, the sector put us to work building tire drags and sand traps. Tire drags were old car tires bolted together and attached to a drag bar with wire cable in front. They are used to smooth the drag roads each day so cutting sign is easier. The sector headquarters was so tight for money that they made us cut the old drags apart with a torch to reuse the washers that kept the bolts from pulling through the tire tread. What a mess! The tires kept catching fire and we were covered in soot by the end of the day. Our boss was an agent named Dale Claiborne. We would have bought new washers out of our own pockets if he'd have let us.

We also built sand traps. Aliens followed the railroad looking for a freight train to jump for a ride to Los Angeles. They don't leave much foot sign on the ties and slag covering the rail bed, so where the railroad tracks went over a culvert agents would mix sand with used motor oil and spread the mixture in a layer over the rail bed. Particularly at night the aliens wouldn't notice what they were walking through and left good sign that could even be followed from the air. A sector pilot supervised our work.

Then we went to the Academy and seventeen weeks later, I returned to work at the old Yuma Station. I worked there from 1978 to 1989. It was all rotating shift work for eleven years. Shift changes could cause a bit of stress as far as processing of aliens went, for "you catch it, you clean it" was the typical attitude, meaning that if we apprehended an alien, we had to process the paperwork. But files for OTMs (aliens other than Mexicans; typically these were El Salvadorans and Guatemalans, and infrequently Europeans or Asians) took several hours to complete. If a big load was caught, the oncoming shift just had to help process them. You wanted to get them moved to camp as early as possible, so you didn't have to monitor them, feed them, take care of them, or worry whether or not they got sick. Plus, we needed the space for the next batch of apprehensions. In the early years, the detention bus ran to El Centro, only sixty miles away. But later the brass started rigidly enforcing the INS boundaries, so we had to transport OTMs to Florence, 160 miles away, at quite an extra expense to us in time and gas. Occasionally there would be a bus traveling the border, picking up deportations as it went along, so we rushed to catch it and put our detainees onboard.

Working in Yuma was a lot of fun. Out east we had the desert that just went on for miles; we could follow sign at thirty or forty miles an hour in some of it. We worked alone in a vehicle, but could call in a partner or two if we got into a chase. There were big groups in those days, and guys would joke that you just stuck one of our front tires in the rut they were making and let go of the steering wheel. And, there were times when we were very selective in what we chased. If there weren't twenty in the group, we'd keep cutting until we found a group that size and not bother with the singles or small groups. Not much dope came across here in my early days, or if there was, we were too busy to notice.

Later, dope got to be a pretty big problem. Not many really big loads, but three or four human "mules" carrying forty or so pounds of marijuana each. By that time the large influx of OTM (other than Mexicans) loads had dried up, so when you chased a pair or threesome you might be dealing with dope, usually marijuana. Sometimes, the smugglers used bait loads. You'd have a large group enter, typically across the Colorado River, and you'd pick up on a smaller trail nearby. They were hoping you'd concentrate on the bigger trail and not chase the smaller group carrying the dope.

When we got FLIR [forward looking infrared] and night vision scopes it was a real blast. The FLIR was originally bought for the helicopters, but it made the operators airsick. The OH-6 helicopter was too small and too unstable, so all the buffeting and bouncing while trying to watch the TV screen was just too much. So they mounted the FLIR equipment on a truck and it worked great. Later, infrared night vision scopes were mounted on pneumatic lifts mounted into trucks and SUVs. You could sit in comfort in a vehicle on the ground in pitch black and see for miles. No alien carried more than just a water jug and maybe a small *triques* bag with a few personal items. A marijuana packer with forty pounds on his shoulders had a hump caused by his body heat dissipating to the pack. So if we spotted them on a scope we generally knew it was dope before we went after them.

One time, we set up on the levee with a scope and watched a sophisticated backpacking operation. One guy had a big, long board with eyelets screwed into it, and then a long piece of rope with a hook. He'd plant the end of the board and have the rope coming down from that top hook, and he'd lower that board. Then three marijuana smugglers would walk across it, and he'd cross and reverse the process—take the hook out of that end, put it in the other end, and walk back across and lift it up. And that's the way they were crossing all the berms, headgates, and canals through the fields so they wouldn't leave tracks. We watched him for a little while. I just drove down there with my headlights out, idling slow so the vehicle wasn't making any noise. I could see them in the moonlight. The guy, after he lifted the ladder, was really careful, trying to put that berm back into shape with a little brush, when he saw me. The four ran in different directions but the scope saw where each one went and all were caught.

When it came time to go to trial, he said he was just going to see his girlfriend and he didn't know what those guys with the marijuana bags were doing. He was the last of the four to plead guilty. Good thing, I guess. When I had gone to the seizure lot to locate the board for trial I couldn't find it, so it was a case of lost evidence. Apparently another agent had lifted it and pounded it full of spikes to bury on a drive-through trail. It became a makeshift tire-spike-strip before the ready-made spikes and stop sticks were invented.

In those days you worked alone in a vehicle, and that's the way we liked it. We'd be assigned an area—five to ten miles of river, or more in the desert—usually with one other agent in another vehicle. The two of us would coordinate with each other to keep the border drag road cut periodically and we'd chase together if we got something of consequence across the drag. Some nights that would be a pair, and some nights it would be a group of twenty or more.

Once I was working alone on the west side of San Luis on the midnight shift. The area was about a mile and a half of border fence just west of the San Luis Port of Entry and another two and a half miles of river, so I was responsible for over four miles of border. I didn't cut any tracks across the drag road that night, but I wound up catching the biggest alien load I ever caught singlehandedly. I picked up on some sign on the levee and just followed it out. I never saw more than three or four different footprints the whole chase, but when I couldn't follow them any more I returned to where I last had seen them going into a wheat field. The wheat was about waist high and as I pushed through the wheat my feet ran into the feet of someone lying down. I yelled at the top of my lungs in Spanish to stand up and the wheat started rustling in every direction. I started swinging my flashlights around and saw people standing up in all directions. When I lined them all up and marched them out to the nearest road, I sat them down and made a count. There were fifty aliens! The kicker is that none of them had on the shoes that matched the tracks I was following. It turns out that the guides were walking them on carpet and using a soft broom to erase the tracks, but weren't doing such a good job of covering their own tracks. The guides had split just before I came onto the big group, so I didn't get the smugglers. I'd seen bigger groups before and afterward, but that's the most I ever surrounded on my own.

We usually worked ten or more hours a day. We had three shifts, but our areas were generally quite a distance away, plus we had to get our vehicle ready, sit through a briefing, and drive to our area, which all occupied at least an hour at the beginning of the shift. At the end of the shift, if you weren't chasing something—and frequently you were—you still had to get your vehicle cleaned up, put it away, and do your paperwork. If you had a hot chase going, you'd stay on it until you caught them. There was a culture in Yuma at the time, that if you started on a chase, you either caught them or determined where they "loaded up" in a car or on a train. If you apprehended them, you had to bring them in and process them.

As young agents, we thought we were invincible. We drove too fast, didn't always wear our seatbelts, went charging blindly into situations, and pulled over cars alone at night without any thought of being harmed. Sometimes the cars we stopped weren't even called into the radio dispatcher, because we hated to misfire, so to speak. We dreaded having to call in and say "10-8" (Back in Service) and not "Got a load." They say many folks have the dream that they're falling, and they say you could actually die if you don't wake up before hitting the ground. Many cops

I've talked to have the dream that they're in an armed confrontation and being shot at, but their gun is firing blanks. So I guess there is a subtle fear of a physical confrontation, but it doesn't come out except maybe in your dreams.

I was later moved up to Assistant Chief at Yuma Sector Headquarters. And in addition to managing agents and operations, we had to contend with immigration policy that seemed designed to fail. The politicians in Congress and in our own agency seemed bent on handcuffing us instead of the aliens we were sworn to apprehend. It didn't seem to matter who was in power, Democrats or Republicans. INS was always a second-tier agency and Border Patrol was second-tier in a second tier. Immigration policy never seemed to be a big item on the national agenda after the 1952 Immigration and Naturalization Act was passed. The next time immigration got much play was in 1986 when Congress put in place the big amnesty fiasco. If they had done everything that was in the act and not cherry-picked the things they wanted enacted, it might have worked.

Our current predicament relates in large part to that Immigration Reform and Control Act of 1986. It caused a *drastic* effect in just about every aspect of the Border Patrol. One of the big things that irked us was for the first time there was legislation that altered the "open fields" doctrine, which had been a point of constitutional law going way back. Anything you see in an open field that you reasonably believe is related to criminal activity is exempt from the search warrant requirement. But, because of pressure from growers and activist groups, Congress passed this legislation that said for the first time immigration officers had to have a search warrant to enter open fields for the purpose of questioning aliens regarding their alienage, except for narrow exceptions — if you had the permission of the landowner, or if you were in hot pursuit. Otherwise, you had to get a criminal or administrative search warrant.

Of course, that provision was activated right away. But what about the provisions they didn't implement, like the telephonic verification system? An employer was required by law to ask for proof of employment eligibility, but he was given no system to verify the documents he was given. And they never provided the manpower to ensure employers were doing what they were supposed to be doing. So it all fizzled. The 1986 Act did nothing to alleviate the magnet of jobs that was drawing foreigners into the country.

The amnesty and the special agricultural worker programs were also implemented immediately. The two provisions were called Section 245 amnesty and SAW, for "Special Agricultural Worker." A person who had a certain amount of continuous presence in the United States was eligible for amnesty—which meant they could go in and apply for a special card, if they had the proper documentation, rent receipts or utility bills, proving that they'd been here for that amount of time. The Special Agricultural Worker provision was much more lenient. A person need only prove that they had worked during agricultural seasons for three successive years. Fraud was rampant. Document mills began ginning up phony documents to substantiate a claim that they lived here or worked in agriculture. And they weren't just making fraudulent documents like driver's licenses. They were printing up fake payroll records, rent receipts, and tax records. People were selling those packages on street corners.

A man named Johnny Johnson, who lived in Wellton, was prosecuted and received eight years in prison because he was ginning up documentation. Because of him, thousands of aliens claimed amnesty and were eventually granted Special Agricultural Worker provision status, with the package of documents that he sold them for a substantial amount of money. But few of those people were investigated or charged, and most of them who obtained status are now long-term resident aliens, or they're U.S. citizens and have been for years, based on fraudulent documents.

Only in very rare cases were the legal documents revoked. In fact, INS rated various offices on how many of these applications they were granting, legitimate or otherwise. Border Patrol took a different approach: every claim that we encountered should be verified. So we were breaking these claims left and right—doing sworn statements, rebutting that these people had worked in agriculture, and discovering that they had first entered the United States long after the amnesty period closed. And we were having a field day denying these claims, putting these people up for deportation proceedings. And boy did we catch the wrath! INS called us and in no uncertain terms said, "You're not here to second-guess the people at the INS offices that grant that status. If they have those cards or those documents, you leave them alone." It deflated the morale of the rank and file agents. We saw rampant fraud, and it seemed INS condoned it.

Then came Family Fairness. Nobody ever considered the impact on the spouses and children of these new temporary residents, whether they were in the United States or abroad. First, they started making inroads administratively. They would grant a temporary status to relatives who were apprehended until they could figure out what to do with these folks. You'd have a breadwinner who all of a sudden had a status—he could cross the border, he could work, and he was on the first leg of his road to citizenship, should he choose to follow it. But these families were still subject to deportation. Lawsuits proliferated, and after a lot of soul searching and wringing of hands, it became clear that the administrative solution wasn't going to work. Eventually Congress stepped in and passed the Family Fairness provision, which granted legal status to all those immediate relatives of the people who were granted amnesty. A little over 3 million people obtained amnesty under the provisions of IRCA [Immigration Reform Control Act of 1986] but an untold number eventually gained status because of the Family Fairness extension to immediate family members.

And that didn't include when those people qualified for LAPR status—Lawfully Admitted for Permanent Residence. Then some more of them were eligible for preference visas, and when they attained citizenship, those persons were eligible for no-limit visas, which meant no numerical limits to how many could be issued. The web of legalization that spread from the original amnesty provisions went far and wide, far exceeding what was anticipated, in terms of the impact and the number of people who became legal residents. And future congresses may take us down the same road, because there's no institutional memory up there. Nobody remembers how bad that was, how poorly that was managed, how much money that cost, or how rampant the fraud was. A program with good intentions turned bad real quick, and nobody had any commitment to do anything about it. Worldwide, U.S. immigration laws seemed like a joke.

That part was frustrating. So day to day the challenge was between us and the border crosser. We'd go out and get the alien—that was the success story. We could walk him back across the border, or maybe prosecute him, or maybe seize the car he was driving. If he had narcotics on him, even better, even more satisfaction. Ultimately, we just didn't concern ourselves with the big picture. It was between us and the alien, matching wits day by day.

One of the highlights of my career was working at Tacna and Wellton. I went to Wellton as Patrol Agent in Charge (PAIC) in February of 1989 and left there in September of 1991. I actually went to Tacna Station, but they had announced the job as Wellton Station, where they planned to move and eventually did. We moved into a double-wide trailer in Wellton in 1990, and the grand opening was April 28.

Being a Patrol Agent in Charge was a great job. You were top of the heap, so to speak. You didn't report to anyone else in the office, just to the Sector Headquarters. Some chiefs, like Gene Corder, were traditionalists who pretty much let the PAIC call his own shots. Others liked to be more involved. We'd make our cuts for sign on the drags, and our air ops pilots would make their cuts. If there were no crossers we'd get on the highway. Checkpoints were often mandated for continuous operation, even though we often didn't have the manpower. Generally we would run two 6-to-2 shifts. I did work some night shifts, just for test purposes. When we had just the two shifts there could be a gap between shifts. I'd go out there and sit by myself. I had visions that the whole country of Mexico was streaming through, bumper to bumper, during our shift gaps. So I'd go out there and sit. Nobody would come through, nothing. That's why it never worried me that we weren't always doing the mandated twenty-four hours. It was impossible with our allotted manpower, so we did the best we could.

At Tacna, lifesaving was the focus from Day One. We made apprehensions like everybody else, but because of the harshness of that desert, the focus was saving lives. When we had entries in the desert all other activities were put on hold until the aliens were located. And Tacna folks felt pretty special about that. But not every chase ended in success. One alien had walked up south of January's jojoba farm, and he was in trouble, taking tiny steps, staggering, and dragging his feet. And when he got to the drag road, he turned around and went back south for some reason, maybe to go lead someone else out. We were trailing him when a vicious dust storm came up, so our pilot had to return to the airport. The rain started pounding through the dirt in the air and splattering us with those little wet dirt balls. I followed the sign 'til it was all blown and rained out. After the storm cleared, we searched that area over the next few days, but it was a lost cause. I don't know if he ever got out of there.

Our Desert Area Rescue Team, DART, felt pretty special about being recognized as some of the better trackers, a skill necessary to save lives. And they didn't just save lives out in Wellton. Once we rescued a guy on the far bank of the All-American Canal west of Yuma. He just couldn't make that last sand hill. That hill turned out to be the bank of the All-American. He was smart, though, easy to follow. He had crossed through the dunes, and had spent some time at a railroad siding, but he didn't catch a train. He headed back, dragging a stick behind him. He obviously knew that would make him easier to find, and we found him on his last gasp under a tree. We rehydrated him and then drove up the hill to show him the multi-million-gallon canal flowing just yards from where he was waiting under a bush to die of thirst.

DART was also called out to do search and rescues for children and for escaped criminals. One time the sheriff was using an inadequate city jail for the county lockup. A judge had condemned the county jail, and so they were trying to squeeze everybody into a makeshift city jail, and nine felons escaped at night. The DART team was called out. The escapees had scattered out all over the city and they had a three hours' head start. One even had gotten into a taxi cab, found a heroin source, and shot up. But by morning we had tracked down every one of those nine, and they were back in custody by the time the public was even aware that they had escaped. That was quite an accomplishment.

When I went to Wellton in 1989 as agent in charge of the station, I wasn't given a whole lot of direction on where to take the station. It was after the Immigration Reform and Control Act of 1986, and the apprehension levels were really low. We certainly hadn't seen an increase in entries at Wellton in particular, because historically a lot of its entries went to the farms in the Gila River valley. But, newly legalized farm workers had those jobs tied up, so there was no reason for illegals to cross. The new workers came through the port with papers in hand, and there weren't any jobs for the people who hadn't received amnesty. In particular, our mandate was to help control the alien traffic leaving Yuma. Manpower was always in critically short supply. Yuma was always considered a sign-cutting station, and agents didn't like traffic check. For years they didn't have traffic check, and when they did do traffic check, they weren't particularly good at it.

At Wellton we were starting with a fresh slate. Intuitively I thought there was a mandate to make those guys good at traffic check. We were going to control traffic coming out of the Yuma Station area of operation. And at one time we had envisioned, and a plan was put forth, to let Wellton handle all the eastbound traffic check duties. I proposed we would run an Interstate 8 checkpoint. We would also run the Highway 95 checkpoint along the road from Yuma to Quartzite, we would control Dome Valley, and we'd also watch the desert. That would free up Yuma Station to do what they wanted to do and did best, and that was watch the line and chase the aliens across the desert near San Luis.

Our desert wasn't very busy then. We had the drive-throughs controlled fairly well with the sensor arrays. That worked well, because we had guys working traffic check near enough to respond to the sensor calls. The desert is so big that our agents were able to intercept any smugglers that might have been tempted to drive through. For the walkers, we had pretty good sensors set throughout the canyons and passes. There weren't that many to worry about. Deaths were almost nil, since those few aliens that did come through were pretty experienced. They didn't come in large groups—they were singles or pairs, and most were not part of an organized group. So we didn't face the specter of any large volume of people getting into trouble out there. The mandate, if there was a mandate, lay in controlling the roads.

I do know we started in interdiction mode, but deterrence became a popular approach under Chief Patrol Agent Wayne Preston, who came right after Chief Gene Corder. To us, deterrence was stopping those cars on the road. In a phrase we borrowed from Customs, we called it "zero tolerance." We knew that smugglers convinced smuggled aliens to drive the load car. And our philosophy became, "If we stop a car, and there are illegals in it, we're going to seize the car. If the driver's deportable, we're going to set him up for formal deportation. If it's a prosecution case, we're going to prosecute him. If there are kids in the car, they're going to Child Protective Services. If there's a dog, he's going to the dog pound." We intended to maximize the deterrent effect through a zero tolerance of smuggling through the Yuma area. And that was juxtaposed to other places along the border where they wouldn't or couldn't prosecute a smuggler, but we had good rapport with the local U.S. Magistrate. We also had good cooperation from the detention camps. We always had good luck seizing cars. We pushed all cases as far as we could, and we called it "zero tolerance," or as some call it today, "delivered consequences."

Wayne Preston more or less developed the deterrent approach. Everybody capable of wearing a green uniform would be in a marked unit to create the maximum deterrent effect. And he strongly believed in checkpoints. Chief Preston believed that part-time checkpoints, bringing them up and shutting them down, doesn't work. You catch aliens that way, but our job is not to catch aliens—our job is to stop aliens. He ordered us to open those checkpoints and keep them open. The checkpoints were mandated to be open 24 hours a day, 365 days a year, whether they were, in the eyes of the agents, productive or not.

In the eyes of the agents, productive meant: "Are we catching anything?" They thought it was much better to surprise the aliens, get them comfortable using a road, and then spring up the checkpoint and catch bunches of them for a few days. But, that wasn't Chief Preston's idea. His idea of productivity was not having a single smuggling load come through the sector, because all the checkpoints were up all the time. That approach was not popular with everyone in those days, and it created friction with the adjoining sectors that were still in the apprehension mode. They preferred to spring a checkpoint on people, surprise them and catch them, and then go back to doing what they were doing, let them get comfortable, and then do another checkpoint.

San Diego and El Paso Sectors applied Chief Preston's denial strategy, but moved it from checkpoints to the border. The philosophy called for placing units in a fixed position across from the most populated areas. They called the position an "X," for the fact that a chalk X on the ground delineated the preferred location. They strung the agents out as far as they would go and denied entry in those areas, and didn't worry about the aliens streaming around the end of the line, just past the last X. The sectors that used Xs started getting more resources, while we got fewer resources. That made our philosophy of permanent checkpoints, but no Xs, look flawed.

Yuma didn't get resources, even though we were doing a good job. Because our checkpoints were open all the time, the alien smugglers used the adjoining sectors where the checkpoints were up-and-down, open-and-closed. Smugglers of course used scouts and cell phones and every method under the sun to take their loads through when the checkpoint was closed. You'd catch a few dummies when it sprung open, but you didn't catch anything that was really professional. We were effective with deterrence and were among the first sectors to be really effective, but we were penalized for it for many years. Finally, Yuma Sector is beginning to receive resources commensurate with the workload, the area patrolled, and the size of the threat.

I got to see the job from both the agent's and supervisor's perspective. In the early days, we thought we were successful pretty much *in spite* of upper management at the Immigration and Naturalization Service (INS). Border Patrol seemingly was the neglected stepchild of INS, an agency that itself got little respect from Congress or the rest of the federal government. We always seemed to get less than our fair share of the resources. At times we had fuel shortages for our vehicles. At times our vehicles were beaten to death and unreliable. We had managers from INS who would say, "I can get 200,000 out of my personal Volvo. I don't know why your Ramchargers are crapping out after 40,000."

Of course, it was apples and oranges. You drive five miles, leave the pavement and then you're on rough corduroy roads for the rest of the day until the last five miles going in. So, you drive 200 miles in a day, 10 miles on pavement and 190 miles out on these rough farm and desert roads, but headquarters thought these vehicles should last forever. INS didn't want to spend the money to replace the vehicles. I remember the days of gas shortages when we were siphoning gas out of the smugglers' vehicles, so we could put a few extra gallons in our patrol vehicle tanks. Supervisors would assign us to drive down and sit on the levee to watch for aliens. It's twenty-five miles to the border and twenty-five miles back, so you've got a fifty mile allocation, no more. Agents would drive down there, park, and do what they could. Some guys, if they wanted to move, would drive backwards so the odometer would take off miles.

And I'll always remember when we drove the vehicles year after year without replacements, and INS had no vehicle replacement policy. They would give you vehicles without any idea how long the vehicles were expected to last. You might be getting new vehicles next year, or you might not be getting any vehicles for ten years. You would hope that after 60,000 miles they would be eligible for replacement, since GSA (Government Services Administration) policy for a four-wheel-drive was 40,000 miles. A vehicle used primarily off-road was eligible for replacement, but you knew there was no reasonable expectation for getting a replacement because it all depended on the budget.

We had vehicles taken out of service at 100,000, and when no new vehicles came in, we went back into the boneyard, pulled out the old ones, and put them back in service. They were rattletraps, sucked dust from every orifice, and broke down frequently. I can remember days when we'd scrape together twenty vehicles to send out the shift, and ten of those would come back pulling the other ten. Then the next shift would take the same ten vehicles and send out as many as they could. A lot of guys doubled up because there weren't enough vehicles for one-man units like we were accustomed to working. So, we had half the coverage.

The next day the garage mechanics would do what they could, putting on "band aids" to get those vehicles back out. That was a big discouragement because that vehicle was our office. We tried to explain it to Headquarters, the wonks, by asking them, "What does it take to keep an INS employee in downtown New York or downtown San Francisco?" They'd reply, "Ooh! That's expensive office space!" They put an agent in that office: it's air-conditioned. He's got a desk, he's got a computer. He's got this and that. What does a Border Patrol agent have? There's a station, but he hasn't got a desk, just a communal work area. When one guy gets up, another comes and sits down. After a fifteen-minute or twenty-minute briefing in a cramped room, with half the guys sitting and half standing, the agents would go out and get in their office—their truck—and work all day long. An agent's vehicle is his office, and he's in it eight, ten, twelve hours a day.

But nobody upstairs ever saw it that way. To them a vehicle was just a means of transportation and if the fenders loosened up and fell off, the frame broke, the steering column collapsed, or the battery box fell out, they assumed it was because the driver abused it. And those roads, of course, beat up not only the vehicles but the drivers themselves.

Another issue in the early days was the use of apprehensions as the measure of efficiency or, more to the point, the measure of who was going to get what meager resources there were. The policy tended to make you want to catch large numbers of aliens however we could, and some managers were always after us to make the numbers swell. The only way you could do that was to recycle aliens, catch the same ones every day of the week. We did a lot of that. The pickers would come across to pick citrus. We'd catch them and take them back to the border. If they were good ol' boys, we'd make sure we got them back early, so we could catch them again the next day. Or some agents would catch "south-bounders," somebody who was going to return to Mexico in the next thirty minutes anyway. Most of us wouldn't stoop to that because it violated our sense of honor, but some guys would catch those south-bounders just to get a tick mark. Another frustration was when you had a load and headquarters would say, "No more budget for jail space," so we'd have to stop booking smugglers, or the camp would be full, so deportees were released into the U.S. with an Order to Appear paper at a hearing at some future date. Most never showed up.

My management style assumed that employees should accept responsibility. I delegated and let them handle it. I operated a lot on common sense, which I think is more important than raw intelligence. I gave them direction and a format so everybody knows what is expected, and then cut them loose. "If it's something out of the ordinary, don't hesitate to call me, but don't call me on the small stuff—look it up or figure it out." I tried to lead by example and always set a good example. I wouldn't expect anybody to do anything I wouldn't do. If I filled the car wash rack full of mud, I'd sweep it up. If I tracked mud in the station, I'd clean it up. I would go out and work a shift whenever needed. And I was meticulous on integrity aspects. Some people probably thought that I was a little harsh or intolerant, but I saw it as setting high standards and upholding them. In essence, all a supervisor has to do is make sure that agents do the paperwork, tidy up at the end of the shift, don't get heavy-handed with aliens, and follow the rules. The trick is getting agents to do all that.

The job itself is self-motivating. The job is fun . . . at least it used to be. You had to be self-sufficient, desire to be outdoors, and to *work* without much supervision. That's probably the biggest thing. If left alone to their own devices, agents do the job well. They catch aliens, because it's the path of least resistance. The day goes faster when you're doing what you're assigned to do, because catching aliens is fun and catching dope is even more fun. Driving a car in the desert looking for people, matching wits with the crossers, matching wits with the smugglers at the checkpoint, trying to pick out a smuggling load out of a long string of cars going down the freeway, or checking a train looking in all those little hidey holes where aliens are trying to hide: all those things are fun. It's like hunting, or playing hide-and-seek for a living. Agents do well at that. Tracking is fun, not so much its monotony but the end result. So, leave agents alone and they will do well, by and large. Some people are not cut out for that, but most agents will take the path that's most pleasing to the soul, which is doing the job and doing it right.

I think the key is hiring motivated people. A guy can pick up tracking and he can pick up the routine things, but he can't pick up that motivation, that independence, that self-sufficiency. I don't think you can teach it. If a guy wanted to be an investigator, he could put in for a job and move off the line. He might not be motivated to do the work that's done in the desert, but might be good in an office setting, motivated in a big city to do the work that's done there. One guy told me, "I'm leaving here because I don't like going home and coughing up little dirt balls" from breathing dust all day. I can sympathize with that. Some guys stayed longer than their usefulness. You could assign them to the border, and at the end of the shift they'd come in with clean boots. We all knew who they were. They hadn't stepped out of the car. You provide a climate where there're opportunities for them to find a niche they want to get into. Opportunities to move up or to move out depend on job openings, which may take time coming.

Later, I did the same job for eleven years as an assistant chief, and that was a grind. The assistant chiefs got a reputation of being sourpusses, but they always saw the worst. I handled accidents and would see the wrecks. I did a lot of proposals for disciplinary action on agents who messed up. And I was the one who got the whiners coming in about not getting their transfer, or this or that. Personal problems—no personal problem is frivolous, but in a lot of cases there wasn't anything we could do about it; there wasn't anything anybody could do about it. Or, administrative problems when agents wanted to make an exception to policy, like changing health benefits outside the enrollment window. And after a while, it wore me down. It wasn't like doing a job for eleven years—it was like doing the *same* job *every* year for eleven years. You see the same things over and over and over again. Different faces, same problems. It became not eleven years' experience, but one year's experience eleven times over. I was pretty disillusioned by the time I finally said enough is enough.

And we needed our own agency to focus on the job at hand. We have had chiefs selected on their ability to look at all decisions from the perspective of "What would Congress think?" because Congress provides the bucks. To me the question should be "How are we serving the public? How are we serving the citizens in our area?" Do the aliens steal cars or clothes off the clothesline on their way through a neighborhood? Are they trampling crops as they head for the smuggling vehicle? Are they running people off the road, or endangering lives by driving on the wrong side of the freeway? Even if chiefs have motivation and the ability for clear independent thinking, there's a danger that they are selected for their ability to toe a political line. They may know how to schmooze Congress or the current administration, but they forget, or never knew, their agents in the field and the citizens they supposedly serve.

Regarding the future of Border Patrol agents, there's a danger that technology can make them lethargic. They may tend to wait for a sensor to go off or for a camera operator to tell them where to intercept an alien, instead of hustling to track someone or staying alert to smugglers who aren't on the camera. But some technology is being better utilized. Border Patrol is using dogs more efficiently than it did. At first, we didn't have any use for dogs, because they didn't come with any extra funding. The dog handler had to have a vehicle twenty-four hours a day, so in effect we lost a vehicle. We didn't have enough vehicles to get our shift out, so why would we want to lose a vehicle for a dog handler to take home? They also trained one day a week, so manpower in the field was depleted by one day a week. And initially we couldn't use them in our primary searches, because headquarters said somebody might sue us over a dog bite or claim a seizure violation. So we'd have to pull a suspect into secondary inspection before using the dog to sniff for drugs. If you develop the necessary suspicion to get a car into secondary, your day is made. You can look it over closely enough to find any dope, so you don't need a dog at that point. Nowadays dogs are worked to sniff out dope in primary and then the vehicle is taken for secondary inspection.

There are still challenges out there. As the aliens get smarter, agents have to get smarter at the same rate. Smugglers are still finding ways to come across, whether it's tunneling under or developing better fake documents. There are any number of things they do trying to beat the system, and Border Patrol can't deter or foresee them all. There will be those that find a way, like a guy who had a homemade hot-air balloon or hang glider to carry marijuana over the border. He fell to his death because of a malfunction. On another day Border Patrol might discover a tunnel under the border or some newfangled compartment inside of a truck or train car. Agents have to expect the unexpected.

ALVARO "MIKE" OBREGON

Alvaro "Mike" Obregon served in the Border Patrol from 1980 to 2002 and at Tacna Station from 1984 to 1986. He currently lives in Tucson, Arizona.

I joined Border Patrol by a fluke. In 1978 I walked into the Superior Court building in Tucson. A poster said, "Now hiring Border Patrol." So I filled out an application and eventually got hired. I was told to report to Del Rio, Texas. I remember calling the airport and telling them I wanted a one-way ticket to Del Rio. They said, "Just a minute, sir." They come back and said, "I'm sorry, sir, but we never heard of it," so I rode the bus all the way down.

I was there from 1980 to 1984 doing mostly sensor activity, city patrol, and highway checkpoint. We normally did the still watches on the crossings on the canal. You've got the river, Rio Grande, the canal, and certain areas. It was pretty interesting. There was a lot of smuggling. But I wanted to work in my hometown, Tucson, so I took a position at Tacna, Arizona, and figured I could then transfer to Tucson.

Tacna was a different area, very hot and dry. At Tacna the bushes are not even big enough to give shade to the lizards. We used to jokingly call them stick lizards. They would carry a stick for a while, and when it got too hot, they would climb the stick to cool their feet off. And they carried canteens. It was interesting down there.

I caught a group of aliens, one time, down there right at the border. They were only about a hundred yards from the drag road with twenty-five miles to go. They only had a gallon of water apiece and I knew they wouldn't make it. We picked up a lot of dead, too many. Women, kids, men. They don't know the area. They can't carry enough water to survive that desert trek—it was just too hot and harsh. You'd find them dead there by the highway. You'd find them dead there by the canal. They just didn't make it. Kids. . . . I remember cutting the lower drag. There were tracks of three women, two kids, and two males. I called Glen Payne, told him what I had, then I went up Papago Well Road and found their tracks. I took the Ramcharger up and found them on top of the sand dune. The little kid had died in his mother's arms. The other one crawled about ten feet and died. The other gal walked away—we found her later, dead. The guys we found out on the highway. They said they had left water. We backtracked their trail . . . they never left nothing. It was tough. Little kids . . . the only way we could track them was because the youngest kid was dragging a little bag with toy soldiers and cars in it.

I've been around that sort of thing. I served thirty months of combat duty in 'Nam, so I've been around death since I was seventeen. You just brush it off. In 'Nam I served all over, from Phu Bai to Chu Lai. You just learn to live with it. Thirty months there with the Marines, and they wanted me to stay in. I said, "No, thank you." I'd had enough.

Tacna was a small, tightknit station. Everybody knew everybody. Everybody knew what everybody else was thinking. We knew each other and how we cut, and where we'd go next, and where the aliens would go next.

Congress and politicians took away our farm and ranch checks and took away city patrol. They said we profile. We don't. After you work the border for a while, you can tell who is here legally and who is not here legally. By patrolling the highway and watching the cars go by, you can tell. It's just the way the driver and passengers look at you. The way they freeze up. It's just an instinct that you pick up. Nine out of ten cars I stopped were loaded with illegal aliens.

I remember a trainee I had at Yuma, named Ramirez. We were sitting there on Dome Valley Road. Cars would be passing by late at night. He said, "That one, Mike?" "Nope." "That one, Mike?" "No." Then a truck passed by with a gal hugging the driver and she waved. I said, "That one." So, we chased them all the way down to Wellton. They bailed out in a hayfield—fourteen of them. He said, "How did you know?" I said, "You'll learn."

How can it be profiling? I live by the Mexican border and I grew up in the U.S. You can ask me any day or stop me any time, and I'll tell you I'm a U.S. citizen. It doesn't bother me, but some people take offense to that. I don't know why. There should be no American citizen, whether he be Hispanic, black, white, or whatever, who is offended if asked where he's from. When you ask some people where they're from, they say, "What do I look like, a Mexican?" "I didn't ask you that. I asked you where you were born."

Mike Obregon. Photo by Bill Broyles, 1985.

It's a simple question, "Are you a U.S. citizen?" "What do I look like?" I don't know what you look like. A simple question takes a simple answer. If we're going by the law, agents must have just reasonable suspicion, not probable cause. If you're an American, you're an American. You can tell Mexican nationals or Swedes or Canadians by their haircut, from their clothing, their mannerisms. It's just something that you learn.

Sometimes Mexican nationals tried to play that game of "You're Miguel Obregon. You must be my friend." I had people offer me their daughters. I've had people offer me their money. I always said, "No." I'd always call for back-up. It's strange, but they said, "You should let us go." I'd say, "Why should I let you go? I'm working. This is my job. If I let you go and they stop you over there in Dallas or in Phoenix, they'll find out someone — me — let you through. I'm not that dumb." No, I would just do my job.

That's why, for a long time, they wouldn't hire Mexicans to work Border Patrol. They thought they would be, how would you say, lenient. And sometimes you *would* feel sympathy for the people. There're a lot of hard-working people who just want to make a better living. But I've got to make a living, too. "I caught you, you're mine, let's go." That's it. End of story. I suspect that Border Patrol's OIG (Office of the Inspector General) sometimes ran sting operations trying to test agents with bribes, but I wasn't tempted.

Now we're getting a whole different type of alien coming in: fighters, runners, smugglers, criminals. They just want to fight, and now they're carrying more guns. And our agents are younger, with less real-world experience. They have more education, but less common sense. In a job like this, you've got to be street smart. You've got to know when the aliens are scheming up stuff because they talk among themselves. You can hear them. Back in Eagle Pass, Texas, I stopped a group of about forty. It was the middle of the night, and one of the guys said, "Aren't you afraid?" I said, "Why should I be afraid?" He said, "You're all alone. There are so many of us." I said, "I'm not alone. I've got my friend here." At that time we were carrying .357s. I said, "The first six of you die. Who wants to be first?" "Well," he said, "You've got a point there." I said, "Sit down." So they all sat down.

But you get people like that. If you're afraid, you've got no business there, because you *are* all alone. You've got no communication out in the canyons, especially out from Tacna or Tucson. Just before you go in there, you've got to let somebody know where you're at and what you're trailing. If it's backpackers carrying marijuana, they'll send some agents out to back you up, but back-up may be four hours away. You're way out there with not enough people working. We'd have two or three agents pick up forty or more crossers. If we had been trailing forty and only picked up thirty-five, then we'd have to backtrack, because we knew that five were in trouble, possibly dead. We did pick up a lot of dead.

We made a lot of rescues. Aliens would get exhausted, dehydrated, injured, lost, sick. We didn't have a trauma team then. It was just us. We carried water and food, whatever they needed. We care. We're compassionate. But we can fight if we have to. I always told my guys, "You treat aliens the way they treat you." They respect you, you respect them. If one mouths off, take that one down. Don't let them start up. A little mouthing off will just get them excited. Cuff him, and sit them down.

Tacna was a nice place, because you had a lot of camaraderie there. I lived on the main drag in Wellton when I was in Tacna. Everybody could see the house and the driveway. When I'd fire up the barbecue, they'd all stop by. I was only going to cook one steak for the family, but all of a sudden I had to go to the store and get more because everybody was showing up. Highway patrol officers, marshals, sheriffs, and Border Patrol agents, we just had a big old party there. "What are you doing, Mike?" "I'm going to cook a steak." "I'll be right back." And they'd join us.

Right now, our agency is so big that hardly anybody knows anybody. We need more gatherings. Let agents get to know each other and their families. Basically the only family you have is your other agents. Just like any police work, you're an outcast to other people, because you carry a gun and badge. They think that you're a different person, but you're not—you're just a regular old Joe doing your job. You get home at night, take that gun off, and you're the same as anybody else.

For our agency you have to bring your work ethic. We had some lazy people. And we had some good people who all they want to do is work. One, for example, is George Gonzales. He goes out and looks hard for trails, and when he gets on one, he won't quit. He'll stay on it two or three days. Some other guys may not even see anything, but there's a few of that kind everywhere.

I started working when I was twelve years old. I asked my dad for a bike. He said, "You want a bike? Let's put you to work." So, I went to work for him. He built houses. There I was working for my bike and I never stopped. I joined the Marine Corps at the age of seventeen. I figured I'd find better pastures, but—whoo!—they didn't offer anything but rice paddies and bullets.

The Marine Corps gives you discipline. They make you and bring out strengths you never thought you had. When they push you and push you, you find you do have something special in you. When they say they build men, they do. That's another family, because once you're a Marine, you're always a Marine.

A good agent has good ethics, strong will, knows the job, and tries to improve every time. You're compassionate, you do your job, and you do it in a fair way. There're a lot of good agents and a few bad agents, but that one bad one makes everybody look bad. Good agents can't tolerate the bad ones, because if you see something happening and you don't report it, you're just as guilty. For example, you stop a smuggler's vehicle. Inside the load vehicle there's a radio, there's watches, or whatever, and you see an agent take one. If you see that and you don't report it, you're just as guilty. So, we police each other. We have to, otherwise we put our own job in jeopardy.

I had an agent come up to me and say, "I just witnessed an agent kick a handcuffed suspect." I said, "Is that a fact?" He said, "Yeah." So I say, "Write me a report." I called the other agent in and had him write a report, too. I made my report to higher up and that guy got drummed out, too. It doesn't take five people to bring down one person like these city cops do, jumping on their neck with three others holding them down and yelling, "Quit resisting!" I've stopped people and said, "Where are you from?" "I'm from Belize" or wherever. I say, "You got any documents?" "No." "Get in the car," and they open the door and get in. You don't have to be a butt-head. Just do your job.

After 9/11, Border Patrol hired so fast that it had little time to check out recruits. When you do that, you're going to get a bad apple in there. Even if their background checks aren't done yet, Congress is pushing to have them hired. I sat on some hiring board oral exams in Minneapolis and was told not to flunk anybody. I flunked one candidate, and they said, "Mike, you're not supposed to turn anybody away." I said, "I can't have him in the Patrol. He's going to hurt somebody or get somebody hurt." They said, "You're going to have to write it up." I said, "I'll write it up. Do you want to work with him?" "No." "I don't either."

The oral boards are looking for common sense and logical-thinking people. We highlight officer safety. No Wyatt Earps. No trigger-happy people. You can't be a John Wayne; that only works in movies. You can get hurt out there. A lot of people have quit because of that fear.

The Border Patrol is hiring more women now. The women are good. Some other supervisors were reluctant to take them. I took the women into my unit and they kicked ass, because they work good, and they're not afraid. Some of the gals were better than some of the guys I had there.

I don't pay attention to minority numbers. I might be Hispanic, but I don't ever worry about race. I grew up with everybody in town. I went to Pueblo High School in Tucson. Black, white, brown, green—they were all my friends. I never knew prejudice until I went in the Marine Corps, then I found out what the meaning of the word was. Some of them had real strong feelings. There was a guy from Odessa, Texas, who served with me in 'Nam. He said, "You know, Sarge, where I come from if we're walking down the street and a Mexican is walking toward us, he better cross the street." I said, "Is that a fact?" But he said, "Sarge, I want you to go home with me and meet my folks." I said, "Your folks taught you that, and you want me to go home with you? No, thank you."

I always treated my people fairly, even when I was in 'Nam in Third Platoon. There was a guy in there from Second Platoon that got a Dear John letter, and I happened to be within range of his anger. He looked at me and said, "You know, Sarge, I'm going to kick your ass." I said, "Fine." Then, the squad leaders stood up and said, "You have to go through us first." The guy looked around and said, "No thanks," and walked away. You must treat people fair when you're a supervisor. There are supervisors that don't do that. They think they're God. They forget that they were down there once.

Border Patrol was the best job that I ever had, and to me, it was so well worth keeping that I always tried to do the right thing. I loved it. I loved being out there and tracking people. What was it Ernest Hemingway said? "There's no hunting like the hunting of man." You know aliens try everything to evade you but eventually you just walk up on them and say hello. "How did you find me?" "You left your footprints behind." One time in Tacna, we went in the orange groves and I found a guy. I asked, "Are you going to run?" He said, "Yeah." I said, "Okay, just go ahead and run." I just walked behind him and followed his tracks. He got tired, climbed up a tree. I walked to the tree and said, "Okay, come on down."

Really, I did more than I expected to do in my lifetime, because when I left 'Nam I was screwed up. I never knew Border Patrol existed, but I found a job and accomplished what I set out to do. I got to be a supervisor. I never hurt anybody that didn't need hurting. I'm satisfied with what I did. I've got good kids who never got into trouble. I enjoyed what I did. I really did. I loved it.

Not everybody is cut out to be a Border Patrol agent, a city cop, or a state cop. If you're in it just for the paycheck, then you're going to get hurt because you get complacent. Border Patrol takes a lot of stamina, a lot of common sense, and wanting to work. A lot of these college graduates have been a little pampered. You don't get spring breaks in this job. It's not a party—it's a job, a dangerous job. If you don't have any common sense, you're gonna get hurt. Not everybody is your friend, especially in this business. College is good. If I could have afforded it, I would have gone to college, but what would I have done different? Probably nothing. I don't think I'd like a desk job.

ROBERT "MAC" McLEMORE

*Robert "Mac" McLemore joined the Border Patrol in
1986 and has been stationed at Wellton since 1991.*

I was born in Eagle Pass, Texas, and didn't learn English
until I went to school. My mother still speaks Spanish at home. When
aliens or my homeboy friends ask, "How can you apprehend and deport
your own people?" I tell them, "They're not 'my people.'" And I remind
them, "We're not against Mexicans or any other nationality, but to deal
with illegal immigration, smuggling, terrorism, and border crime, we've
got to control our borders. Mexico regulates its borders too."

Just this morning we picked up a grandma, something like ninety years
old, and she was barefooted. It was a family group from Oaxaca. I think
only one individual—he must have been the son—even spoke Spanish,
let alone English; the rest of them didn't know how to speak either one.
And the little ones probably, one and two years old, they were just dragging
them along. We received a call reporting them crossing the highway out at
milepost 46, so I went out there. They were walking towards Tacna. They
were tired and they were lost, they didn't know where they were. They got
left behind. They had the three or four kids and grandma.

We hear aliens are paying anywhere from $1,000 to $2,500, depending
where they're going, depending where they're coming from, depending
what nationality. Now the emphasis is on the terrorists. We've heard as
much as $10,000, $20,000, $30,000 per head, if they're Arabs. All these
arrangements are made down south in their little hometowns, and frequently someone else pays the money for them, a relative or employer.
For the most part, the aliens don't get released until the smugglers get the
money in their hands. We had aliens we picked up last week that were
claiming to be on the way to Georgia and Virginia.

Mac McLemore. Photo by Bill Broyles, 2005.

Wellton's in the big leagues. I recall back in the early 1990s, we'd get groups coming out of the desert, and they were all headed for the same agricultural communities. After developing all the intel, we'd go out there and hit the farm or ranch with warrants. Now I guarantee you that Yuma is loaded with people hidden in stash houses waiting for our checkpoints to shut down. You hear on the news all the time in the Phoenix area and Tucson area that Border Patrol has found someone or a load of dope and backtracked it back to a stash house. That's common.

Officially, the penalties for smuggling are pretty high. I think it's three to five years. They're pretty substantial on paper, but realistically, they're not. It's not deterring smugglers—they still keep coming. Several things are factored into the fines or the imprisonment: was there endangerment, were the aliens being smuggled in closed containers or trunks? This raises the ante for the smugglers when they get caught, as opposed to somebody who just has them in the back seat. So it varies. Immigration law has a big bark, but no bite. As in the past, you get the juveniles or pregnant females who are driving or guiding, and they get cut loose by the magistrates. The smugglers know that. They know who they can snag into doing the dirty deed, and they know if we catch them, more than likely they'll be released, unless they have a prior criminal record.

We were a small station at Wellton when I came in 1990. Many a time we only worked two shifts, days and swing. It had to be a special operation with overtime funds available for a third shift. A good shift had three agents. We used to do some farm and ranch checks, and we've gotten away from that for various reasons, mostly politics. We don't go checking people out in the fields unless we're actually in pursuit of certain individuals, and we actually see them go into the field. We don't aggressively patrol farms anymore.

At Yuma, aliens go straight north, and in a matter of minutes they're in the groves or on good roads where they can blend in and hide. Depending on where they come across, they walk only a couple of hours, as opposed to trying to come across through Wellton, *our* area, where they've got thirty to forty miles of desert before they can hit any decent road, and of course there's not very many places to hide out here. So it was easier for them to come across through that area near Yuma, but as more and more agents are assigned to Yuma, aliens are starting to filter back through our side.

Statistically speaking, there're many more people crossing. Fifteen years ago, we had 20,000 people crossing, and perhaps one-tenth of one percent, 20 people, died. Now we're getting 2 *million* people crossing, and perhaps 200 of them die. Even though the ratio is lower, it seems much worse because of the total. I don't remember the count on the deaths this year or how many were women. We certainly did our best to deter them or find them.

I don't think it's that we've gotten that many more aliens recently — especially since Texas seems to be drawing them in. I always ask them, when they show up here, "What are you doing here in Arizona? Why didn't you go through Texas?" I think we just get the stragglers or the uninformed. In Texas they're just walking in the front door, and they're being released out the back door, because their facilities are so overwhelmed with especially the OTMs [other than Mexican aliens]. Texas kicks them loose. They don't have the bed space and can't keep them at all. I was speaking to somebody from my hometown, said that in one month's time they apprehended something like 4,000 OTMs, and every single one of them was processed and then released from custody, but not returned to their homeland. That was just at one station out of that sector. They don't have the bed space. But if we catch them here, they're goin' to jail, they're gonna be detained, they're not gonna be released.

We're accepted in the Wellton community. They like us. Once we started expanding and our workload started increasing, we started using more air operations, assists, and more helicopters landing at any given hour of the day. Those folks who initially were complaining about noise and dust got used to it. We haven't had any problems at all. We haven't had anybody come knocking on our doors here, complaining about noise or any issues that I would expect. They want us here. There were some issues when we briefly discussed moving the station, but people in Wellton said, "No, we *want* you here."

I'm always out recruiting. This is a good job. Where else, outside the military, do you get to "go out and play" in the desert, and you get a car and all the gas you need? You go out there and chase people. It's a good job, a good career, pays well, and has good benefits. I'm always recruiting. Having worked in Yuma and in other areas, I'm happy at Wellton. I'm not going anywhere.

I joined Border Patrol because I was looking for a career and it has been good to me. If you've kept your nose clean, this is the job; you can't beat it. A few years back, you never heard about the Border Patrol. You heard about some immigration issues and the problems, but you never heard about the Border Patrol. The "big leagues" was the FBI and the DEA, and now it's kind of turned on them and favored us. It's rare that you don't watch the news on TV and there's a story showing a Border Patrol marked unit with agents. We're at the forefront, without a doubt.

I come to work every day, because I enjoy it so much. I've gotten my hands into all sorts of different collateral duties and seizures and interesting assignments. I like to think I make a difference. There are days that you don't think so, but I believe in the long run, we do. I've been in shoot-outs and I'm still here. I guess my biggest accomplishment will be to get through this unharmed and enjoy my retirement with my lovely wife.

I've noticed changes in the demeanor of the undocumented aliens that come across. I think the reasons are the same for wanting to come across, but their attitude, their perspective, is different. They act like it's their right to come up here, at any cost. I think they're meaner now than they used to be. We're getting a whole different kind of people now, as opposed to past years. We get a lot more druggies and all-around bad people with attitudes. They'd shoot their own mother if they had a chance. A lot more are gang-related than before. Nowadays smuggling humans is about big money, and the aliens are a saleable commodity.

I expect all of them to be armed. That doesn't mean that they *are*, but that's my attitude going in there, when I encounter them, and I would hope that all the rest of the agents do the same thing—treat them like they were armed. I don't suppose that one comes to work with the intention of getting in a shoot-out. We had a drive-through that had drugs in it, and when the vehicle was found later, we were able to identify it because of the bullet holes in the back. They were trying to get across, we saw it, we chased it back, and it almost got stuck in the mud. About the time those guys were holding the fence open for the truck to get back, a passenger jumped out and shot at us. So we shot back. The last thing from my mind was that somebody would actually jump out and start shooting, but that's the way it happened.

We're probably *the* identity of Homeland Security. There was a lot of confusion even within our ranks as to what we were. We didn't want to lose our identity—we had worked too hard for it. We're very proud of our green uniform. Now we're at the forefront. We're in a high visibility state. Nobody knew who Border Patrol was. The Border Patrol as a whole will continue to grow. I must say, we put a lot more bite into the immigration law. The only way that you can keep *some* kind of control, without letting it get way out of hand, is to keep the manpower up. The way it's going right now, I can see us being a 20,000-agent force, and we'd *still* need people.

There's gonna be a whole bunch of us Baby Boomers retiring soon, so the Patrol is shifting towards inexperienced agents. Of course, they probably said the same thing about me when I came in. We're always talking about "the old Patrol." But it's a different attitude with individuals nowadays and a whole different outlook on life. They want to start at the top, not work their way up the chain like the rest of us. I refer to them as the "Microwave Generation." And the academic standards have also been somewhat relaxed. There's a lot of stuff that's no longer memorized—you just need to know how to apply it. And nowadays the individual has to screw up really bad to be fired, whereas it didn't take much before.

I can say that there are very few Border Patrol agents who have actually gotten to go to a foreign country and meet with our counterparts—and I'm one of them! That was an experience. I got to see a whole different aspect of border patrol work and a different mind-set. For us, it's about smuggling people and narcotics. For other countries, it's about perishable commodities, such as cigarettes and coffee, and they're just as serious about it as we are. It was an eye-opener for me, and hopefully for them also. I had a preconceived notion of where I was going and I was very surprised. I guess it's our fault for not knowing any better. I assumed, "This is the U.S. and everybody else is Third World." That couldn't be further from the truth. It was a very good experience for me to visit Lithuania, Latvia, and Estonia. Budapest, Hungary, was even more interesting, because I was teaching a class on fraudulent documents to criminal investigators from Kazakhstan, Kyrgyzstan, and Uzbekistan at the International Law Enforcement

Academy. They had an idea of what the American Border Patrol was, or at least a preconceived notion. In what little news they got out there, they heard that America doesn't control its borders whatsoever. Everybody asked me, "How many agents do you have?"

The most interesting question I heard from them was how much we *paid* to get hired. How much was our bribe? So I explained that our hiring system is based on merit and performance. They said, "Look, somebody has to get the money." I told them, "No, that's not the way it works." Some of them had connections, friends or family; some of them had paid to get a foot in the door—that was their opportunity. It was kind of hard for them to understand our hiring process: we apply first, and then somebody checks that list, and then they send us over to a different agency and they check out our background. They were just in awe of how things work— especially when I'm telling them about federal law enforcement. And then they also were very curious about the experience of my wife being a police officer. I explained to them how officers work on the local level, and that was eye-opening for me and them.

In 2004 we opened a camp down along the border. We call it Camp Grip, and it gives smugglers something to think about besides where to eat in Phoenix at the end of their run. In the early days of Grip the smugglers were surprised to see anyone in the area. Several times agents faced off against smugglers who tried to figure out who they were. When they did, they hightailed it back across the line. Grip makes a huge difference. Attempted drive-throughs are down 90 percent and the other 10 percent are apprehended. Even if we just drive back and forth along the line, we make a huge difference.

Camp Grip started as a result of the fourteen aliens who died in the Granite Mountains area back in 2001. That event started the ball rolling. The remoteness of the area where they got lost necessitated us having a 24-7 presence in that part of the desert. We were forced to try to stem the flow and divert it elsewhere. Prior to Grip, that door was open in that part of the desert. All the illegal alien and the drive-through smuggler traffic pretty much came in unimpeded, free reign, unless we would catch them up along the interstate.

The camp itself progressed from a two-man unit working 12-hour shifts down there for two-week rotations. As I recall, one individual patrolled while the other one slept. And then they'd swap out. Then we upped it to four for "officer-safety" reasons, and then it's grown ever since. It started off small, in a little travel trailer. It was kind of warm in the summer during the day, to say the least. In fact, I think some of the folks that were down there were actually sleeping outside, because it was cooler than being inside, even though we had air-conditioning powered by a small generator. Then the second year we obtained some military ConX steel boxes and outfitted those, turned them into living quarters and a kitchen. It's kind of nice to have a little bit of running water for sinks and showers. The travel trailer had been limited to a small water buffalo with a spigot on the back. The present-day campsite seems pretty luxurious compared to the first couple of years. It's still not an easy detail, what with working 12-hour shifts seven straight days, but the guys enjoy going down there and getting down to the grass roots of Border Patrol work, away from the office.

The illegal activity down there stopped for a while after the fourteen died. That worked in our favor. Then soon thereafter we had 9/11. So again, everybody was up in arms and illegal traffic slowed down. Then it started picking up again. We got a *lot* of illegal entries, large groups and vehicles again, some crossing in within a mile of the camp.

A vehicle barrier has been built and it limits the drive-throughs, though it won't completely stop pedestrians. I think we were pretty successful apprehending the drive-throughs prior to the barriers coming in, because the terrain itself works against them. It's a long way to drive. Most of the vehicles break down, whether they're new or not, or they get stuck. Lately they've been using stolen late-model four-wheel-drive and dualie Fords and Chevys, stolen out of the Phoenix area, for the most part. But those break down also, because it's pretty rough terrain out there, especially when they know that more than likely we'll be on the road, so they try to go off-road. That works in our favor. So I think most of the traffic we've been having lately drives north as far as the Camino del Diablo, drops the aliens off, and then returns to Mexico, so then the aliens or dope smugglers are on their own to walk out.

Now we have calmed it back down. Prior to the camp being there, our response from Wellton Station was a minimum of sixty miles, but now at camp, the sensors go off or the agents find the sign going across the road, and we're on it in a hurry. And if the aliens are walking, they're still very catchable. Grip has definitely cut down our response time. Plus the agents are patrolling actively and frequently down there, 24-7-365. If it's fresh sign, we chase after them cross-country. But if it's older sign, then we don't; we'll just go to the next available drag road to the north and try to find their sign there.

And the aliens are getting wilier. They're tying foam, rugs, or carpet under their shoes, or laying down those Mexican blankets to cover their tracks. Or, if you've got a road that has banks on both sides, they may put ladders across and step on the rungs, anything so they don't leave a footprint. It's amazing what they're doing, and it's getting a lot tougher to catch them. Eventually all of our young agents are gonna learn the tricks, too, and improve their sign-cutting skills.

Most of the aliens are guided by somebody, a *pollero*. The people we're catching are from the interior, down in Oaxaca and Morelos, southern Mexico. Every once in a while we'll catch a large group of, say, Oaxacans, and then a couple of them in the group are locals from Sonora or Baja California. Polleros know what they're doing. It's very structured and very organized. The only time I've seen aliens actually "give up" the guides is when someone is hurt or left behind for dead, and we happen to rescue them. Then the aliens are willing to give us names and identify them. Other than that, aliens don't reveal the smugglers, because they may try again another day or because they're threatened. I would imagine they're threatened, because it's a lucrative business.

I think we first started toying with the idea of Camp Grip after the fourteen died. Even before that, we were detailing people out there. If the fourteen hadn't gotten lost and walked around in circles, they'd easily have made it up to I-8. But they got all turned around and loop-de-looped south and east and west. I think the guide was incompetent. I think he got turned around in the dark or something, because one of the guides almost made it out to I-8 before we apprehended him. He was able to figure out which way was north, but he probably would have died out there, too, because he was still a good six or eight miles away. He was headed up towards the rest area at Mohawk, but he wouldn't have made it.

Smugglers use LPOPs, listening-post-observation-posts on hilltops. Without a doubt, they're up there in the mountains inside the U.S. watching for us. They're organized. But we'll catch them. We've had them come off the mountains during hot weather. In fact, at Camp Grip last year, we had one come out. He died out there north of the camp. The only reason we found out is because his family and some other people drove across the border illegally to look for him, and they were easy to catch. They said, "No, we're looking for my husband who's out there." And we started searching. Yeah, he was out there. He was dressed up in cammies and was a spotter or scout, but things went bad for him.

We've actually had them come off the mountains here and activate our rescue beacons, because they're in dire straits. But, we had one who looked fresh, and I think he set off one of the rescue beacons just to see what kind of response time we had—he was gathering intel on our response time. We eventually caught him again coming across on an ATV with foodstuffs. But that first time, he said he got left behind by a group and had been in the desert for several days. He was clean as a tourist, but claiming to be lost in the desert.

The Camp Grip toilet system started off as a coffee can that headquarters decided was good enough for the troops out there. Then, we had the port-a-potties, and those worked fine. They get kind of warm inside, so if you're going to do your business, try to do it late evening or early morning, because it's unbearable inside during the summer. It's so hot that the liquid chemical dries up—it doesn't take but a couple of days for it to just evaporate.

And then we had the "atomic toilets," the "atomic crappers." Those were pretty good! They're cast-iron pots with toilets built around them, and they work off propane. You'd go in there and do your business, and the next guy, and the next guy, and the next guy, and every other day you would incinerate the waste, burn it for about four hours and then scoop up the ashes with a kitchen spoon—but not the one we used for cooking. Those were pretty practical out there, other than they used a lot of propane. One was tested at headquarters and it caught on fire. Imagine an outhouse burning at the headquarters compound—brand-new toilet and there's an outhouse fire. There was a lot of funny discussion among the agents about which assistant chief had used it last. Now we have a septic system with flushing toilets. That's pretty nice and makes all the difference in the world.

The way things are going, Camp Grip is there for the duration, unless new policies come out. But right now, there's no inclination towards removing it or going back to seasonal operations—it's there year-round. The name Grip probably came from trying to get a grip on that area, which was not really our area—it was our country, but we didn't have control of our real estate out there. We had to go out there and get a grip of things. Today Camp Grip may seem like a "spa," but some of us knew it as a real rough campout. Some of the guys used to have to sleep outside—especially the guy working days. The guy working nights had no choice but to sleep inside in that little travel trailer. Of course, you had people walking in, other agents coming in and cooking, and the radio was always blaring. It wasn't exactly comfortable. That was roughing it. I was there the *first* year. The only gripers we have down there are folks who have never been out there before, but if you were there those first years, it seems pretty damned nice now. When new agents gripe at me, it falls on deaf ears.

RANDY HERBERHOLZ

*Randall "Randy" Herberholz joined Border Patrol in
1986 and now serves Customs and Border Protection Air
and Marine in Albuquerque, New Mexico. He was a
pilot in Yuma from 1999 to 2006.*

Isn't it funny, the diversity of people that end up in this
occupation? It becomes such a tight brotherhood that the diversity is *tremendous*. Take me. I left Spokane, Washington, and left a job that was
probably paying me about three times what I signed on for. When I signed
on as a GS-5, Step 1, starting salary for the first year was $13,100 per year,
and out of that came taxes, insurance, and uniforms. Back then Border
Patrol told recruits to show up with $400 in cash to buy your uniform.
Now when they show up, they're issued what they need for the first year.
I had to sell my boat so I could buy a gun belt. Selling your boat really
hurts. That's how it went back then. Somebody looked at a seniority list
today, and we're up toward 20,000 Border Patrol agents, and I'm number
1,200.

I entered on duty in September of 1986 in McAllen, Texas. It just doesn't
seem like that long ago. I can almost give you a weekly play-by-play of what
I did at the Border Patrol Academy. I ended up in the Border Patrol by de-
fault. I didn't intend to go into the Border Patrol. I was looking for something to get me out of Spokane. I was single, twenty-eight years old, and
looking for something to do, to kind of pull me away from Spokane. I was
part of a big family in Spokane, so I'm still the prodigal son. I'm the only
one who left Spokane, and I have no intentions of returning. But I owned
a small business in Spokane, and on weekends I started flying airplanes
just for fun, just to pull me away from work for a few hours. I got pretty
involved in flying and belonged to a flying club. Somebody told me, "You

should look into maybe air traffic control. Certainly that would pull you out of Spokane, at least for a few years."

So I went down to the federal building and I applied to take the test for air traffic control. As I came out of that basic civil service exam, across the hall they were testing for Border Patrol. And I thought, "What the heck, I'm here." I walked in, took that test, and thought "There's no way," because law enforcement had always been something that was kind of more of a dream than something that I really wanted to pursue. And luckily for me at that time, all that was required was a high school diploma and a clean nose that you weren't in any trouble. So when they called me six or eight weeks later and said, "You passed the exam and we'd like to schedule you for a medical examination and an oral interview," I thought, "Wow, there's a glimmer of hope here."

I started getting excited about it. I was one of those busy kids: I had a job when I was thirteen, and I worked all through junior high, all through high school. I was working fifty hours a week when I was eighteen years old, so I couldn't really make the time to study criminal justice or go to college. When this was offered to me, I became pretty excited. I went to the oral interview in Spokane, and I remember those guys looking at me and just kind of shaking their heads like, "What is this kid doing?" I never studied a second language. I had a high school diploma, with a three-point-something grade average—not really *that* great—but I was a good kid, played sports, and stayed out of trouble. Anyway, after the oral board, they said, "Well, we're gonna recommend you to the academy. Have you ever lived outside of Spokane?" I answered, "No." "Have you ever lived anywhere remotely near the Mexican border, or do you know anyone that's ever lived near the Mexican border?" "Well, no." "You are in for a *big* surprise. And for that reason, we'll give you the opportunity." And I knew I was in trouble.

After selling my boat, I had money to buy a one-way airline ticket to McAllen and the $400 in cash to pay for my uniforms. I had a couple hundred extra for hotels and expenses and meals and that kind of stuff, and that was basically all I had. I was kind of walking away from life in Spokane, Washington, and moving on to bigger and better things.

I did have a backup plan. For a while I had worked as an auto mechanic, so I had my tools and stuff in my mom's garage back in Spokane, and I always figured, "If I flunk out . . ." or, more likely, "*When* I flunk out, I can always be a mechanic, and it's pretty transient, so I can load up my toolbox and go to work just about anywhere." That was my backup plan for when they told me to go home from the academy at Glynco, Georgia.

Randy Herberholz 169

Randy Herberholz. Photo by Bill Broyles, 1990.

At McAllen the senior said, "We're gonna send you to the academy and it's a real paramilitary thing, and there's physical training, and there's immigration law, and there's Spanish." They're filling our heads full of all kinds of doubt, making it seem like there's a 1 in 8 million chance that you're probably going to succeed if you're not already in this kind of life-style or into this type of thinking. I was pretty discouraged, to say the least. They put us on a plane at like 6 p.m. in McAllen, and we flew to Jackson-ville. And then from Jacksonville, they put us on a bus—I think it was a prison bus. It was already nearly midnight, and when they put us on that bus and started driving us towards Glynco, it hit me about what a gigantic, *gigantic* mistake I'd made, that I'd made this *horrible* error that I was never going to be able to recover from, that I probably wouldn't last three days at the academy, and I'd be hitchhiking my way back to Washington state, because I had nothing left.

But that kind of worked as inspiration for me, because I knew no one and I had no friends or relatives or anybody in that neck of the woods, or anywhere near there. I told myself, "You did this for a reason. Now it's time for you to man up and get with the program here." So I did. Actually, I ended up enjoying my stay at the academy as a trainee. I was a little bit older, and I think that helped. I was twenty-nine years old when I went to FLETC. And they warned me about that, "You're gonna be around guys that are twenty-one, twenty-two, and you've got a few years of life experience that they don't have. That might work in your favor, or it might not. We'll see." But it did. I committed myself to the fact that, "Okay, this is what I'm gonna do, and I'll give it a shot. Here we go!" I did quite well at the academy.

For once I had time to study. I had nothin' else on my mind. So I actually came out of it pretty good. After going back to McAllen, I really started liking the work there. When I'd talk to friends or relatives back home, they'd ask what it was like. And the first thing I would say is, "This is like the job that everybody dreams of having, they just don't know that this is it." They give you a set of keys at muster at 6:00 A.M., and they say, "Have a good day. We'll see you about 3:00 or 4:00." And that's it, and you're totally unsupervised the whole day. And it says right in the job description, "Must be able to manage themselves in an unsupervised condition for long periods of time." So basically you're working unsupervised all day long, with the knowledge that they've given you at the academy.

Not everybody can handle that freedom or responsibility. It does take a special kind of person to do this job, and I'm surprised that the failure rate isn't higher than it is. But people think we have an astronomical failure rate—within three years 40 percent quit. It takes a particular kind of person to be a Border Patrol agent. You have to fit in a mold. You have to be a willing participant; you have to be "in the brotherhood." You must understand what your partner's thinking, what he's gonna say, and what he's gonna do before he even does it. And some people just don't think that way. It's a lifestyle, not just a job.

McAllen was my first duty station, and I loved working there. You got a set of keys at 6:00 A.M. and they wouldn't expect to see you until 3:00, 3:30. You could be as busy or as *un*busy as you wanted to be. Even back then Border Patrol had a misunderstood public image that all we did was round up illegals and herd them back to the border. But there was a lot more to it than that. I said "yes" to everything that came along. As a Border Patrol agent I learned to drive a road grader, water truck, and heavy construction equipment. They asked, "Anybody know how to operate this?" And I said, "Sure I do!" I had never been in one in my life. "Can you drive a backhoe?" "Oh, yeah, I can drive a backhoe." I had no clue how to drive a backhoe, but these opportunities would present themselves all the time. We also had horse patrol, ATVs, and dirt bikes.

Other than working in the field, I best loved working with the sensor crew where I'd come to work every day in jeans and a tee shirt, and I'd go out and try to out-think aliens and smugglers, outsmart them, and outplay them by putting the sensors somewhere the groups will set them off, but cattle won't, or people out for a stroll along the river won't set them off. So you gotta play a little bit of a mind game to do that. Plus I got to go to work every day in jeans and a tee shirt, which was kinda cool, after having been in uniform for five or six years.

At the other end of the scale from that, I did prosecutions in McAllen. I *loved* that, too. Most people would say "no" to that, because it was coat and tie. But I'd go to the courthouse every day and talk to the U.S. magistrate. We had a little routine that we did every day, where I'd come in and present the cases to him in his chambers before we went into the courtroom, so that nothing would blindside him. He wanted to have a heads up on the whole thing. So I'd get to go up there and present, "Okay, here's Juan Martínez. He's been charged with statute 1325 U.S. Code the third time." He'd say, "It's time to do something besides just send this guy back home." And that's kind of how it would go. And in the process of that, then you meet everybody in the whole food chain, from the U.S. magistrate down to the assistant U.S. attorney and U.S. Marshal Service. It was a happy family that shared the same pie, and it felt good. It made me feel good to see how many good people were actually involved in all of that.

I guess one of the most discouraging things about being a Border Patrol agent is catch-and-release, catch-and-release, catch-and-release. It makes you feel good when a guy who deserved to go to jail went to jail. You could go to the assistant U.S. attorney or have the attorney tell the magistrate, "Hey, look, this guy needs to go to jail." And instead of just the automatic "ninety days suspended, time served, and back to Mexico you go," the judge says, "This guy has been in trouble on more than one occasion, and he deserves to go to jail." The bad guy is standing up there, and because he's played this game several times before, he thinks it's gonna be ninety-days-suspended-and-back-you-go-to-Mexico, but the judge looks at him and says, "I'm gonna have you serve these ninety days," and all of a sudden his eyes get the size of saucers. "Wait a minute! What happened? What happened to my ninety-days-suspended sentence?!" Instead of thinking that my job was a merry-go-round with the aliens, it turned into so much more.

Also, I was a post-academy instructor, which made me feel really good, that I actually had guys that were where I was not so long ago, now looking up to me for advice and my wisdom and expertise and knowledge.

I was trying to get into the pilot program in McAllen, but while detailed to FLETC at Glynco as a law instructor, I was offered a permanent position teaching at the academy and a pilot trainee slot at McAllen at the same time. I was stunned. I called Patrice, my wife, who has a psychology degree, and told her the whole story. She said, "Okay, let's do this. Five years down the road, which of these two scenarios would probably bother you the most: sitting at Glynco wondering how good of a pilot you could have been, or sitting in the pilots' office in McAllen wondering how good of an instructor you'd have been? Which one of those two scenarios causes you the most discomfort?"

I said, "If I was to really think about it, I'd probably be sitting out at Glynco wondering if I'd have been a good pilot." She says, "Sounds to me like we're staying in McAllen." So we did. She ended up getting a better job and I ended up in air operations. I had been on the ground for ten years. And if you talk to most of the pilots, none of them do that much time on the ground—none of them. Joe Dunn may be the exception. But normally, most of our pilots are already licensed when they join with the intention of going directly into air ops at the first opportunity, usually in three years.

I was a little apprehensive about doing that, because I wanted to keep flying as my hobby. I thought that if I started flying for a living, the day might come when I didn't enjoy flying, and I didn't want that to happen. I always wanted to have flying as fun. At that time Border Patrol was flying Super Cubs and Cessnas, which I didn't care that much about. But then along came the OH-6s, and not too long after that, we bought those new A-Stars. And along came an "H" model Huey. And I started talking to Patrice, and I said, "You know, if I was over there, I'd be flying that stuff. That's stuff that I could be flying, instead of a Piper Cherokee on the weekends. I could be flying an 'H' model Huey right now." So anyway, it came to the point where I decided I wanted to go over to air ops, and luckily the chief over there in McAllen, Jimmy King, he wanted me there as well, and that helped.

At McAllen I bought a plane to maintain my ratings and my currency requirements. There was another agent there at McAllen Station, Gus Gonzalez. We were partners, we bought a little Beech Sundowner, and we flew it to maintain our ratings and stay current, and get everything we needed done here in McAllen. And he ended up going to El Paso as an assistant chief patrol agent for air operations.

So that's how it all started. That seems so long ago, and yet it's such a short time. And, this is really unheard of in the aviation community: I had accumulated 8,200 flight hours in those ten years. And in the aviation world, that's unheard of. There are colonels in the Air Force who retire with 4,000 flight hours. I thought I flew a lot in McAllen before I came to

Yuma. In Yuma, we used to get in trouble if we flew more than a hundred hours a month. Howard Aitken, our chief pilot, was forever writing memorandums to El Paso Flight Operations explaining why Randy and Joe and Howard each had flown over a hundred hours every month. That's roughly five hours a day of intense work above the ground without a net. Finally he got a waiver. It just made it easy for us, so we didn't have to worry about that anymore. We religiously flew a lot of flight hours.

In Yuma, we had time to cut sign. We cut sign out in the east desert every day. And we didn't start chasing aliens until we finished the cut. The cut alone would take three hours. By the time you flew all of those washes between Yuma and Ajo, it'd take you a good three hours. And then you'd go back and follow up whatever you spotted along the way. In Tucson there's no time to cut sign. As soon as the ground agents hear that a pilot is 10-8, they call him, "We have work for you. I need you over here, I just scattered a group." "We just had a vehicle bail out on us." "We're tracking guys that are packin' dope." I say, "Okay, you're number 5 on the list, you're number 6 on the list, you're number 7 on the list," and that's pretty much how the day goes here. It's nonstop. You have to make yourself go home.

Our apprehensions are still tops, but as you would imagine with any other type of organization as large as Customs and Border Protection Air, some guys like it, some guys don't. Of course the Border Patrol pilots love it, and that's why we're doing it in the first place. They say that they're professional pilots that have moved into law enforcement. The Customs mind-set was that they're professional pilots that have chosen federal law enforcement as their field of operations. Guys like me, we're really Border Patrol agents who use a vehicle with a fixed or rotary wing.

We're still the old ground-pounders, and at this point we still do it. More so now than ever before, we'll land south of Sells, or land south of Ajo, and get out with a group of aliens, and place them under arrest, and wait for two hours for a ground vehicle to arrive and pick them up. During that time, they're in our custody. If we weren't Border Patrol agents, if we didn't know how to enforce immigration law, and if we didn't know how to speak Spanish, we would be in a world of hurt.

Therein lies a problem. This intermingling of agencies is gonna have its headaches, and that's a problem, one of the biggest ones. It's more mind-set than anything else. The Border Patrol pilots all still believe through and through that they are Border Patrol agents. After DHS combined Border Patrol and Customs pilots, they're not! They're now in CBP Air and Marine. They were traded from the Cubs to the Yankees. We're actually not part of the Border Patrol anymore, but guys like me, in my twenty-first year of doing this, "bleed" Border Patrol green. That's just the way it's gonna be. I don't like it and I don't understand it. That's all in the eyes of the beholder. But I like to think I know what I'm doing out there. And I know what I'm doing, because I spent twenty years in the Border Patrol.

Flying our new A-Star B3 helicopter is just like being in a Cadillac Coupe de Ville after driving around in one of these OH-6 Jeeps. But I flew an old OH-6 today, and it's funny what you miss. I guess if you drive around in a Cadillac for a really, really long time, it's kind of fun to get back in a Jeep once in a while, because I had a really good time out there today. I was flying closer to the ground than you do with an A-Star. I was landing in places that of course I couldn't land in my A-Star. And I think the ground agents love seeing an OH-6. There's something about the sound of an OH-6, and seeing an OH-6 coming, that makes you feel good. It's like the cavalry's here; "I'm not alone anymore." It's a good feeling.

Two weeks ago one of our horse patrol guys in Casa Grande actually fell off his horse. He was going up the side of a mountain south of Sells, his horse tripped and fell, and he fell down into a cholla bed. He was trapped; he could not move. He was not badly injured, other than cuts and bumps and scrapes, but he was actually trapped in a cholla bed. He had so much cholla in and on his body, he couldn't move. It probably took me thirty minutes to find him. He was calling on the radio, and he didn't actually know where he was and couldn't get to his GPS. It took me a little while to find him but I did, and I got help up to him. Another horseman rode up and extricated him. I was reduced to tears as the agent was forced to "say goodbye" to his faithful horse, right there in the middle of the desert. Later he wrote a letter and said, "Boy, when I heard the sound of that helicopter, it was just like my guardian angel had shown up." It's such a great, great feeling to hear that helicopter coming.

And that's the part that means the most to me. These guys remind me on a daily basis of how important we are to them. And to me, that's as good as a paycheck. That's the part that makes you feel like you want to go to work tomorrow. People ask me, "After twenty years, how can you possibly look forward to going to work?" And that's how—I'm gonna make some guy's day today. That's the whole purpose of me suiting up and going out there: some guy is going to be really, really glad to see me, and that's what it's all about. I can save them hours of walking. I can turn four hours into forty minutes for them. And that's what these guys all look forward to. It's a long tedious task when you're following aliens footprint by footprint by footprint, down through gullies and washes and back up the sides and over the tops.

The other day one of our ground agents had a Blackhawk with a Customs pilot out there with him in the area, but he heard our Border Patrol OH-6 pilot sign on. He said, "Hey, I think I just heard Fox Trot 11 take off from Ajo. See if he can come down here and get on this foot sign for us." The ground was up over mountains and down through gullies, and it was gonna take them a long time to push it. The Blackhawk pilot in the area said, "Hey, I think I can help you with that. I'm probably about ten minutes out." The ground agent said, "Thanks, but honestly, we need a sign cutter."

Therein lies the difference. Howard Aitken had that problem over there, where the Customs guys were working nights, and the Border Patrol guys, sign cutters, were working days, and they wanted to rotate to night. They did and it lasted one day. Those pilots unaccustomed to sign cutting said, "This was too low, too slow, we don't want to do it. We'll go back to flying 500 AGL at night. This is a little more labor intensive than we care to get into, so we'll work night shift from 500 feet." Sign cutting is a skill acquired with years of practice. We've gotten so used to low and slow, that it's just how we do the job.

Good Border Patrol agents are the ones that love it the most, guys who like going to work. They are the guys that really put in the effort to do a good job. And that's what they work for. They get paid to do it, too—so how great is that? The most skilled, the most professional, and the most successful guys at this job are the ones who really enjoy it even after all these years. That's what makes the difference.

A lot of guys, like Glen Payne or Joe McCraw, would have stayed longer in the Patrol if they'd have let them go beyond age 55. And there're a lot of guys that are happy to retire. But it's hard to give this up. I would imagine that retired Border Patrol agents are probably the grumpiest people to be around, because it's giving up something that they really love. And sometimes they have to retire from a physical standpoint, because the body just won't take it anymore.

Howard Aitken's a great boss. And he's one of those guys that is very, very loyal to his troops, and always has been. He always sticks up for the guys that work for him. He'll go toe-to-toe with management on any given issue, if it's in favor of his guys and if it's the right thing to do. He's not intimidated by management at all. Howard's not afraid to tell them, "That's not gonna work. We can't do that. No can do." Headquarters tried to institute a 7-day-a-week, 24-hour-a-day flight ops with only six pilots when I was over there. Howard just said, "That's not gonna work. We can't do it." Plain and simple. "You can have X-number of flight hours per week. I'll put them anywhere you want them. You want them at 2:00 A.M., you want them at 6:00 A.M., you want them at 10:00 P.M., I'll put those hours wherever you want them. But we don't have enough pilots, we don't have enough equipment, we don't have enough maintenance staff to give you 24-7 coverage. So there you are."

And that's one thing that I've always respected Howard for: he knows the right thing to say, and it's always what needs to be said. Whether the guy's wearing triple-cluster oak leaves on his collar, or just a plain old grunt like me, if it needs to be said, Howard will say it. He's some good guy to work for.

Learning to fly a helicopter seems impossible at the time. It is a totally different experience. You have to be open to the idea that it's not an airplane, that it doesn't operate like an airplane, and that most of the time the helicopter is out-thinking you, or it's ahead of you. The biggest thing that they teach you in flying helicopters is "stay ahead of the aircraft. Always anticipate what it's gonna do before it actually does it. Think of what your game plan is gonna be." It isn't tough to learn to fly. It is tough to continue to fly and not become complacent—especially the more modern aircraft. The OH-6 will constantly remind you that it's a machine. That never goes away. It always makes funny sounds that keep you on your toes. I don't think anybody flies it these days without realizing that they're flying a forty-year-old aircraft. Every time you do a preflight in the morning, it tells you about its age. They're just old aircraft, old *reliable* aircraft. So you're constantly on your toes. And if you have a component failure, you land.

Border Patrol pilots have done a gazillion practices for emergencies. No other agency trains as hard as we do for current training or emergency procedures training. We know how to put them back on the ground. Look how many times we've proved it. Of all of the accidents we've had, very few—I mean, a handful—have been fatal. Only a handful have even re-quired the guy to be hospitalized for more than a day. But I think the reason is because of the recurrent training we get. And, everybody keeps in mind that they're flying an old piece of junk that was supposed to be turned back into Budweiser cans about ten thousand airframe hours ago.

The OH-6s were supposed to be deadlined at 5,000 airframe hours. It was built as a throwaway aircraft. It was a disposable aircraft, built specifically for Vietnam. And when they produced them at Howard Hughes's factory there in California, they were built with the idea that they were cheap aircraft, easy to build with quickly replaceable parts, and when you're done with them, you throw them away. And here we are, forty years later, still flying them. Most of them in Tucson are at 10,000, 11,000 hours. I've flown four-zero-kilo [40K] that has 12,000 airframe hours, *and* it has a Navy Cross for being shot down in Vietnam. These things were supposed to have gone away a long time ago, and here they are, still doing our day-in, day-out flying. When the A-Stars can't fly, which is more often than it should be, and when the 600NS can't fly, there's always an OH-6 available — always.

The respect, the admiration, that pilots get from the guys on the ground is tremendous. And it's heartfelt. They don't call you and say, "Hey, thanks a lot for coming by, we're certainly glad we had a helicopter." They call and say, "Hey, Randy, we wouldn't have been able to do it without you. We want you to know that. Once again, as always, you saved the day." And it's heartfelt. You saved them a lot of physical pain, for starters; you kept them from having to climb up the side of a mountain, or getting lost. One agent got turned around out in the middle of the Mohawk Mountains and didn't have a clue where he left his vehicle or which way to go. Without an aircraft there, it would have been a really long day. We've done it on numerous occasions. Even with the advent of GPS, agents still sometimes ask, "Hey, would you do me a favor and hover over my truck on your way out of here, so I can at least get a line back to it?"

Sometimes I come home and complain to my wife. "Oh, I had a horrible day! It was long and hard and hot, and my back hurts." But I know that tomorrow's gonna be another one of those days when somebody's really gonna need me out there. Somebody's gonna be grateful that I went to work and that I didn't call in sick. I mean, even on the days when you get up, and your feet hurt and your back hurts and "today would just be the perfect day for me to just 'bah,' take a sick day." Take a sick day? I've got 1,500 hours saved up in sick time that I'm gonna retire with and not get paid for. Tomorrow's gonna be the day that some guy is really gonna be glad that I'm out there. And that's what does it for me.

The exhilaration of flying is still there. The best hours of my day is the time between start-up and shutdown. I don't look forward to going into the office and generating my preflight paperwork for my mission. And I look forward even less to coming home at the end of that mission and having to do paperwork to tell everybody what I just did. But I can't imagine *not* flying.

What we do is hazardous. It carries a very high degree of danger, compared to what some of the other people do, but at the same time, I think your degree of professionalism probably determines how big of a predicament you're in. There are go-getters out there who fly hard and fast with their hair on fire. But I think those are the exceptions. The good Border Patrol pilots that have lasted, that have survived the test of time, are the guys that always knew, "Hey, there's a right way to do this, and there's a wrong way to do it." And you can be very successful doing it the right way. Again, I think that's why our numbers of fatalities and stuff are so low, especially considering the number of accidents that we've pushed ourselves into. You know, at a hundred feet and a hundred knots, you're really hanging it out there. And there are professional pilots who would consider that sheer insanity. A number of our Patrol pilots have over 8,000 hours skimming the treetops with their skids. That's what they've done their whole career. It's not as inherently dangerous to them, or they don't see it as dangerous, but they're probably more cautious than the guy that's at a thousand feet, buzzing along up there.

There can be no compromise when it comes to safety. If you feel that you're in a position that you don't want to be, then you've already gone too far and exceeded the safety limit. The best advice that I can offer new pilots is, A, be safe, be as safe as you can possibly be. And B, have fun, because this is the best job that you will *ever* have, ever. But A always comes before B.

I did a lot of rescues in Yuma. Joe Dunn was the pilot and I was the co-pilot in the Huey when we picked up a girl out in the desert south of Wellton. One alien had walked out and said that they left someone in distress back in the Gila Mountains. A ground unit found her and called us for help. We were airborne before they found her. We weren't very far from Wellton at all. They found her, and we got into the area about the same time. They said, "This one's gotta be evac'ed. We don't have time to call Tri-City Ambulance or one of the ground agencies. She's gonna have to go." We landed, put her on board, and took the two BORSTAR agents who had EMT training with us. We no more than pulled the skids up off the ground than she coded, her heart stopped. These guys went to work real quick on her back there, and we were cooking for Yuma Regional Medical Center. As a matter of fact, en route, I called dispatch and told them to get in touch with YRMC and tell them what we were coming in with. Dispatch said, "They're not gonna send a gurney out to the helicopter until you're completely shut down." I said, "Do you know how long that takes in a Huey?! We're not gonna do that." I said, "We'll offload her and haul her in. You tell them to leave a stretcher out there where we can get it, and we'll do it." By the time we landed, they'd changed their mind. They came out and got her as soon as the skids touched, and hauled her inside. The last I heard, she made it, but I wouldn't have bet a nickel.

And of course we've had the other end of the scale, too, where we've already found them when it was too late, and it's so sad. It makes you think. The desperation factor is way up there. A percentage of them walk out into that desert knowing that there's a chance they won't make it. It's sad to think that the desperation level is so high that they're actually willing to take a higher than normal chance of losing their life. That's where a good professional pilot comes in mighty handy.

I've never met a self-serving Border Patrol pilot, one who wasn't more about what he had to give people than what he got for himself. We're all very concerned about making sure that the other guy is taken care of. Even the agents who don't appear to be so friendly, they're a public servant in their hearts. And their paycheck means less to them than the respect of people that they work for. And I think they're all like that. I like to think that that's what keeps my clock ticking. We don't say no to the paycheck, but at the same time, nobody does this job for the money. The guys that are good at it have the feeling that "I'm helping somebody else by doing my job."

Each individual Border Patrol agent that you talk to has a heart, and that's the most important part. I have seen—and you've heard this a hundred times, too—I've seen Border Patrol agents take money out of their wallets or take a sandwich out of their lunch box for the people that were hungry or down. You would have a hard time finding an *un*compassionate Border Patrol agent. I haven't found one yet who's not touched by a story, or a little kid, or somebody out there in need of help. The first person to provide that help, more often than not, is a Border Patrol agent. And to me that's a legacy that I hope carries on *forever* in this agency.

I did go back to my mother's and get my auto mechanic tools. They're out in the garage, but so far I haven't needed them.

WENDY CONDE

After joining Border Patrol in 1991, Wendy Conde worked at several stations. She has been at Wellton since 1998.

I'm Wendy Conde, and I've been at Wellton since 1998 as an intelligence agent for the station. I do various jobs, including statistical gathering, information sharing, multiple agency liaison, and so on.

I'm not from this area. This is my husband's side of the country. I actually grew up in Calexico, California. My dad was an inspector at the port of entry in Calexico from 1970 to 1991. He started in the Border Patrol at the Blythe Station and was in academy class 48. His name was Windle G. Roach. After Blythe, he went to New Orleans, where he worked under Attorney General Bobby Kennedy and deported mob boss Carlos Marcelo, a big-time Mafia guy that they thought had a part in the Kennedy assassination.

My husband's family is all here in the Yuma area, and he wanted to come home after being away for nine years, so we did. I love this place. It's wonderful—peaceful so far, and we're hoping that it'll stay that way. I love this desert. You've gotta go out and actually sleep out there under the stars, and see the desert change color as the sun rises. It'll start in gray hues, and then it'll turn into like pinks and purples. The rocks literally change color. And then it's all green once the sun is up higher. It's just an absolutely beautiful sight to see.

I was the first female assigned to Wellton Station. It was difficult because the male agents didn't know how to relate to the female agents, but we all soon adapted. The first three years were real tough for me, trying to get into the men's mentality and the men trying to get used to the way *I* thought. Women and men do think very differently. Women think a lot

Wendy Conde, with photo of her father, Windle G. Roach, on the monitor. Photo by Bill Broyles, 2009.

more on the emotional side; men are more logical. So what I may think is illogical, to them is logical.

I butted heads with a few of the guys, but I think I've gained their respect, because I've hung in there, and I treat everybody with respect no matter how they treat me. Now it seems like they can't survive without me, and they are at my office door saying, "We need your help!" Now I feel very much a part of the Wellton Station, and the women here have a very close working relationship.

The main thing that I've learned is that building a family atmosphere at Wellton is the key to high morale. I learned all the systems and all the policies and procedures at Wellton, so I feel comfortable and effective here. I've learned so much and it's because of Wellton's staff moving me and teaching me. I'm the type of person that if you're strict with me, I learn more. I don't know why, but I think it's a challenge to me. If somebody tells me I can't do it, then I'm gonna show them I can, and if they give me a project, I work on it until it's perfect. And that, to me, made me a better agent, because I can honestly say I can stand up with some of the best from the Wellton Station. I love the Wellton Station. It's great working here.

Glen Payne asked me to be the federal women's program manager.

With every female who came into the Wellton Station, I had what I called "the girl talk." And we would sit down and I would help them understand this is not just another job—it's a career! We're all *agents* here. In this dangerous job we must work together. When women don't feel confident or they feel threatened, they don't perform as well. So if I could help them, I would.

I also would tell them that if they needed someone to talk to, I was always available. The best thing to do is talk about what's bothering them. "I gotta get this off my chest." Once it's off their chest, then they can go on. They've talked about it and they're done with it. And so I try to help the women with that. This is a stressful job. We work very long hours, and it can affect your home life.

My husband is in law enforcement and I'm law enforcement. Many spouses and agents need counseling, whether it's from a friend or a professional. So I used to talk to the new trainees who came in. "Hey, if your wives are ever feeling like they don't understand what you're doing, they are always welcome to call me. Tell them about me; tell them that I'm the women's program manager here, and a wife to a law enforcement officer. I can help." I'll be more than happy to help the wives, because it is hard on the wives. Their husbands sometimes don't realize how their wives feel. They think, "My wife's home all day, so she's not doing anything."

Personally, I'm not just a full-time Border Patrol agent, I'm also a full-time mom with four kids. When I'm *off* duty with my kids at home, my work never stops. I tell my agents, "Guys, I know you're tired when you get home, but how do you think your wife feels? When you get home, she's gotta take care of *you* too, and if you're not listening to what your wife's telling you, then you're gonna start having marriage problems. They'll resent the job and then resent you, so you gotta listen." Listening is a big thing, and guys have a hard time doing that. Sometimes my husband says, "You don't care about *my* job, do you?" And I reply, "I just came from my shift, and now I'm doing laundry and I'm making dinner. I care, a lot, but not right now." And then he feels bad because he has a lot to talk about, so I have to try and be a good listener, too. It goes both ways at our house.

I had never cut sign until I got to Wellton, although I always heard my dad talk about cutting sign. There's a technique to it. The real experts can follow tracks over rock. That malpais rock is hard to track on. I remember some of the hints that my dad used to give me. "If it's fresh, over rock, you're going to actually see the oils from the shoe on the rock.

But you have to have the sun in the right spot in order to see it. If you have the sun in the right spot and it's old, it's going to be more faded, but you can still see it." I have yet to see it, but I'm still looking.

And, I try to look for the things Glen taught me. I look for anything that's been moved. Glen says, "You might not be able to see the footprint itself, but you can see the little rock turned up, or you can see the piece of grass bent. And then you find what they're guiding on, and you keep that in line, in the same line that you're looking for which way they're going, and you see the little disturbances here and there, and then finally you come to a road, and there's their sign." That's when I feel, "Oh! Wow! I can *do* this!" It definitely requires patience. There have been times I've lost the trail, so I move in circles, systematically going back and forth to where I last had them. Finally I get on them again, and away we go. But it's definitely a technique, and some guys have incredible skill.

We had a deceased person out there by the Mohawk Mountains. The group he had been with said he couldn't keep up, so they left him behind. We backtracked the group to the exact spot where they left him, but he wasn't there, so he obviously got up and walked away. We were out there on foot, on ATVs, and in fact I went out on horseback on my day off with my friend Cindy Cedar. On horseback we covered a lot more ground than on foot, but we still couldn't find any sign. And it still haunts us. I wonder where he can be every time I pass that location.

I remind the guys that whatever they do follows them through their career. For example, your casework follows you through your career and people are gonna know your name, good or bad. The federal attorneys will learn your work and know your name. If they see a prosecution report coming in with your name on it and your prior cases have been terrible, they don't even want to look at your case.

To me, a person must put forth the extra effort to do these things, to make their station look better. If you make the top shine, the bottom's gonna shine, too. But the top can't shine unless the bottom's shining. If my chief doesn't look good, then I don't look good. We accomplish this by doing everything correctly and by the book. Then we all look good. Individual agents make or break all of us, not just themselves. It takes only one bad apple to make the station look bad and have the public look down on us all.

We're getting some real good apples in the Patrol now. Some get discouraged because they've been here a year and don't know it all. But I've been in fifteen years and still don't know it all.

I used to give our agents the old desert survival speech, what to take out there, what to do, and what not to do. My husband still gives classes on that, and he's got good information. A lot of the aliens will be really thirsty when they come into the station. I remind the agents to only let the alien sip the water. If you let the aliens gulp water instead of sipping it, it could cause them to throw up. We had these two guys that came out of the desert and they'd been there three days without eating, so we gave them little Dinty Moore tins. One alien asked, "Can you give my brother a couple of these? You don't have to give me anything, but give my brother . . . he's very hungry." And I said, "I'm gonna give your brother one can now, and in an hour I'll give him another one, because if I give him too much now, he's gonna throw it all up. You're both dehydrated." Their lips were parched and their skin taut, so I told them, "Here, I want you to drink this, but I want you to sip it and drink it slow." The best advice for agents and aliens alike is, "Constantly take sips of water until your body can handle more."

One group that was brought in out of the desert—and I'm not kidding—had uncooked chicken after days without refrigeration. And we were going to toss it in the garbage, but the woman was insistent, "I *have* to take my chicken with me." And I told her, "It's no good." And she wanted to cry, because she wanted to take that *uncooked* chicken, spoiled, smelly chicken with her. She didn't want to give it up. I told her, "You're gonna get sick if you cook that."

When Cindy Cedar and I were riding out there, she asked, "How many people do you think are walking through this desert right now?" I replied, "It could probably be a whole bunch of them. What I'm wondering about is how many *dead* people there are in this desert that we'll *never* know about."

KENNY SMITH

Kenny Smith currently lives in Albuquerque after serving in the Border Patrol from 1980 to 2003. He was at Well- ton Station from 1991 until he retired.

I spent twelve years in the Border Patrol at Yuma Station and then was able to step into a supervisor position at Wellton, a smaller station. After coming to Wellton I realized a smaller station could really work together better. We could always find something to do. We covered such a big area that we could go somewhere different every day, so we stayed very busy. I loved it.

After I had been in Wellton several years, the brass decided, on some level above our station, that they would pull out everybody at Wellton, except for Glen Payne, our Patrol Agent in Charge, and send them to run a checkpoint at the old agricultural inspection station thirty-five miles west of Wellton in California. The result was the total abandonment of the Wellton area for a period of time. While Wellton Station personnel were working at that checkpoint, the number and size of groups walking across the desert south of Wellton's area ballooned. And vehicle loads of aliens were getting away untouched along the back roads and highways through that area. They were finding no resistance. All these aliens were getting away, one group after another. The pilots could count most of the walkers entering across the line but who knows how many smuggling loads drove through our area. The Wellton area was full of apparent illegal aliens; the trains were loaded with them, too. Local residents and other agencies were phoning in like crazy with reports. PAIC Payne had to tell them, "I don't have anybody to send," and he didn't! There was nothing he could do. After four or five weeks our Chief Patrol Agent consented to let us leave that checkpoint and return to Wellton. The only catch was that we had to divide our manpower with the roads and the checkpoint on Highway 95.

During our first week back, I was headed up to the checkpoint in my truck and saw a loaded pickup coming right at me. He saw me and turned off towards a canal bank to try and get away. I knew where he was headed and raced to head him off. The driver stopped, and his load of aliens bailed out and ran. I caught three of them before they could get away. Pilot Howard Aitken was flying the helicopter that morning. I radioed him and asked for help, telling him there were twelve to fifteen running from me over east of the Snake Pit, where an old bar used to be near Dome Valley Road and Highway 95. Howard got there quickly and circled the load vehicle, looking for the rest of the group.

As we searched for the aliens, another loaded vehicle, a van, passed by me before I could even get on the roadway from the canal. I said, "Howard, I've got another load here. I'm gonna have to bail off for a minute." He said, "I'll help you after I try 'n' gather these up." While Howard searched for the rest of that first load, I quickly chased down the second vehicle, ran the plate, and even before the plate came back I could tell it was a smuggling load. I lit it up with my red and blue lights, and pulled it over. I jumped out of my truck and quickly secured the driver and the keys. Meanwhile a DEA agent who was headed to meet with me that morning at the checkpoint, stopped to give me a hand. He and another agent with him kept the rest of the illegals in the van for me until we could get a Border Patrol van to take the aliens to the station.

While those two watched that load, I went back to the north side of the area where the illegals had first run from me earlier that morning. Howard found them and herded them to where I could pick them up. Glen brought a van from the station, and we loaded the aliens from the second vehicle into the van and put the drivers from the three load vehicles into my truck. Once we had all the aliens under control, the DEA agent and his partner went back to town, postponing our meeting to another day. One of our agents, Greg Dushane, came from the checkpoint to drive the service van with all the aliens from that loaded van the DEA agents held for me. Glen took the empty load van, and he and I started to follow Greg back to the station. Luckily, we had everything under control and Howard went on to cut the border line as the pilots did every day. Up to that point we had already caught about twenty-nine illegals.

But, as we drove through Dome Valley, on the way to the station, I looked up, and just ahead of me was a pickup with a piece of plywood

Kenny Smith. Photo by Bill Broyles, 2007.

covering up something in the bed. The driver had come from a side road, I guess trying to avoid us earlier. Knowing from experience what that plywood meant, I knew it was a smuggling load. I picked up the mic and said to Glen, who was listening on his walkie, "Glen . . ." My voice trailed off. He had seen it too and responded on his walkie, almost before I was done, "I know." So we pulled in behind it and I ran the registration on the plate as we followed it down the road towards the freeway. The driver of the pickup was driving erratically, looking back at me in the mirror, and he suddenly pulled into somebody's property and stopped, a mile or so from where we got behind them. I picked up my mic and said to Glen, "They don't live there," and he said, "I know." We slid to a stop next to the truck, boxing it in. I jumped out and went to the truck, quickly raising the plywood sheet a bit to take a quick peek. As soon as I could see under it I said to the bunch of folks hiding under the plywood, "Buenos días," and lowered the plywood back down for a minute. I knew we had to make sure the driver couldn't try to bail out or try to drive away, so I quickly approached him and said in Spanish, "Give me the keys and get out." He handed me the keys and I took him to my truck. We got the rest of the illegals out and finally got them all loaded up. We had to put them in the empty load van Glen was driving and come back for the pickup truck later. It was a long day and I still hadn't made it to the checkpoint twenty miles away to the north. That resulted in about forty illegal aliens and three vehicles in one shift.

Aliens were everywhere during that time. Call after call would report, "We've got a bunch along the tracks or over at the canal or hiding in a grove." There were aliens everywhere on the loose. There were groups just coming across this desert, one after another, and they weren't piddly little groups of threes, fives, and sevens—they were groups of fifteen, twenty, or thirty-plus. For a week, we had three or four groups a day of twenty-seven, thirty, thirty-five. Finally, it started to taper off a bit, but until then we were getting load after load after load through Dome Valley. Every morning the guys headed to the checkpoint would catch at least one load before they got through the valley.

The cars never had any guides. Most of the smugglers relied on one of the people in the group to drive. The smugglers would ask, "Which one of you guys wants to drive the car? If you drive the car, you don't have to pay." The car—load vehicle—would be brought to some pre-arranged place in the U.S. to wait for the group to cross the border on foot. Then one of the aliens would drive the vehicle, and the guides would leave, or sometimes a guide was in the group, but often we didn't know who it was. We'd always prosecute the driver of the vehicle, because who else are we gonna prosecute? After all, whoever drove was assisting the rest of the group to enter illegally. The driver was just as guilty as anybody. And we needed to prosecute somebody on every load, as a deterrent, hopefully. The guy driving was usually just a dumb slob who decided he was gonna get smuggled for free, but in effect he was getting paid, so he was guilty. Nobody gets a free ride.

We worked the desert a lot those first few years I was in Wellton, and with a small amount of manpower we caught a lot of aliens. A shift of two or three agents sometimes would catch a hundred a day. Those were hard, long hours, but cutting sign and chasing are fun. Sometimes in the hot summer it's less fun. Finding dead bodies, like we did at times, was never fun.

When I started out in Border Patrol, we were lucky to have our own assigned Jeep. Whatever you drove in the field was called a Jeep. You usually had to be a fairly senior agent before you had your own Jeep. The rest of the agents drove motor pool vehicles, but having three shifts a day share vehicles creates problems. It's harder to make two or three guys be responsible for one piece of equipment and to keep it properly cleaned and maintained.

Walkie-talkies were a similar story. Nobody had a walkie-talkie assigned to themselves until about 1986 or '87. We could check them out of the armory sometimes, but most were old and didn't work very well. Some of them had just come in from the prior shift and hadn't been recharged, so they'd be dead. Or, you'd go out in the field and an hour later your battery's dead. They didn't have replacement batteries. You were lucky if you had one that worked.

The patrol used to issue us flashlights, plastic or little thin metal ones. Guys would break them all the time. Most guys eventually bought their own dependable Kel-Lite, but they still had the problem of batteries. Flashlights eat batteries really badly. The service would supply batteries, but the government was buying old military batteries, and sometimes your freshly issued batteries would last about twenty minutes before they went dead—sometimes not even that long. You'd be chasing a group for a couple of miles on foot, and your flashlight would peter out, and you'd be a couple miles from your truck in the pitch dark. You couldn't see a thing, so guys started buying their own batteries so they wouldn't have that problem. A lot of guys carried two or three flashlights, but it was recommended that you not hold one in each hand as you cut sign. If you ran into somebody who wanted to shoot you, you'd be a sitting duck.

Well-known author Luis Urrea wrote a book called *The Devil's Highway*, and it was completed just before I left the Border Patrol. At his request and by authorization of the patrol's upper management, I drove him all around the desert. He wrote about the incident where twenty-six aliens became lost and fourteen died while crossing the desert. The press called the ones who survived "The Yuma Twelve," and sometimes the group that died was referred to as "The Yuma Fourteen." Urrea's book sold like hotcakes.

Urrea told me that when he was younger, and even just before his work on the *Devil's Highway* book, he was kind of afraid of the Border Patrol. He had heard the old stories from friends and family members about how corrupt and mean *La Migra* was and how we had allegedly beat up aliens, or that we even shot and buried people in the desert. He had heard all the bad stories and misconceptions and was a little concerned. He halfway expected us to be aggressive and compassionless when he met us. As he was introduced to us for real, he realized most of what he had heard was hype. When we offered to show him the desert and openly discuss the tragedy of the Yuma Fourteen, he came to realize, "Hey, these agents are just like every other person. This agent is just like a cop doing a job." He realized he didn't have a true perspective. That bothered him, so he researched it further and talked to more people.

I was on duty when we discovered that we had those twenty-six people down or lost in the desert. The agents were not in a panic mode, but we know we only have a small window of opportunity in rescue situations, which is what this was. Commands were coming from upper management to make sure certain protocols were being met and they were at the same time asking for information about what was going on. The station supervisors had to ensure that everyone at the station was at work, every shift, until this was taken care of. We had a lot to do, in a short amount of time. We had to send supervision to the field with the agents and at the same time keep people running the show at the station. Nobody likes to find dead bodies, especially of young people. We reacted with urgency and ran this like any rescue. We asked questions of those we found initially, sent agents to their last location to backtrack, had the helicopters fly a line as quickly as possible, and kept track of all the different footprint sign that we found. When the group splintered, we put agents on each group until the trail ran out, the persons were rescued, or dead bodies were located.

Our station, being small with limited manpower, was stretched too thin to deal with the logistics and backtracking for so many aliens in an area the size of Delaware for an extended period. Yuma Station sent some good people to help for every shift, and Tucson Sector sent some of their agents to give us a hand. The Tucson agents didn't really know the area, and they worked situations a lot differently than we do. Everyone tried to help to the best of their ability, but sometimes we got in each other's way. Not meaning to and not knowing the area that well, they were ruining our sign, and that added to the confusion. The sign or tracks in these cases are the evidence and tell the story, but tracks are a fragile thing and it's hard to get the whole story from them. So there couldn't be any immediate or absolute resolution to the situation. Sometimes it was hard to find out what was going on, because of the extra agents running around on quad runners and in trucks, so we had to tell them to "be more careful. If you ruin the sign it will be that much harder."

Headquarters wanted answers now. Our supervisors in the field kept the station and the upper management as informed as they could. Our agents were often on foot with low-powered walkie-talkies, so messages had to be forwarded from them to the station by agents in trucks or by the pilots. We had to call upon the Marine Corps Air Station rescue helicopter to transport people to the hospital. There were agents at the hospital and in the field, our ground agents, Tucson ground agents, two Border Patrol helicopters, the Marine Corps helicopters, sheriff's deputies, and coroners for the deceased. It was a circus.

Management constantly wanted to know if everybody was accounted for and the condition of anyone we found alive or dead. This was a high-profile case, and Washington felt the need to pester us constantly for answers and updates. The press was everywhere with live-feed trucks for the TV networks, and Washington wanted to know how many aliens came in, how many did we get, and how many died, plus all the details. Headquarters wanted an absolute resolution, right then. So did we, but we couldn't give it to them.

Until it was all over, we had an unknown number of people spread over a thousand square miles of area from near Ajo on the border all the way to near Mohawk Pass. Walking from there requires walking about eighty miles, if everything goes right. This group became lost and walked a long distance out of their way. Where we found the first couple of illegals was on a sandy drag road on the eastern edge of our patrol area, almost as far as one can get from Wellton Station on any road. It is essentially a jeep trail passing along and over many arroyos in the middle of nowhere, thirty miles from Wellton Station.

As a crow flies, the border is at least fifty miles from the interstate. On the ground the problem is the number of small mountain ranges, patches of sand, and large areas of cactus that walkers must detour around. You cannot even see any landmarks of civilization or lights until you have gone almost forty miles of that trip. The aliens start out with only one or two gallons of water for a sixty- to eighty-mile trek that takes two or three days, depending upon their endurance. This group entered south of Ajo, and in the first couple of hours of their trip they saw the lights of what they thought were Border Patrol agents from Ajo, so they ran and hid. Afterwards, when they got back together, it was pitch black and they had taken a wrong route, ending up lost and miles west of where they intended to be. In interviewing survivors from that group, we had to figure out what really went on. They left the border with a rookie smuggler who got them lost, and sometime on the second day, at least two of the original group turned back. We never did determine whether they made it back to Mexico or not.

In a lost-person situation the public might think that more searchers will help. But in the manner we work, one inexperienced person can do a lot of damage. And, initially it's not considered a crime scene, but often it turns out to *be* a crime scene, so we need trained agents to do the work. Moreover, the evidence of where that person has traveled and where you're going to find him is pretty fragile. A whole lot of people running around, bouncing their trucks across the desert and the like, can obliterate the only record we have of the situation.

The job of a rescue brings up a lot of questions that need immediate answers. It requires that we know the first place that survivors are encountered. This is usually how we know there is a problem to begin with. We then need to try and find out or estimate the entry location at the border and send agents and/or a helicopter to the border to find where they originally crossed the border and get the description of the foot sign for everyone in the group. We need to find out how many were originally in the group and what direction they traveled. Did they all stay together or where did they split up? And at the same time, we need agents to backtrack from that first place of encounter with survivors. When the tracks we have don't add up to the number of people we know to be in the group, we need to find the place where they split up so we can look for stragglers. Answering all those questions requires patience, concentration, and common sense.

Humans suffering the latter stages of dehydration do not do things that make sense. Dehydration starts to break down the body, and the mind does not work correctly. It kind of shorts out like your car battery when it runs out of water. That's why people near the last of their lives strip down, try to dig holes to get into, or walk or crawl in circles.

The logistics of an extended rescue like this require transporting aliens we've apprehended, bringing extra fuel and water, and shuttling fresh tires for flats. We seldom set up a stationary command post, but our command center usually moves with the agents and the people being searched for. Upon the discovery of a dead body, the local county law enforcement and the county coroner are needed before the bodies can be moved. Like many crime scenes, there is no specific time element that can be adhered to. It takes as long as it takes to determine if everyone is accounted for, where they came from, who they are, where they were going, and if there are people within the group who are criminally liable for this happening. In this case, one of the two smugglers was caught and prosecuted. He almost died out there too, but he is in prison for a long time because of his part in it. Others were traced to Mexico and even some in the U.S. These kinds of cases can take months and years to completely settle and close.

This whole incident, though a crime scene, wasn't like the confined scene of a house fire or homicide in an apartment—this was more like the swath of a hurricane or the chaos of an earthquake in a major city. We did what we could, locating all the sign that we were certain was in the original group. Up to a certain point, we accounted for it all. Everyone we could account for had either been apprehended and sent to the hospital, or they died and their bodies were sent to a staging location.

There were a lot of dead bodies, fourteen in all. Anytime you encounter dead bodies, it is personally difficult. It is even worse when you encounter children, because they usually have no choice in such matters. They are following adults. Of the ones that died in this group, one was a boy, a teenager. While I was there at Wellton, every year we located people who had perished in that desert. It was never pleasant.

The long and short of the big rescue is that it was a tough, stressful time over a two-day period. It was a bad place to drive, so agents kept getting flat tires, and agents unfamiliar had a hard time finding their way around. We had to put everybody on every shift out there for fifty-six hours before we could say it was over. Agents often worked twelve hours at a stretch under miserable summertime conditions, but we got it done.

People might ask why we didn't use K-9s to help. The desert air is too dry to hold a scent and it requires special dogs to do such a search. It would take too much time to get them. Dogs that do this sort of thing usually need something to give them a scent to begin with and we didn't know how many aliens there were, who they were, or where there might be something to use to give a scent. Time is very important. If we wait for others to come and use specialized skills, it will often be too late. The difference between the ones that survived and the ones that did not was often only a couple of hours.

As far as rescues and assisting other agencies, the Border Patrol has spent many years trying to train the local agencies to understand that if you've got something going on and you want us to help you, don't send twenty-five of your guys to trample the tracks and then ask for us to figure them out. We'll *try*, but sometimes it's impossible.

In the hot summers of Wellton, we had a number of bad days, "cluster days" as we called them. One of them was right down on the line before we built Camp Grip. In this incident we encountered seven vehicles smuggling people, and each vehicle tried to outrun us but ended up with all of the aliens bailing out of the vehicles and trying to get away on foot. Fifty-four aliens—little kids, women, men—all ran away in open desert. It was hot and they had little or no water, and they didn't have any idea where they were running to. The truth is, fleeing is just an impulse. For this little caper we sent every agent from the whole station down to the line, but it can easily take two hours to get there. We had to round up as many trucks as we could and not leave the oncoming shift afoot in the process. We managed to gather all of the aliens, put them into our vehicles for transport, and get out with only one of our trucks stuck once. In the end we tied up two shifts—and all of our available vehicles—to haul out fifty-four aliens. It was a real mess.

On another "cluster day," one of our agents was going to stop a load vehicle on Palomas Road, an unpaved road on the north side of the valley next to the hills. The agent, I forget his name now, radioed in saying, "I've got a load vehicle coming up Palomas Road. Wait a minute, there's two. No. Wait. There's four. I'm counting seven, eight, nine!" A jacked-up red 4x4 pickup was in the lead. The agent, really excited at this point, was almost yelling on the radio, "There're nine vehicles here, I'm gonna need a lot of help!" He tried to stop them but they tried to get away. When the aliens realized they weren't going to be able to get away in the vehicles, the vehicles slid to a stop, all the doors opened, and everybody tried to run away on foot. Some of them got up in the hills, but after we hustled every available agent out there, we caught them all, except the two guys in the lead pickup. The whole station got involved, and we packed seventy or eighty aliens into our station to process them all. We towed and seized nine vehicles from that mess. That was definitely an all-day sucker. When the guides bailed out they picked their spot well. They ran into a nasty ol' salt cedar and scrub brush thicket where a guy couldn't track anything very easily. We wasted a lot of hours looking for them. That was just one of a number of days like that while I was at Wellton. Days like that made Wellton an interesting place to work, but those days were intense and took a lot out of us.

There's been so much published about Border Patrol that the public doesn't know anymore what's real and what's not. We're out there—we as the Border Patrol—trying to get a job done, and a lot of people choose not to recognize us or acknowledge who we are. A person taking a poll could stop twenty people on the street and probably only a very few would be able to tell you what we do. I've been referred to as a park ranger, a sheriff's deputy, a highway patrolman, an MP for the local military base, and the list goes on. Many look at the uniform and can't get past the badge and gun.

I have heard many reasons why people don't like us, and occasionally I have heard compliments about the fact that we are there and what we do is important. Sometimes I've heard it said by people, "I'm glad I don't have to do your job," or "I know a farmer who works a bunch of wets." Often people don't think what goes on around them is any of their business. That's one of the reasons we're having such an alien problem now in this country.

I saw a report from Louisiana or someplace where a cop stopped a vehicle because the tail light was out, and the vehicle was just loaded with illegal aliens. But the local police didn't have a procedure to take care of something like that, and there were no Border Patrol agents in that area at the time. So he wrote them a ticket and let them go. If I remember right there were 27 illegal aliens in that vehicle.

There are a lot of special-interest groups all over the country—and there's a special group for everything nowadays. We're having to fight everybody's perception of what the Border Patrol should be doing. We enforce established laws that are part of the U.S. Code. Our law for Border Patrol is mainly in Title 8 of that U.S. Code. We have been accused of mistreating people we encounter. We do not mistreat people. We enforce the laws, no matter what their socioeconomic level is. If they break any law, especially the federal statutes under Titles 18, 19, and 21, which covers immigration, customs, and drug enforcement, we arrest them and turn them over to the courts to decide.

At times folks will say, "All those illegal aliens want to do is get a job," or "They just work in the fields." I've heard that a lot. A lot of citizens need jobs, too. Not all of the jobs that an illegal takes are field-worker jobs. The reality is the illegal immigrants start out working in the fields, then they move up as carpenters and electricians and mechanics. It's unusual to find a guy anymore that's worked in the fields for longer than a year. Even the ones that used to work in the fields are now working in meatpacking plants and/or construction sites, and they're making a lot more money than they could in the fields. So, the farmer is still out looking for hands, and the cycle continues.

The Wellton Station and Yuma Sector for many years had hardly any violence. In this area you often caught what everybody called "the good ol' boys." Most of the time you could just open up your truck and tell them to get in, and they would. But this isn't always the case. We were issued an order by the Chief Patrol Agent: "You will search all of your aliens before you put them in the trucks." Most guys searched their aliens anyway. But over time, guys got lax. One agent caught a group in the railroad yards, and he just had them get into his truck to go to the station. At the station, he started writing them up, and he said to the aliens, "Take everything out of your pockets and put it up on the counter." One guy brings out a comb, a couple of Mexican coins, a gun—"GUN!" He laid a frickin' gun up on the counter and everybody's hitting the floor and running for cover. What the hell is he doing with a gun?! He calmly laid it up on the counter, just like it was a comb, pencil, gun.

He had killed a woman on a horse farm. He worked there and he went to the main house and stabbed her to death, but then he found a .22 magnum pistol loaded with .22 long-rifle bullets. It was a five-shot pistol, and he had put two shots in her, so he only had three bullets left. We questioned him later, "Why didn't you ever try to use it on anybody else?" He said that there were always too many officers around. He had been taken off a freight train by Union Pacific cops, and a Border Patrol truck was there, so he was counting two UP officers and two Border Patrol agents.

Aliens are cagey and that's why you can't depend on anything—you never know what kind of a guy may be dangerous. The quiet guy that you stop for driving a load car might run over your butt, not for meanness but because he's scared stiff. But he'd kill you for sure if you got in the way. The next guy may be so scared he can't even talk to you.

I chased a vehicle one day in Dome Valley. After I put the lights on him, I had to follow him for a mile and a half, but he wouldn't yield. I had to call it in and say he's not yielding. Several other agents joined the chase. Eventually he did pull over and we pulled the aliens out. We got twenty-two out of that van. They were crammed in like sardines in a can. We often apprehend between twenty and twenty-seven people in a van load. If they averaged a hundred pounds each, twenty people would weigh a ton. And I know they're gonna average probably between 120 to 130 pounds a piece. That's well over a ton, and probably closer to a ton and a quarter, in a vehicle that's only designed to carry a half a ton, or a thousand pounds, including fuel. These load vehicles are coming down the road with the suspension completely bottomed out, and that's dangerous. How many miles can they drive? Who knows? But none, safely.

But, look at that van in Louisiana. After that patrolman released that van, it could have driven up the road and gotten into a serious accident. Over the years in the southern border states, there have been numerous fatal accidents involving overloaded smuggling vehicles killing both aliens and innocent third parties who happen to get in the way of desperate, dangerous drivers. Everyone on the road is at risk. When will the public finally realize the problems that our citizens face as a result of what some call "illegal immigration"? What is it going to take for us to put a stop to it?

JOE BRIGMAN

*After joining Border Patrol in 1987, Joe Brigman came to
Wellton Station in 1991. He plans to stay until he retires.*

I was born and raised in Ajo, Arizona, and went all through
school there. My dad worked in the mine. I actually worked in the mine
ten years before I even came in the Border Patrol. Four of those ten years,
we worked twenty-six days in a row and got two days off. I did that for four
years, working in a crushing mill, so I knew what it was like to hump it up
and work for a living.

Actually, I didn't even grow up in Ajo—I grew up seven miles north of
Ajo in the middle of the desert out there at a cluster of houses called The
Well, which was the company well that pumped water for all the mine and
town. That's where I grew up, right there. House Number 2, Route 2, Box
22, was our address. So going to town, even one as small as Ajo, was a big
deal for us. I'm probably about as much of a desert rat as you could find
anywhere around.

When I came into the Patrol, thirty-five was the cutoff age, and I turned
thirty-four in the academy, so I was an old guy, the oldest guy in my class.
But I grew up around Ajo and there were a few Border Patrol agents stationed there at the time. They had four or five guys working out of a little
single-wide trailer out there at the highway "Y." Paul Waterman was a
supervisor and we talked a lot. At the mine we had gone through a strike
and some layoffs, and things didn't look good for the copper industry, so
Paul talked me into applying for the Patrol.

I had a background of being outdoors and in the desert. As a matter of
fact, my first trip on the El Camino del Diablo was 1969, when we were
in high school. I graduated in '71, so I was out there many moons ago, way

Joe Brigman. Photo by Bill Broyles, 2007.

before I was even in the Border Patrol patrolling the area. As I remember, it was a rough road, but it was just as natural as it was about the day God made it. When I was living in Phoenix, I got my letter offering appointment to the Border Patrol at Sanderson, Texas. I couldn't even find Sanderson on a map! But we scurried around the next day, went down to the library, and ended up in Texas. I stayed down there from 1987 until 1991.

But Sanderson Station was a hardship station, one of the very few in the Patrol back then, as was Tacna at the time, so that was my opportunity. When our hardship rotation finally came available, I put in for every Border Patrol station in Arizona. I would have taken any of them, and boom! here came Wellton. And I said, "Hell, I'll go to Wellton in a heartbeat. That's close to home." After I received my travel papers out of Sanderson to Wellton, I flew a couple of my buddies down to help me drive. I had a U-Haul truck, my '78 Chevy truck that I still have, and my boat, and we drove from Sanderson all the way to Willcox, Arizona, home of Rex Allen, the Arizona cowboy. I told them, "Boys, I'm not spending another day here—not in Texas, and not in New Mexico. I'm going to Arizona!" So we stayed the night there in Willcox and had quite a celebration. So that's how I ended up here, came here to Wellton in 1991 and have been here ever

Desert Duty

since. It's the best Border Patrol station in the entire United States Border Patrol, guaranteed.

Here in Wellton we do lots of different things. You might be checking freight trains, you might be doing traffic check, you might be cutting sign on the lower drag, you might be checking sensors, or you might be flying in a helicopter. Now, with this new Patrol stuff, you might be on an ATC (all-terrain motorcycle), you might be in a sand rail, be down at Camp Grip, or you could be detailed to sector headquarters as a public affairs officer, which was a great experience I had, too, by the way. I've done all that stuff. But Wellton is its own little microcosm.

But that's what makes Wellton unique: the desert. You've got traffic check out here on Highway 95 or I-8, you're searching canals and groves, and you're rescuing aliens and arresting others. I mean everything that you want to do out here is available, big time. And we try to schedule these guys so they're not doing the same thing, because it can get monotonous. But we're not sitting on an X like some stations. You can go out there and work by yourself most of the time cutting sign. But what makes it unique is the diversity of types of work that you can do.

Things are done in Wellton for specific reasons—whether it's cutting drag, or the way you work aliens, or the way you work dope. And the reason they're done that way is because guys like Joe McCraw, Mark Haynes, Glen Payne, and other old-time Border Patrol agents have looked and modified and fine-tuned this beast out here down to the point where that's the way the job gets done correctly and efficiently. It works. That's the way you catch the dope, and that's the way you catch the aliens. We know where they're coming in, we know where they're going, and we know how to get them in between. The variables are manpower, resources, and money. We can catch them.

People tell me a million times, "You can't shut that border down; you can't stop illegal crossings." And I tell them, "Nonsense! You *can*. If you've got the political willpower to do it, and allocate the number of Border Patrol agents that we need, the U.S. Border Patrol can shut the whole border down, and do a damned good job of it!" I believe that wholeheartedly—I damned sure do.

I can speak for myself and most of the old-timers here. Once you come over here, and you're from Wellton, that's your station. I don't like to think that we're any better than Yuma or Blythe or anybody else, but we do things a certain way out here. The fact that they're done a little bit different doesn't make them right or wrong, it's just the way we do it. I get pretty protective of Wellton. As a matter of fact, I shot a message off the other day to a guy that kind of inferred that we weren't quite up to snuff on some stuff, and I was accused of getting a little too sensitive. I said, "You're never too sensitive when you're protecting your troops." And that's the way I look at it. We take care of business out here—big time.

I don't know anybody who comes out here without realizing, "Wow, this is a whole different creature. You guys have got a huge area," especially when they fly over it. I've had people say, "It's amazing you catch *anybody* out here." And I say, "Oh, no, no, no. No, we can catch them. They're *highly* catchable. It's just a different way of going about it." At San Luis aliens can be over the fence and into a safe house in a matter of minutes. Out here, they come in along the borderline and they're looking at two to four days walking to the highway. You get on them, and track them. Back in the old days, we only worked two shifts out here. If you worked swing shift and you got onto a group coming out of the lower drag, you couldn't just say, "I've got my ten hours, eleven hours, *twelve* hours in," and go home. Because there was no midnight shift, you were gonna stay on their trail until day shift came in. We spent many, many, many nights out there at the top of the sand dunes at Mohawk, working that sign, on foot, over the top of it, and we caught them. We took pride in working as hard on a pair or a single as we did a group of six or eight or ten. There's no difference. Those people need to be found.

That was the mind-set back then. "This is America, this is *my* desert. You guys come in here in the wrong part of the world. You're gonna be caught." And we did. A single was just like a group of fifteen or twenty. Of course twenty was a lot easier to track, but we spent a lot of time on just those pairs and trios. It takes years to train the new agents and the new trainees to go out there day after day after day in the desert. On every group, you learn something different.

But nowadays we just don't have the time to take the trainees and new transfers and teach them how to look for sign and how to read the sign once they find it. We look to see if the footprints are bugged in or there's wind trash in the toes so we can get an idea and a feel for when they came in. A lot of times now, they walk on foam. So? Or they're "rocked up" at a waterhole. So? Or, "I don't know how many there are." There can always be an excuse for not getting out there and just busting your ass, but not at Wellton Station. We don't accept excuses. Let's catch these folks! Some new agents see things differently, but our job is to train them.

When I went to work for Phelps-Dodge down there in Ajo, I made $28.16 a day. That was good money back then. And then when I came in the Border Patrol, I think I made like $14,000 a year, or something like that. I took an actual pay cut, going from the mining to the Border Patrol. For a while I was detailed to sector prosecutions, and I was working Saturday mornings overtime. I'd go in at 5:00 A.M. and get off at 1:00, which on a Saturday is like having a day off. But I still got my eight hours of overtime, and sometimes I'd work Sundays, too. One day my boss at prosecutions asked me how many days I had worked, and I'd worked forty-two days in a row—and I didn't care! I was making money, having fun, and catching aliens out there. Sometimes when I worked both in the field and in prosecutions, I'd chase guys out here in the desert and then see them two days later in the prosecutions office. They'd look at me and you could see that look on their face, "Aren't you that guy I talked to in Wellton?"

We got 878 pounds of weed last night just east of the lava flow. Then recently they got 766 pounds from eleven backpackers. There's a *ton* of bad guys over there. There's a lot of dope coming through that Growler Valley. When we finish those vehicle barriers along the border, we'll see a huge difference.

I was working up at the Highway 95 checkpoint one time, and it was midnight shift. It was two or three o'clock in the morning, and here came a set of headlights with the guy going real slow. I'm thinking, "Boy, he's gonna throw a U-ey on me here and flee." He just kept coming. Finally he cruised up there about fifteen miles an hour, and the driver is a little, skinny, ratty-haired guy, and he's drunker than a skunk. They pulled up there and stopped. And I looked over in the back, and there's a guy—same kinda looking dude—he's in the back seat, passed out, mouth open. I looked over there in the passenger side, and the guy is wearing a pair of shorts, a tee shirt, and some sandals, and he's got a red-and-white cane. He's blind. So I asked the driver, "Hey, bud, where you goin'?" "I'm going to Parker." And I could see the beer cans and smell the beer. I said, "Parker?! You ain't never gonna make Parker."

A Department of Public Safety officer just happened to be working back down the highway, so I said, "You know what? Give me the keys to the car." So I got the keys, got him out, and pulled the vehicle off the road. But now I've got a guy that's drunk that's driving, I've got a passed-out dude in the back seat, and a blind guy with a red-and-white cane in the passenger seat. I asked, "Whose vehicle is this?" And the blind guy said, "It's mine." I said, "What are you doing with a car?" "Well," he said, "I'm from Massachusetts and I've been down here, and I'm a little out of my luck, and I just got my check, and I met these two fine guys"—fine guys!—"and they're gonna drive me up to Parker." The DPS officer arrived, and she cuffed and stuffed the guy that was driving, woke up the passed-out dude that was in the back seat, and ran some records checks on him. Come to find out, he had outstanding warrants. What does that leave me? A car and a blind man.

DPS takes the two guys. I asked the officer, "What am I supposed to do with the car and a blind guy?" She said, "I don't know. You're federal; you guys can handle it." So I ended up calling down to the Crossroads Mission, got somebody down there, and I said, "This is what I got. Can you guys help me?" At least we'll get him back to Yuma and his dad can come. They said, "Okay, we'll send a wrecker out there."

When the wrecker driver got there, he saw what I had. Plus, the blind guy had these great big ol' pussy sores all over his legs and his arms. It was really pretty nasty. The wrecker driver said, "You know what? I'll tow the car, but that dude ain't getting in my wrecker." So I said, "Well, where's he gonna ride?" He said, "Well, he can ride in the car." So we got the blind guy in the car, and the last thing I saw was the blind guy sitting behind the steering wheel in a car being towed back toward Yuma.

But I also remember the Fourth of July in Ajo when all the El Salvadorans died down there in 1974. I was also at Wellton when those fourteen died out there in 2001. As a matter of fact, my crew actually located the last two people, one guy that died and the guide who barely lived. My crew found the guide and got him sacked up. I'll tell you something on that deal: those BORSTAR (Border Patrol Search Trauma and Rescue) guys literally brought him back from death. He was foaming green stuff out of his mouth, had almost no pulse, and those BORSTAR guys started sticking those IVs in him, and I stood there and watched them. It was just like adding water to a sponge. Pretty soon he started coming back, and he survived enough to go to jail for sixteen years.

It seemed like there were twenty-six, and fourteen of them died. They call them "the Yuma 26." That was back when we didn't have a lot of traffic out there, so we didn't get out there every single shift because of low manpower. But I sent a guy out there, and I said, "Ed, just go up there and make a cut, and just take a look and see what's out there." And there was nothing, no footprints. And then the next day, Dave Fagin went out there, and he found those first guys there on the Vidrios Drag out there. That was a hell of a mess—big time.

Oh, it was crazy with agents and vehicles. We'll never have as many flat tires as we did on that. We had forty-five or fifty flat tires. We were bringing them from the garage, and it was a pretty massive undertaking in itself. I'll brag on the Wellton agents—we called in Tucson BORSTAR, because Yuma Sector didn't have one. BORSTAR does an absolutely fabulous job now. They're highly trained, dedicated. Those guys are absolutely the cream of the crop, bar none. But in the early days, they were imported into an area that they didn't know anything about, and they weren't used to cutting sign like we were. I had myself, and I think four other guys down there, and I put two guys on the sign of one alien's tracks to backtrack him to see if there was a larger group; and I put two guys in separate vehicles to backtrack the dead guy.

The BORSTAR guys were out there to assist, I guess. And we'd be on the sign and those BORSTAR guys would be looking at the ground, and our guys would come and just leave them in the dust. And it got to the point where we were pushing the sign so fast and so hard that the BORSTAR guys just followed along in their little high-powered ATVs (all-terrain vehicles) and all their fancy equipment. They could not get up in front of us. If they did, we would just blow right on past them. They were looking for the sign, and we would come right by, and they wouldn't even see it there. But overall they did a good job out there, and they busted their butts, like everybody did, but they couldn't hold a candle to those Wellton boys, no way.

You gotta find aliens before you can save them. You can lose a lot of hours if you can't track. All of the BORSTAR guys are motivated, and as good as they were, weren't always the best sign cutters. If you get them exclusively in a rescue situation, they're always the best choice. In a lot of cases, the only guys that could go and pass the physical standards of swimming and running and stuff were the young guys. Most of the time the young guys hadn't been in very long and didn't really know how to cut sign. But you could take some of them old fat boys that'd been around a long time, stick them out there on that sign, and they'll be like white on rice—they're *not* gonna get off that sign. They might not be able to stick an IV in, and they might not be able to do all the medical stuff or run five miles, but they can get on that sign and track those guys anywhere.

There are old-time agents who would absolutely be a good addition to teach the new guys how to cut sign. Now we've got cameras, and sensors, and aircraft, and helicopters, but there's no replacing that Border Patrol agent on the ground looking at sign, and reading everything that it has to say. Unfortunately nowadays there're a lot of skills going by the wayside, because they're not doing it anymore. Few stations cut sign like Wellton does.

There's not probably an area in the whole Border Patrol that faces rougher terrain than Wellton. The roads absolutely destroy a fleet in no time. Just the sheer fact that we're running 24-7 on the long, long miles of dirt, and in a lot of cases off-road, will destroy a fleet. They haven't made a vehicle yet that can withstand the rigors of Wellton Station. They're coming close, and some vehicles are better than others, but we've gone through the Humvees and all these special off-road vehicles and others. There's just not a perfect one made for Wellton. A Tahoe, if it's got the right size tires on it and you lower the tire pressure, can go just about *anywhere*.

The Humvees are good in *some* respects—they're big and tough—but have you ever tried to change a tire on a Humvee? It'd take two big ol' fat boys to do it, and it's a tough job. Are you gonna do it by yourself? We've got these "K" trucks now, with the slide-in boxes. They're great in a lot of ways, but they're heavy and have diesel engines that you can hear a mile away. It's got the bells and the whistles that go off when the doors are open. As they come from the factory, when you turn on the ignition, your head-lights come on. Now what the heck is going to happen if you're watching for a load of dope at night, and your headlights come on automatically?! That's the kind of stuff that we deal with, but there hasn't been a vehicle made yet that can withstand the rigors of the patrol. And a lot of it has to do with the terrain. A lot of it has to do with the basic design of the vehicle. Hard-charging guys get out there, and the vehicles take a toll.

Some of the less suitable factory vehicles would start showing stress damage at twenty thousand miles. The most suitable ones can probably go thirty thousand, sometimes forty thousand. Most of the vehicles don't end up with high mileage on them, because they're physically destroyed before they can get there. Within the last couple of years, we've really had great support as far as getting additional vehicles that we need. Probably an average vehicle out here, probably reaches forty, fifty thousand miles tops. That's running 24-7 with three shifts, and the only rest they get is when they break or when they're due for service. We've got a great vehicle maintenance program with vehicle control officers, and that's one of the reasons why they even last as long as they do.

And tires? We've gone through every single make, model, manufacturer, tread design, special deal, test this, test that, and fill them full of goop. They had a goop that was supposed to keep tires from deflating whenever they had punctures or cuts. The only thing is, the tires with that goop weighed about forty pounds more than they normally did. You could hardly pick them up. Then you couldn't put air in them! The goop clogged up the valve stem, so you had a nice tire that was full of goop. It was okay if you had a puncture wound, but if you ram a piece of ironwood into the side-wall and tear out the whole sidewall, whatta ya' got now? That goop's all over the place. You'd get it on your hands and couldn't wash it off, or you'd get it all over your uniform. Oh, it was a mess. Without mentioning brands, some of your basic standard six-ply or eight-ply tires that you can buy off the shelf work just as well as anything else. None of them will survive an ironwood in the sidewall.

Not very many places in the Border Patrol have the same situation that we do, and the toll that it takes on the vehicles is pretty extreme. On the other hand, our terrain takes a toll on the *agents*, too! When I first came out here, my girlfriend would say, "You wanna go four-wheeling?" I said, "Are you crazy!? I do that all day! I don't wanna go out in the desert!" But now we do, because we love it so much. Wellton is a great place to work.

Here's what I tell the trainees, "You've got to cut sign slowly enough that you can actually see what you're looking at. Anybody can drive down a road and look out the window, but you've got to be able to *see* what's there. You've gotta drive slow enough for your mind to register all those little things that you're looking at." I tell these new trainees, "If you're not seeing animal sign, if you're not seeing leaves inside the heel prints, or if you're not seeing ant hills and what the ants are hauling up, then you're going too fast. You've got to slow down to be able to analyze all this information that your eyes are seeing." We try to teach them here, wherever you're going, cut on the way down there and cut on the way back. You should always be looking.

The alien groups have gotten so commercialized now. Back in the old days where you had the old-timers that worked at the same ranch or the same farm, and he would bring his family, his kids, a friend. They knew the route and routine. But gosh, now, smugglers are bringing people up from the interior, from Chiapas and Yucatan, who don't have a clue about this desert. Now there's so much money involved, that almost without exception out here, you've got commercial guides that are getting paid by the head. "If you walk this group in, we'll pay you X-number of dollars per head." The really crazy thing is that everybody's got cell phones. All of the guides, almost without exception, have cell phones. Now if the guides or pick-up drivers see us working an area, they change plans on where to meet. They have absolutely excellent communication. In the old days, aliens would just walk to a place, put a marker out, and might lay there for six, eight hours, or all night waiting for their ride. Sometimes we'd come by, see the marker, and bag them up. But now, they're constantly on the move. Unfortunately, you still have those folks that either can't afford the guides, or don't want to get involved with smugglers because they don't trust them. Smugglers are dangerous bastards, absolutely ruthless, but people without guides get lost and do goofy stuff.

We don't really have many walking loads of drugs coming across now here in Wellton's area. Almost without exception, ours are in vehicles. They drive our roads or go cross country. If they hit it hard and fast, there're places they can run forty or fifty miles an hour. If we don't have anybody in the area, the smugglers can make it out to the interstate. What's amazing, though, is they'll steal these one-ton dual-cab pickup trucks right off the car lots in San Diego, load those things up with 1,200, 1,400, 1,500 pounds of dope, come down here, never get on a road, and will drive fast across those flats, and just completely demolish those trucks. We've had them launch themselves like Evel Knievel over the railroad tracks by Dateland. They go airborne, land, and just keep on going. And we've gotta go out there and try to catch these guys. It would destroy our fleet to try to chase them, which is why our sand rails work well, as do our helicopters.

Over in Yuma's area, smugglers often put aliens in the back of a truck when going across country. We came upon two people laying on the side of the road, a Brazilian and a guy from China, who actually bounced out of the back of the truck, and were just laying there stunned. The smugglers were driving so crazy that there was no way to hang on.

It's not very often that people can go into a job and absolutely love what they do. To be able to do that as a man in today's society is priceless: you absolutely love what you do, don't mind going to work, work as long as you have to, and really, really take a lot of pride in doing the job the way it's supposed to be done. Too, we maintain traditions of a proud history, with each agent trying to play his part to be a good Border Patrol agent, following in the footsteps of people like Glen Payne, Mark Haynes, or Sterling Smith, my first PAIC down in Sanderson. One of these days I'll hang up the belt and badge, but I'll always be one of those old Border Patrol guys. Being part of this is important for me as a person, and for me it's an accomplishment.

And then, you've got the mission of service, protecting America. I talk to every brand-new class of trainees, and I tell them, "Not only does Wellton Station need you, but America needs you. We need people like you who care about America, who care about protecting our country." Besides all the politics, we play a vital role in making sure that 9/11 doesn't happen again and that we keep the drugs and the dope and the criminals out of our country. I guess maybe I'm just an old-fashioned guy from Ajo, Arizona, but to me that's important. That's part of being a responsible citizen. And to be able to roll it all up in one deal and get paid to do it? Man, you can't beat it with a stick.

About two weeks after 9/11, Bob McLemore and I went for a sixty-day detail at headquarters in Washington, D.C. We were right in the middle of the war room with a number of sister agencies. Border Patrol set this whole thing up, lock, stock, and barrel, but it was done so well that INS [Immigration and Naturalization Service] and all these other people started moving in. The next thing you know—and this is true—they had us relegated to a little bitty table over in the corner. And that's where we operated. But it was very interesting in there every single day.

The chief of Border Patrol at the time, Gustavo De La Viña, would come in every morning for a briefing. And the first thing he did was walk straight over to the Border Patrol and talk to us, "How you guys doing? What's going on?" And every Border Patrol agent assigned to that situation room was in dress uniform, had their weapon on, and was standing tall. The other agencies were wearing Levis, sandals, and tee shirts, and they looked like a bunch of misfits. Those guys weren't even armed, and we were. You could tell who had their stuff together.

Part of what makes Border Patrol different is leadership. The Border Patrol is structured, and has people within the structure who are capable and experienced. They have picked up the traditions and experiences from the people before *them*, and they've passed it on. Border Patrol is different because we're squared away, we take care of business, and we take pride in our uniform.

My uniform is important to me. I "dressed down" a trainee this morning. He showed up with a black tee shirt on. I explained to him that that black tee shirt is not uniform. The uniform doesn't belong to him, it belongs to guys like Glen Payne and Mark Haynes and Sterling Smith. That's *their* uniform; even though they're retired, that's still their uniform. I told him, "Don't you show up at *my* muster, mister, and denigrate that uniform. Why would you even show up wearing a black tee shirt?" "Well, I've got a cold." I said, "If you're sick and you can't come to work, you call in sick—don't denigrate my uniform." So, that young man probably will never again show up with a black tee shirt on. But that's what makes us different—it's structure.

The academy teaches you that we're gonna take care of business, we're gonna survive, and there's tradition. It's more than just you—it's the Patrol. And that needs to be carried on and passed on, but it's harder these days. I'm just one of those old-timers who will eventually pass through like everybody else, and there'll be somebody else to replace me. But that's what makes us different. The Border Patrol takes care of business.

We try to set the trainees straight the first week in the academy. In comparison with the other agencies, we now have our own facility, and it makes for a better agency. In Glynco, for instance, when I went through, we were there with all the other federal agencies, it was a multiagency atmosphere, but we're the Border Patrol and we wore our uniforms everywhere we went and everywhere we marched. We didn't lollygag around in twos and threes. We marched, and we had our standard bearers, our flag bearers. We did our chants and sang our songs. When we were going down the sidewalk, you'd better get out of the way, because we're not moving onto the grass for anybody. The Capitol Police was the only other agency in uniform, and they were doing the same thing. And one time, boy, they were coming down the sidewalk, and we were coming down the sidewalk, and man, it was getting ready to be a head-on collision. Fortunately our guy and their guy told everybody to scoot over just a little bit, but every single elbow hit when we went by.

As a supervisor, I don't have women or men—I've got Border Patrol agents. If they come out of the academy and they come down here to work for me, and they pass their seven-month and their ten-month exams, gender doesn't make any difference to me. If I need an agent over here or an agent over there, then load up and get after it.

If you're a Border Patrol agent and you've come this far, you should be able to handle yourself regardless of your gender. That's the way I look at it. In specific instances where you've got a load of dope, for example, you're gonna send your most tactically sound people and the agents who know the area, but gender plays no role in it. There are female agents that can handle the weight, and there're some that can't. There're male agents that can handle the weight, and some that can't. But we're all agents.

Unfortunately, as the Patrol has gotten bigger and more complicated, a lot of different issues are involved. What I try to do as a supervisor is try to make the process go as smoothly as it can, and still stay within policies, regulations, and guidelines. But there are always ways that you can make the system work a little faster, a little better, a little easier, or a little more humane. I tell my guys, "The number one thing that we're gonna do out here is go home to our families at the end of our shift. The second thing we're gonna do is take care of business as safely as we can. And the third thing we're gonna do is have a pretty good time while we do those first two things. If you do it right, all that can happen."

But we've gotta be strong on the administrative end of the thing to make the rest of it work. Nobody likes doing payroll, nobody likes doing the memos and things like that, but that's all necessary, because we have to be accountable for what we're doing, whether accounting for hours, or servicing vehicles, or logging fuel at the end of a shift. All that has to be done. It's all part of the whole system. And it's all important. It's like processing aliens: there's more to the Border Patrol than just catching them. You've got to process them and take care of them. And you identify the criminals and the bad people, and separate them from the people that would probably make good American citizens.

I could have left Wellton many times back when they were offering promotions. I had high scores. But I didn't want to leave. Why would I want to go anywhere else, except the desert that I grew up in? Any time you can get paid to go out there and hunt human beings, catch dope, and at the same time be involved with Mother Nature, and watch the most beautiful sunrises in the world—and sometimes on the same shift you watch the sun go *down*—you've got the whole thing. Working in the middle of the whole desert makes it unique and worthwhile.

RONALD S. "RON" COLBURN

Ronald S. "Ron" Colburn joined in 1978 and was chief of Yuma Sector, including Wellton Station, from 2005 to 2007. He served as deputy chief of Border Patrol in Washington, D.C., until he retired late in 2009. His family represents four generations of border patrolmen.

Being sort of a history buff, I went through some of their old sign-cutting logs during a slow moment at the Douglas Station in southeastern Arizona. They had used the old green government ledger books: one for the arrests made, and the other one to write down the intelligence-related information about the sign "cuts," as the guy would say back then, going way back into the late 1950s and early '60s. I'd look back into the record from the earlier officers when it was a ten-man station or smaller, and the monthly apprehension totals back then were numbers like "7, 12, 1." It was amazing, because during my time there in the 1980s, we were real busy, getting three to four hundred arrests a month. Then fast forward to the late 1990s, and they were getting one thousand a *day!* And I thought we were busy at four hundred a month!

I remember one record where an agent—or PI, patrol inspector, as they were called back in those days—had sign "cut" a single walker across the Geronimo Trail east of Douglas and had followed him up the San Bernardino Valley, and then finally arrested him by the salt flats near Willcox, Arizona. Can you imagine having that luxury of time to walk for days at a time and follow someone? I imagine he walked probably for fourteen or sixteen hours a day, went home, slept, came back out where he last left the sign, and continued the chase until he finally got his one man. Back in the 1950s and '60s, that was the way it was done.

With one of my sign-cutting and tracking teachers, Dwayne Hudson, we tracked a group that we presumed were OTMs (other than Mexicans) by the trash left behind, the size of the group, and where they were walking some rough, rough country in the Chiricahua Mountains north of Douglas back around 1980 or '81. We tracked that group for three days. I had the time of my life. The unfortunate end of the story is, we tracked them all the way to the point where they were picked up by their smugglers, so they got away. But to this day, I'll never forget the pure fun of staying on a group for three days straight.

Also, I've been doing a search of my family's history trying to nail down my grandfather, because he was in a mounted guard unit in Arizona, before the Border Patrol, somewhere between 1917 and 1920. It was over in the Naco-Douglas stretch, and he was in a cavalry-style unit when they patrolled the border. In the 1920s he was listed as a resident in Douglas, Arizona, and his profession was tower man for a mining company. His job, according to my dad, was to go down to Sonora and look at ore samples in mines at Nacosari and Cananea. My dad said he also manned a water-cooled .30 caliber machine gun on one of the hills there overlooking the mines of Bisbee, toward Naco, during the Battle of Naco with Pancho Villa and the *federalistas*. His orders were if the battle begins to bleed over onto the U.S. territory, open up on them, and get them back, no matter which side it is. Chase them back with the machine gun.

My father entered on duty with Border Patrol in 1956 here at Yuma. My earliest memories as a kid four and five years old are like snapshot pictures. I see the white arches of the old sector headquarters building, while I was tagging along with my dad to check his mail drawer or having to fill out his weekly work-hours reports. I remember seeing welders and mechanics in the back working on equipment or road graders. I remember the old Jeeps. We have a photo with the canvas bags that they would drape over the front radiator to evaporate and help cool the radiator system, and also to have potable water available, if they needed it, while running the dunes. I still remember seeing those. I remember playing with my little toy soldiers in the sand, while a line of Border Patrolmen were out doing PPC [Practical Police Combat] shooting competitions on weekends. My dad was a competitive shooter. I spent my earliest days with the old patrol, with the empty .38 caliber shell casings in my ears to shut out some of the loud noise of shots being fired.

In 1978, I started in Douglas, Arizona. I truly consider Arizona my home. I was born in Pasadena, California, and within days, as a small infant child, was moved to Yuma, because that's where my dad entered on duty. I think I was born the day after he graduated from the Border Patrol

Ronald S. Colburn. U.S. Border Patrol official photo.

Academy in '56, which was held at Fort Bliss, El Paso, Texas. It was an eight-week course back in those days. He talks about a lot of beans and tortillas, the fare of the day that they got fed at the academy.

After Douglas Station, I went to the academy to teach law for a couple years, and back to Arizona, at Nogales, as a supervisor. Then I went to Watertown, New York, so I did the Canadian border, too. I came back down to Texas and ran BORTAC field operations. BORTAC is Border Patrol Tactical Unit, our version of SWAT (Special Weapons and Tactics) for special operations. Then I went as Patrol Agent in Charge to Sonoita, Arizona, the jewel of the Southwest and an eight-man Border Patrol station. Soon I went to Nogales, then up to Tucson Sector as assistant chief, then to Washington, D.C., as associate chief.

The day I arrived in Washington, they took me into my office and said,

"Here's your office, but don't move in, you're going over to the White House." This was just after 9/11. Unbeknownst to me, the White House had called the day I interviewed for the job and said, "We need a Border Patrol agent"—this was the White House—"to help manage this transition to a concept that we are now calling Homeland Security, should it pass Congress."

And it passed. That was all confidential at the time. I didn't know any of that, except that when I went to Washington, D.C., from Arizona, for my interview for the job, Chief Gustavo De La Viña of the Border Patrol asked me, "Why do you want to come to Washington, D.C.?" I said, "Truly, it's 9/11. It's calling upon me to come to Washington, D.C. I feel like I need to be here to help manage the change that we're about to experience." There was a sense, I think organization-wide, that we were about to experience grand change, we just didn't know what it was, and I wanted to be a part of that and the War on Terror. The chief and the other interviewers exchanged glances. I didn't think anything of it at the time. After I got the job, they told me that I had just "volunteered" to go over to the White House. I spent the next thirteen months there during the passing of the bill and the creation of the Department of Homeland Security.

My intention was to be a navigator, so to speak, and to have an interested voice on behalf of the Border Patrol, not knowing whether I would be heard or not. During that period of time a little committee of five sequestered themselves in the White House and literally wrote the Homeland Security Act. I was just coming on board at that time. The guy driving it, as the appointee of the president at that time, was Governor Tom Ridge. He had not yet been appointed secretary. Basically I went to work for him. The title changed three or four times while I was there, but it ended up as the Director for Law Enforcement for the Homeland Security Council. The Homeland Security Council was set up similar to, and parallel to, the National Security Council, only significantly smaller in number. At first it was called the Office of Homeland Security until the bill passed, and then they decided to make it a council and make it more permanent inside the White House.

Tom Ridge, about half of the organization, and the Office of Homeland Security went with him to the new Department of Homeland Security headquarters to become his immediate staff, while he began setting up an entire department. About sixty-six of us remained behind in the White House. As the Director for Law Enforcement, I worked for a senior director for Border and Transportation Security, who was also on loan to the White House. Most of us were not permanent staff or political appointees—we were governmental executives from our respective disciplines. My boss was an admiral in the U.S. Coast Guard, and he worked for a two-star general, major general, from the U.S. Army, who later went on to become first chief of staff for Secretary Ridge. There was a constant transition of leaders and political appointees.

We came into a newly formed organization, a bureau called the U.S. Customs and Border Protection. They brought together Department of Agriculture inspectors for ports of entry, Department of the Treasury, U.S. Customs support personnel, and others, and we had to put them together. The president's hand-picked team—the Asa Hutchinsons, the Robert Bonners, the Tom Ridges, the Gordon Englands—basically was told, "Okay, you guys, it's your new secretariat-level organization. Stand it up and form it. Here are your twenty-two agencies. Make it all work." They decided that they needed a one-face-at-the-border concept and a 360-degree border security net. So it included the lawful ports of entry—maritime, air, land—and the ground between ports of entry. That's where they came up with the concept of one bureau called Customs and Border Protection. They still felt a need for interior enforcement and investigation, and that's where ICE, the Bureau of Immigration and Customs Enforcement stood up. But you had to truly rend apart a couple of different former large agencies to do that, one being INS, the old Immigration and Naturalization Service. The mantra of the group was "no redundancy, no overlap, no gaps." So, we began to try to devise how to work all of this out. At times we had shouting matches in those working groups as decisions were being made.

Keeping Border Patrol's identity and its strength was truly a challenge, and to this day, as DHS continues to evolve with its twenty-two agencies, it continues to be a challenge. They refer to identity as "branding." We in Border Patrol prefer to call it "tradition."

Well over 90 percent of all arrests of removable foreign nationals from inside the United States or those attempting to come in are done by or detected by the U.S. Border Patrol. So of the 1.2 million arrests of removable foreign nationals from the U.S. in 2005, 1.19 million of them were done by the Border Patrol, and that last ten thousand or so were effected by ICE and other organizations that feed in. But ICE ended up with the responsibility for holding, feeding, and detaining them long-term, and eventually for physically removing those people. But their best and first-served customer is the U.S. Border Patrol, because we're the ones that capture them and temporarily hold them. I foresaw some very difficult times ahead if ICE was not in the same organization, if they answered to different bosses, and that is what occurred. To this day, we're still trying to work that out.

Another piece of the puzzle was realignment of the air operations. I think they're getting it right, although change is difficult. We've taken the Customs, ICE, air, and marine operations and joined them as one entity within the air and marine operations into one entity of Customs and Border Protection [CBP], the same bureau that Border Patrol is in. We modified their mission to more clearly state border security and law enforcement focused along the border between ports of entry. We can still go out, for example, and support U.S. Forest Service rangers in destroying marijuana crops on a national forest somewhere in a remote area, but that's not our priority mission. Our priority is antiterrorism along the border, defeating mass migration, and mass illicit cross-border trafficking, especially on the southwest border. And that's where we're redirecting those air assets. So far, some of it's working out very well.

But if you are one of those Border Patrol pilots, you may see it quite differently. They are no longer Border Patrol agents. They actually now have a different assistant commissioner that they answer to, even though they grew up in the Border Patrol, they were ground-pounders before they qualified as pilots, and they still see a loyalty to the U.S. Border Patrol. They may still "bleed green," but technically they don't work for the Border Patrol anymore. As a sector chief, I'm their tactical commander and I still call the shots on how they deploy, but a completely different administrative entity, CBP Air and Marine, hires them, feeds them, and repairs them.

People still don't know what to call us oftentimes, other than Border Patrol. And the traditional green, the branding, has survived very well. Some of the working groups would say, "You're all going to go to navy blue uniforms for everyone, you're going to have a gray background, you're going to have silver and navy blue highlights, and that's just it. No arguments. That way we're all the same." I said, "Okay, the U.S. Coast Guard is now a part of DHS and has very nice white dress uniforms and white boats with an orange slash. They're all going to this uniform, too?" "Well, not them. They're retaining their tradition and their branding." "Okay, how about the U.S. Secret Service. Are they going to this new uniform?" "Well, no, they're retaining their old uniforms and emblems." "Why?" "Well, because it's very important. Since the 1800s, they've been the protection to the president and administration and they've been the ones to find the counterfeiters. There's a history there."

I said, "Okay, now that we've established that precedent, here's the U.S. Border Patrol," and I "flew" the Border Patrol flag. Chief Gustavo De La Viña and then later Chief David Aguilar also fought with the bureaucratic leaders to retain our history and tradition. There's actually now an expectation from the public of who and what the Border Patrol is. So far, we've been able to defend our position on why the uniqueness of our branding and our tradition must be retained. In the spring of 2009 DHS Secretary Janet Napolitano announced that there would be no new branding, uniforms, or emblems within DHS. The operative word was "new." Border Patrol's brand is eighty-five years old and should withstand scrutiny. It is a fight worth "dying on the hill" for.

We're very proud that we're able to carry on the mission of the Border Patrol. Since 9/11 our mission has not changed. In the transition to DHS, the one agency that truly has an unchanged mission, other than a stronger emphasis on antiterrorism, is the U.S. Border Patrol. We have always been that single agency assigned to protect America's frontiers between the ports of entry. That didn't change.

One way I used to put it back East was, "The FBI and Department of Justice did not transition over to the Department of Homeland Security. They're still *the* lead domestic antiterrorism agency in America, even though they're not *in* DHS. Their challenge truly is, within the domestic United States, to find the needle in the haystack, that one sleeper cell terrorist, the one that's here somewhere. Now, in the Border Patrol, we face outward to protect our borders, and our job is to capture not the needle, but the entire haystack wherein lies the needle."

When I arrived in 2005 as the Yuma Sector chief, which includes Wellton Station, we had about 330 deployable personnel in Yuma. We now have, counting trainees at the academy, well over 600, and soon we'll have close to 800 or better. So we will have doubled and nearly tripled our staff. Along with that, we will have doubled our air force, the CBP air and marine operations.

Historically, our agency was called for the race riots in the desegregation movement in the early 1960s, deputized as U.S. Marshals. Former Yuma chief Elmo Rainbolt was on the cover of *Life* magazine, misidentified as a U.S. Marshal, but he was a U.S. Border Patrol agent, escorting a small child to his classroom during the desegregation days. During the Cuban Missile Crisis, when they needed a surge of forces out in the Florida Keys, who did they send? They sent the Border Patrol. The first ever scuttling of an attempted domestic hijacking in the air in the United States was by a Border Patrolman. The agent gave the hijacker the old overhand right and knocked him out cold, ending the hijacking attempt by a Cuban national. During the Gulf War in 1991 we sent teams to all the major U.S. international airports to be the first ones to put ourselves in harm's way for a terrorist that might roll the proverbial hand grenade into a crowd at a terminal.

The men and women—the agents—truly are the most important asset that the Border Patrol has. The men and women who are out there on those lonely canyons and trails on a night shift out in the desert, walking alone, hearing a heel kick a rock up ahead, knowing that they're about to get into it, but not knowing what *it* is. They are the very most important asset. That was also one of the challenges I had inside the Washington Beltway. I had to convince the bureaucracy that the men and women out here, just like in the military, don't work for *them* in Washington, D.C. The bureaucracy must work so that the men and women out in the field can get the mission done.

That's why training is so important. We have the toughest training academy of all the eighty-plus federal law enforcement agencies in America. The Border Patrol has the longest, and possibly the most complex and difficult, law enforcement police training, as well. I say that not just because of the Spanish language requirement. There are probably very few laws, other than maybe some of the Internal Revenue Service's tax laws, that are more complex than the U.S. immigration laws. So it's quite a challenging academic requirement we ask of our people. As the Marines have been to the Department of Defense, the Border Patrol was the proverbial "knuckle-draggers" of the Department of Justice. Time and again, we disprove those erroneous images and those invalid theories about who we are and what we do. Yes, we go out and get our boots dirty every day. That's what we're supposed to do. But yes, we also speak a minimum of two languages, and can basically repeat, from rote memory, more variations of case law and statutes than most criminal law organizations are required to. It's the nature of our business.

I'm a believer in transparency. Whether it's good, bad, or ugly, we're servants of the people. I think we are the foreign legion to America, as the French Foreign Legion is to Europe. We're that exciting place to run off to. And it really is an adventure. The more people that learn about us, the more excited they feel about us and the more supportive they'll be. Critical? Of course, some are, and we've had our embarrassments. But as far as I'm concerned, if we err at all, we're transparent, and that builds trust.

With Homeland Security's growth, one of our fears is that somehow we'll lose our small familial feeling. I can't go anywhere without running into somebody I know or know of. The *esprit de corps* is truly there. Border Patrol has some traditional programs that we built ourselves, such as the way we do our employee assistance program, the way we do our peer support, and the Border Patrol Chaplaincy program—all of these programs were looked at suspiciously by the new parent agency, DHS. They were truly asking us, "Convince us that this is good." The first death in the line of duty within Homeland Security, unfortunately, was a Border Patrol agent, James P. Epling, here in Yuma, Arizona, in December 2003, who drowned while trying to save the lives of illegal crossers foundering in the Colorado River. When DHS leaders saw us go into action, taking care of our own, the family, the extended family, and the community, I think that they began to understand, and they said, "There's something new, unique, and different about this Border Patrol organization that we adopted. They cry for their own." Much of the federal government didn't do that. They didn't see themselves as one big family. They saw themselves as, "It's a job. You go in, you go home, no hard feelings"—but with no close or warm feelings, either. With us in Border Patrol, they saw people hugging in the hallways, they saw people who knew the first names of each other's children, people who cried when there was a death, and people who were willing to give a kidney or to die, literally, for each other.

Right across the street from our new Border Patrol headquarters in the Ronald Reagan Building at 13th and Pennsylvania Avenue, just three blocks away from the White House, is the bronze statue of Black Jack Pershing in a park named for him. I walk people across the street—visitors, reporters, Homeland Security personnel—to see the statue of Pershing and say, "This is the origin of the Border Patrol uniform." There's Black Jack in his jodhpurs, he's got on his campaign hat, and he's wearing our coat and our Sam Browne belt. You look at that, and you see the history of the Border Patrol uniform. It's obvious that we patterned ourselves after the *first* guy that was enforcing border security, Black Jack Pershing. It's the same uniform. To this day we still wear green as part of that tradition.

CARLA L. PROVOST

Currently in charge of Wellton Station, Carla L. Provost joined the Border Patrol in 1995.

I was a college student and interested in law enforcement, but back in the 1980s I thought I've got to go to college. I came from one of those families that values earning a degree. So I went in as a business major and, lo and behold, I found out my school offered a criminal justice degree. I was attending Kansas State University and in my sophomore year changed over to criminal justice. I became a police officer in Manhattan, Kansas, in 1992. It was about a hundred-man department, Riley County Police Department, but I was looking to enter the federal world, not really knowing what I wanted to do. It was actually a U.S. Marshal who told me about Border Patrol, because growing up in Kansas, I didn't know anything about the Border Patrol.

I checked out the Border Patrol and went through the hiring process with all good intentions of using the Border Patrol as a stepping stone to move on to something such as FBI. I got into the Border Patrol in January of 1995. Within a year, I knew there was no way I would ever leave the Border Patrol. I was assigned to Douglas, Arizona, right when it was becoming a hot spot. By '96 we were getting hit really hard. I loved every aspect of the job. Being outdoors, working out in the desert. I absolutely adore the desert. I've done my whole career in Arizona for a reason, because I really love the desert and this is a great job.

I did eleven and a half years in Douglas. It was a great place to work. I promoted to first-line supervisor there. I did a lot of time on the bike patrol unit, which I loved. I was a firearms instructor as well. There were many opportunities for me while I was there, and then I promoted on to field operations supervisor. My last couple of years in Douglas, I went to

Carla L. Provost. Photo by Bill Broyles, 2009.

Washington, D.C., did some special details there, and started branching out looking for something new.

I worked for Chief David Aguilar and Deputy Chief Ron Colburn in Tucson Sector. Then I was detailed to headquarters back in 2002 when Ron Colburn was in D.C. When I was ready to return to the field, I applied to Tucson and Yuma sectors. I love the desert, I love Arizona, and I wanted to look somewhere in Arizona.

At Wellton Station, we're over three hundred agents now. And we've got a lot of youth, a lot of inexperience. Right now the average time-in-service of my agents is two to two-and-a-half years. They're great agents, hard workers, dedicated, and really excited, I think, about being in a station like Wellton where they can get out and work the desert. And we have excellent general knowledge that we can tap into, such as experienced agents like Jerry Wofford, Joe Brigman, and Bob McLemore, who have been around here a long time.

Since 2006, Yuma Sector has more than doubled the number of agents. That rapid growth is a key issue that we deal with: keeping enough supervisors—first-line supervisors and field operations supervisors—and being able to fill those positions. From the outside some agents see Wellton as a small town and don't think they want to come out and work this area. They've never seen the desert that our area of responsibility encompasses, and our job announcements are not as full as I would like to see.

For day-to-day operations, I have Jerry Wofford as my second in command. He is just outstanding. He knows the area like the back of his hand, he's a great leader, and he has known operations for a long time. Wellton runs very well. I've got great managers. My first-line supervisors are my eyes and ears. They're the ones that know what's going on in the field, because, unfortunately, I can't get out there day in and day out like I would love to do, like every PAIC would love to do. The supervisors are the ones who know what's going on and they provide a solid experience base.

The agents are outstanding. It's just the inexperience that I seem to deal with the most, and getting things that the agents need is sometimes difficult, considering tighter budgets. My senior managers and I have a good working relationship with the young agents. They're excited to be in the job, excited to be out here working.

I'm the first female Patrol Agent in Charge of Wellton Station and one of the few in the Border Patrol. We already have more female agents since the time I came into the Border Patrol. I think we're sitting at a little over 5 percent of women in the Patrol nationally. I think you could find average statistics in regular law enforcement run around 10 percent. I'd like to see Border Patrol get up to that level of 10 percent, and we do targeted recruiting, but I don't see it growing dramatically. It does not seem to be a job that attracts a lot of women. The desert can be harsh, and the shift work is difficult for a family. We have a lot of mothers in the Border Patrol. I have a three-year-old myself. We have a lot of husband-and-wife teams in the Border Patrol as well. We are growing and I think it's a good thing.

Recruiting is very big right now for both women and minorities, and we've done an outstanding job, but there are groups within Customs and Border Protection that are considered underrepresented: women, African Americans, and Asian/Pacific Islanders. It partly comes down to who resides in border communities. Obviously in the desert Southwest, you've got certain populations that live here and I think you see that reflected in who applies. I came from Kansas, but if you look at the majority of Border Patrol agents, the majority of our applicants are people who grew up along the border region and really know what the Border Patrol is about. Whenever I get a new class of interns—they're no longer called trainees— I always ask where they're from and I'd say a good 50 percent are from the border region, but now we're starting to reach out and we're getting people from across the country. I think our numbers are going to improve when it comes to minorities.

I've never had any issues as a woman. I've been welcomed from the beginning. I have seen some women struggle. But as a whole, I don't think anything's harder just because we're women. Women go through the same physical training at the academies, and as long as you can get through that and can handle the fieldwork, you'll do fine. It depends on the individual person as opposed to being male or female. Whether they're males or females, I've seen people struggle to get along with their peers in the field or to master the many tasks of the job. Whether you are male or female, if you are capable and can show it, then you shouldn't have any issues. When I first started in law enforcement, you would see more athletic females who had played sports, but today we see mothers who have raised their children and who just decide, "Hey, I'm coming in and doing this."

As a female out in the field, when you come across alien women and children you feel compassion for them and realize their situation. Women would quite often talk to me and say, "Please, please, please . . . ," but I just explain to them, "This is my job. This is what I'm here to do. I understand your plight, but I have to do my job." They seem to understand that, as well. It may be the same for male agents.

When I look at the generation differences, I do see differences in attitudes and skills between older agents and younger agents. Managers, like myself, try to look at those generational differences and apply them. Young people today seem to need more feedback than, maybe, we needed. They want to know "Why" about everything. It used to be, give an order and go do it. The newer generation seems to want to know why—"Why am I doing this?"—which is a good thing. The younger agents are very much a Why-generation and want to know why they're doing things and what's behind it. I still think that you see very dedicated agents, just as those who have been around for a long time. They really have an interest in what they're doing. They see the importance of what they're doing. I just think it's a difference in the way they approach the job. And, the young guys still go to the experienced agents for information, knowledge, or advice.

First and foremost a good agent has honesty and integrity. But he also needs to learn from mistakes. Even if you mess up, and everybody does once in a while, you must come back and you say, "Hey, this is what I did, and I messed up." In law enforcement, that's very important, because that honesty and integrity is your career. All it takes is one time of not being truthful and you can never stand up in a court and be heard again. I think that's the most important thing that stands out. You've got to be honest and have high integrity. Cover-ups and denials only make things worse, not just in Border Patrol but across the whole law enforcement field. Time and again, when I've seen people lose their jobs, lose their careers, it's been in those scenarios.

A good leader must be respectful of people no matter what the situation. If you have to give them bad news, if you have to be hard on them, or if they've messed up, you can still lead them if you treat them with respect. I also believe that you can be firm and make yourself very clear without yelling. You sit them down and say, "Here's what you need to work on." Explain yourself. Too, leaders must give praise. You can't just give criticism. You've got to give well-rounded appraisals, especially with this generation. Talk to them. Come in and have a cup of coffee with them. Because our agency has grown so much, it's sometimes hard to be close to the agents working the field. I take time, when I can, to just make it more personal, find out about their families, what's going on in their lives, or what makes them tick.

I'd like to get our new station built, so we can have the space that we need. Beyond that, I want to make it a place where agents want to come, and where they want to stay and work. If you really like to get out and work, this station is a gem. We have sixty-four linear border-miles of amazing desert to work in and opportunities to do so many different things. Part of what I want to do is get that message out across the Border Patrol: Wellton Station is one you want to work at. What a great place to live and work: Wellton, Yuma, Roll, Tacna, the whole area. I want to make sure it's a place that the agents are happy being at. Wellton still has that family appeal about it that the Border Patrol has always prided itself on.

As good Border Patrol agents, we want to keep our legacy going. The patch on my right shoulder says CBP and DHS, but that patch on my left shoulder is Border Patrol. We "bleed green." The names, the breakdowns of DHS, CBP, and the Border Patrol under it, can be confusing to the public as a whole, but I think we've done a good job of keeping our Border Patrol identity as well as integrating into DHS.

I absolutely loved being a first-line supervisor and running the bike patrol unit in Douglas, working a special unit, being able to do good case-work, and seeing some people get some prison time on smuggling cases. I love the job I'm in right now. The Border Patrol has given me so many opportunities throughout my career. I love to work with the agents, to be in the leadership position with them and, hopefully, to gain their respect and make this a place where they will continue to enjoy working.

Apprehensions in the sector as a whole last year were down 78 percent from the year before, which wasn't even our high. Our high was in 2006. Wellton Station is down 27 percent for the current fiscal year from what we were last year. But success brings administrative challenges so we can continue to remain successful. Lessons learned in the past show that Border Patrol as a whole is looking at the importance of sustaining what we gain and getting better support. Now we've got to convince others beyond Border Patrol that they can't just strip our assets and expect the border to stay under control. Whenever I drop below three hundred agents, I say, "No, no, no. You need to keep us at least up to this level to be able to handle everything." It's a battle to sustain the resources necessary to do everything America expects of us.

CONCLUSION:
BEFORE THEY DIE

The Border Patrol has come a long way from that early job announcement back in 1925, and today recruits must show up with more than a horse, pistol, and bedroll. But agents still must bring along all of their honesty and intelligence, gumption and courage. Modern recruiters are looking for people who are "independent thinkers who can work alone, team players who everyone knows can be relied on, people who take personal responsibility for everything they do, and people who believe in America and want to protect it." The minimal requirements are be of sound mind and health, be a U.S. citizen under forty years of age, have a high school education plus another four years of higher education, equivalent experience, or military service, be of good moral character, and have a valid driver's license. Applicants must pass a medical exam, drug tests, physical fitness tests, and a background investigation. Within their first year recruits must pass rigorous tests for fluency in Spanish and immigration law. With few exceptions, agents retire by age fifty-seven.

Time after time agents tell of just looking for a job and discovering a whole career, a lifestyle, and lifelong friends. One of the themes running through Studs Terkel's revealing book *Working* is that many jobs are not big enough for people. One less-than-satisfied office worker told Terkel, ". . . most of us are looking for a calling, not a job. Most of us . . . have jobs that are too small for our spirit" (page xxiv). Convincingly, Border Patrol is a calling big enough to fill a person's spirit. The tasks and skills, regions and terrain, equipment and technology, and nature of the work are sufficiently varied and challenging to keep people interested and excited about coming to work day in and day out. The agency offers upward mobility and diversity of assignments. It is a risky job with adrenaline rushes of pursuit, catching criminals, and at-the-edge training. We're reminded of Carla Provost's comment that was echoed by others, "Within a year, I knew there

David F. Roberson (1941–1989). Photo by Bill Broyles, 1983.

was no way I would ever leave the Border Patrol." Most agents will tell you that the job is "everything I always wanted and more."

Another universal theme in Terkel's *Working* is the quest to find a job that "shows I did something on this earth" and better yet, I even "helped save somebody" from dying (page xxiv). Border Patrol is a hero job. Saving people and saving one's country make agents feel good about both the work and themselves. It is spiritually rewarding. As Joe McCraw reminded us, "The thrill is tracking 'em up before they die. It's a rough ol' way to go—run outta water in this desert."

While agents acknowledge that paychecks are a way of keeping score and do make the job worthwhile, they admit to loving the chases and puzzles that police work provides. In more private moments, most talk of patriotism—service to country and fellow citizens, and of a strong moral sense of right and wrong. Foreign-born agent George Boone sometimes has people ask him why he of all people works for Border Patrol catching illegal immigrants. His standard reply has become, "It is good to serve and protect my country." Invariably their conversations drift to rescues, saving people who face death by thirst, exposure, or criminal assault. As Jim Runyan explained it, "I've always felt that the only people who really care about the aliens, truly care about the aliens, is them ol' guys and gals wearing green Border Patrol uniforms. Good or bad, day or night, the only ones that really care about their welfare are Border Patrol agents. We want to pull 'em out of the desert."

Like other police work, the torrent of ever-changing technology, laws, and policies brings stress to already difficult tasks, for even routine situations can quickly become complex, confusing, and potentially lethal. Above all, agents are border police and must manage people, few of whom wish to be managed. Too, many agents see ways to improve the agency. Their complaints roughly fall within three categories: agents who don't do their jobs, take bribes, or abuse aliens; agency leaders who are more intent on advancing their own careers than benefiting the agency or serving the public; and politicians who profess to want strong border protection but then vote to weaken laws or diminish budgets. This stress—the distance between reality and high expectations—may bounce between cynical-sounding complaints and head-shaking laughter. Yet, most agents find the job itself highly rewarding and voice respect for the aliens they deal with.

And, like other police agencies, Border Patrol agents enforce law: they do not make it, and they rely upon courts to administer it. When arrestees are released or given apparently light sentences, agents may wonder, "Why have I been risking my life to chase aliens and smugglers in the middle of the night if the nation doesn't really want them caught?" But they try not to dwell on this, for it is disheartening. Nor can they compensate for poorly funded or lenient prosecutors and courts. Historically, for example, few federal prosecutors press first-arrest cases against criminals who smuggle people, and few federal prosecutors take cases against drug smugglers who import loads of marijuana less than five hundred pounds. As one can imagine, this leads to galling levels of scorn by the smugglers and understandable levels of exasperation by agents.

Police work in general is very active and strenuous physically, and it relies heavily on street smarts as opposed to book learning, though many agents eventually earn college degrees. Agents must be highly self-reliant and practical. Sound judgment, decisiveness under pressure, and fairness are crucial not only to success but survival. A memory for faces and names is highly beneficial, as is a tolerance for routine, enduring those sometimes monotonously repetitive shifts of checking and rechecking places and people. It is seldom glamorous or exciting, but in rare moments the job can turn terrifying in an instant. Hand-to-hand combat, shootouts, high-speed chases, and foot pursuits on dark nights provide memorable moments that are told and retold. The job requires a combination of physical and mental toughness that comes from unwavering belief in one's country.

Border Patrol agents are "green-collar" workers, who tend to be equally at home in the office and the field. In the office they must operate computers and other "white-collar" technologies and must appear in court to present testimony. Yet they must also be "blue-collar" workers who don't mind getting their uniforms dusty and their hands dirty. In a day's work an agent may handcuff a dozen people, change a flat tire, walk a mile through a field or across open desert to cut sign, and help a citizen dig out a stuck vehicle.

In essence, Border Patrol agents are federal officers assigned to police the borderlands, much like FBI agents are federal police assigned to protect the nation inside the border. The patrol has grown to nearly twenty thousand agents alongside several thousand support personnel. Today, as ever, they stand alongside the Coast Guard, U.S. Customs, and U.S. armed forces ready to defend America's borders.

With the assurance earned from countless apprehensions and rescues, and with resolve tempered by heartbreaking failures, there's pride in being an agent, a pride in one's station and oneself. Veteran agent Jerry Wofford explains, "There's something special about Wellton. I think it's the vastness of the desert, the sheer size of it. It's one of the few places in the Border Patrol where a few agents cover so much area. In some parts of Texas you have expanses, but you also have ranches and windmills. This is just wide open desert. There's an appeal to it." He pauses as if remembering the lure of daily chases and fevered races against relentless heat. By now he is sitting on the edge of his chair and he leans forward, as if to share a secret. He speaks for a legacy of agents at Wellton when he softly adds, "I can find people out there."

OUR APPROACH, AND
ACKNOWLEDGMENTS

We interviewed more than sixty Border Patrol agents for this project. Our guests range from journeymen officers to chiefs, active and retired. Sincere thanks are given to all those who took the time to participate. No one asked to be included, but without exception those we approached agreed to suffer the intrusion on their time and privacy. We hope that access to this work will stimulate others to record their remembrances for posterity. Most historical societies are eager to assist in this endeavor.

This project really began in 1984 when one of us (BB) began interviewing Border Patrol pilots who were friends of David F. Roberson. After Mark Haynes retired from the Border Patrol in 2002, we teamed up for this larger project. Our goal has been to let Border Patrol agents tell their own stories in their own words. Our basic theme is "What does it mean to be a Border Patrol agent?" and we employ a list of general questions. No interview ever stuck to the script, but we were able to start people talking and then guide them to essential topics and common themes.

Our method was to tape a session, usually one to three hours in length. Then the tape was transcribed and the transcription sent to the agents for their review, changes, and corrections, especially spellings of names. Following that, we edited the transcript into an essay, and ran that past the interviewees for approval. Generally, they offered additional information and saved us from errors of editing, fact, or spelling. We appreciate their patience and enthusiasm.

Kate Garmise and Barbara H. Jardee have ably and cheerfully handled the onerous job of transcription. The transcriptions and tape recordings will find a home in the archive at the Arizona Historical Society.

None of these agents speaks officially for the agency. In alphabetical order those included in this book are:

Mac McLemore south of Camp Grip. Photo by Bill Broyles, 2005.

Howard Aitken. Interviewed by Mark Haynes and Bill Broyles, December 2, 2005.

George Boone. Interviewed by Bill Broyles, February 15, 2009.

Joe Brigman. Interviewed by Mark Haynes and Bill Broyles, December 1, 2005.

Colonel R. Child. Interviewed by Bill Broyles, December 15, 2005.

Ronald S. "Ron" Colburn. Interviewed by Mark Haynes and Bill Broyles, February 7, 2006.

Wendy Conde. Interviewed by Mark Haynes and Bill Broyles, December 2, 2005.

Mark Haynes. Interviewed by Bill Broyles, December 2, 2005; April 26, 2007; February 14, 2009.

Hank Hays. Interviewed by Bill Broyles, February 17, 2006.

Randy Herberholz. Interviewed by Bill Broyles, April 12, 2006.

Jackie Mason. Interviewed by Bill Broyles, January 26, 2006.

Joe McCraw. Interviewed by Mark Haynes and Bill Broyles, December 1, 2005; by Bill Broyles, April 12, 2007.

Robert "Mac" McLemore. Interviewed by Mark Haynes and Bill Broyles, December 1, 2005; by Bill Broyles, August 2004.

Alvaro "Mike" Obregon. Interviewed by Bill Broyles, March 21, 2009.

Glen Payne. Interviewed by Mark Haynes and Bill Broyles, December 1, 2005; by Bill Broyles, February 15, 2009.

Carla L. Provost. Interviewed by Mark Haynes and Bill Broyles, April 7, 2009.

Jim Runyan. Interviewed by Bill Broyles, February 19, 2006, and February 16, 2008.

Kenny Smith. Interviewed by Bill Broyles, February 17, 2007.

Ed Tuffly. Interviewed by Bill Broyles, February 17, 2006; letters of March 13, 2006; April 25, 2005; and May 12, 2005.

Chet Wilson. Interviewed by Bill Broyles, February 17, 2006.

We encourage readers to support grassroots spoken history projects at their local historical societies. We continue to work with Carol Brooks at Arizona Historical Society–Yuma, and Kate Reeve and Bruce Dinges at Arizona Historical Society–Tucson. This project began under the encouragement of David Hoober, Don Bufkin, and Adelaide Elm Kimball at the historical society.

We also greatly appreciate the encouragement of our wives, Patty Haynes and Joan Scott; our friends, especially Charles Bowden and John Annerino; and our editors and production staff, Bill Bishel, David Hamrick, Nancy Bryan, Lynne Chapman, and Teri Sperry.

SOURCES AND
SUGGESTED READING

Aguilar, David. 2005. Statement Regarding Border Enforcement and Technology between the Ports of Entry. U.S. Senate Committee on the Judiciary, Subcommittee on Immigration, Border Security, and Citizenship, and Subcommittee on Terrorism, Technology, and Homeland Security, April 28.

Altshuler, Constance Wynn. 1983. *Starting with Defiance: Nineteenth-Century Arizona Military Posts.* Tucson: Arizona Historical Society.

Annerino, John. 2009. *Dead in Their Tracks*, 3rd edition. Tucson: University of Arizona Press.

Bourke, John G. 1891. *On the Border with Crook.* Reprint, Lincoln: University of Nebraska Press, 1971.

Bowden, Charles. 1986. *Blue Desert.* Tucson: University of Arizona Press.

————. 2008. *Exodus/Éxodo.* Austin: University of Texas Press.

Braddy, Haldeen. 1966. *Pershing's Mission in Mexico.* El Paso: Texas Western Press.

Ellingwood, Ken. 2005. *Hard Line: Life and Death on the U.S.-Mexico Border.* New York: Vintage Books.

Haley, J. Evetts. 1948. *A Good Man with a Gun.* Reprint, Norman: University of Oklahoma Press, 1982.

McChristian, Douglas C. 2005. *Fort Bowie, Arizona: Combat Post of the Southwest 1858–1894.* Norman: University of Oklahoma Press.

Metz, Leon. 1989. *Border: The U.S.-Mexico Line.* El Paso: Mangan Books.

Perkins, Clifford Alan. 1978. *Border Patrol: With the U.S. Immigration Service on the Mexican Boundary 1910–54.* El Paso: Texas Western Press.

Roberts, Dan R. 1989. "The Border Patrol—65 Years of Action." *The National Tombstone Epitaph* 16(2): 1, 12–14.

Smith, Cornelius C. 1970. *Emilio Kosterlitzsky: Eagle of Sonora and the Southwest Border.* Glendale, Calif.: Arthur H. Clark.

Spilken, Aron. 1983. *Escape!* New York: New American Library.

Terkel, Studs. 1972. *Working.* New York: Pantheon.

Thrapp, Dan L. 1967. *The Conquest of Apachería.* Norman: University of Oklahoma Press.

Trafzer, Clifford E. 1980. *Yuma: Frontier Crossing of the Far Southwest.* Wichita, Kansas: Western Heritage Press.

Urrea, Luis. 2004. *The Devil's Highway: A True Story.* New York: Little, Brown, and Company.

U.S. Border Patrol website: www.cbp.gov, as viewed on May 21, 2009.

U.S. Code Title 8, Chapter 12, Subchapter 1, § 1101.

Woodward, Arthur, ed. 1941. *Journal of Lt. Thomas W. Sweeny, 1849 to 1853.* Los Angeles: Westernlore Press.

THE EDITORS

Bill Broyles has been walking the desert south of Wellton and Tacna since 1972, and many of his favorite memories are there. He taught high school English and physical education for thirty-one years and now is a research associate at the University of Arizona's Southwest Center. His books include *Sunshot: Peril and Wonder in the Gran Desierto*, and he coedited *Dry Borders: Great Natural Reserves of the Sonoran Desert*. Border Patrol pilot David F. Roberson helped introduce Bill to his wife, Joan Scott.

Mark Haynes was born in Yuma, Arizona. His family members were longtime residents of Gadsden, a farming community on the Colorado River south of Yuma; his paternal grandfather first moved to Yuma County in 1904. Haynes joined the Border Patrol in 1978—he spent three years as Patrol Agent in Charge of the Tacna-Wellton Station and also served as Assistant Chief Patrol Agent of the Yuma Sector—and retired after twenty-five years of service. He has an abiding interest in Arizona history and is currently on the Board of Directors of the Arizona Historical Society. In his spare time Haynes leads historical society tours in southwestern Arizona.